NOV 15 2022

DISCARD
CADL

Deer Man

GEOFFROY DELORME

Translated by
SHAUN WHITESIDE

Deer Man

SEVEN YEARS OF LIVING IN THE WILD

GREYSTONE BOOKS
Vancouver/Berkeley/London

First published in North America in English by Greystone Books in 2022
Originally published in French as *L'homme-chevreuil:
Sept ans de vie sauvage*, copyright © 2021
Les Arènes, Paris. Published by special arrangement with Les Arènes,
France, in conjunction with their duly appointed agents Books and
More Agency and 2 Seas Literary Agency.

English translation copyright © 2022 by Shaun Whiteside

22 23 24 25 26   5 4 3 2 1

All rights reserved. No part of this book may be reproduced, stored in a retrieval system or transmitted, in any form or by any means, without the prior written consent of the publisher or a license from The Canadian Copyright Licensing Agency (Access Copyright). For a copyright license, visit accesscopyright.ca or call toll free to 1-800-893-5777.

Greystone Books Ltd.
greystonebooks.com

Cataloguing data available from Library and Archives Canada
ISBN 978-1-77164-979-7 (cloth)
ISBN 978-1-77164-980-3 (epub)

Editing for original edition by Nicolas Torrent
Copy editing by Paula Ayer
Proofreading by Alison Strobel
Jacket and text design by Jessica Sullivan
Jacket photo composite: JMrocek/iStock.com;
fotooboi_kld/Shutterstock.com
Interior photographs by Geoffroy Delorme

Printed and bound in Canada on FSC® certified paper at Friesens. The FSC® label means that materials used for the product have been responsibly sourced.

Greystone Books thanks the Canada Council for the Arts,
the British Columbia Arts Council, the Province of British Columbia
through the Book Publishing Tax Credit, and the Government
of Canada for supporting our publishing activities.

Greystone Books gratefully acknowledges the xʷməθkʷəy̓əm (Musqueam), Sḵwx̱wú7mesh (Squamish), and səlílwətaʔɬ (Tsleil-Waututh) peoples on whose land our Vancouver head office is located.

*To Chevy, my best friend.
You taught me to live, to feel, to love,
to believe that everything was possible,
and to become myself.*

Dawn

Nature is all that we see,
All that we want, all that we love.
All that we know, all that we believe,
All that we feel within ourselves.

It is beautiful for those who see it,
Good to those who love it,
Just when we believe in it
And respect it within ourselves

Look at the sky, it sees you,
Kiss the earth, it loves you.
The truth is what we believe
In nature it's yourself.

GEORGE SAND

PROLOGUE

IS IT A MAN OR A WOMAN? My eyes long ago lost the ability to spot that kind of detail from more than thirty yards away. Is that an animal running along beside them? Oh no, please, not a dog! I've got to stop them before they scare my friends away.

Like them, I've become very territorial. Anyone who enters my territory is seen as a threat. I feel as if my privacy is being violated. My area of the forest has a radius of three miles. As soon as I see somebody I follow them, I spy on them, I collect information. If they come back too often, I'll do everything I can to scare them off.

I emerge from the undergrowth, determined to keep the walker from advancing any farther. A strong smell of very sweet violets assaults my nostrils. My walker must be a woman. As I climb back up the little forest path, I realize that it's been months since I last addressed a word to a human being. I've been living in the forest for seven years, communicating only with animals. For the first few years I went back and forth between human society and the wilderness, but over time I ended up turning my back once and for all on what they call "civilization" to join my real family: roe deer.

As I advance along the path, feelings rise up in me that I thought I had completely eliminated from my life. What must I look like? My hair hasn't seen a comb for years, and it's been cut "blind," with a small pair of sewing scissors. Luckily my face is beardless. So that's something. My clothes? My pants, completely covered in soil, could stand up all on their own like a sculpture. Well, at least it's dry today. At the beginning of my adventure I would sometimes check my reflection in a pocket mirror that I kept in a little round case. But over time, with the cold, the damp, the mirror tarnished and, to tell the truth, I no longer know what I look like.

It's a woman. I have to be polite so as not to frighten her. *But stay on your guard, you never know.* What word should I start with? "Hello"; "hello" is good. No, maybe "good evening." It's already the end of the day.

"Good evening..."

"Good evening, *monsieur*."

I

AS A CHILD, even as I sat in the warmth of my primary school classroom discovering the foundations of my future human life—how to read, to write, to count, and to behave in society—I could easily find myself looking out the window, contemplating the nobility of life in the wild. I observed sparrows, robins, blue tits, any animal that passed through my field of vision, and I thought about how lucky those little creatures were to enjoy such freedom. While I was shut away in that room with other children who seemed to like it there, at all of six years old I already aspired to that freedom. Obviously I was aware of how rough life out there must be, but when I observed that existence, simple and serene despite all its dangers, I felt a tiny germ of mutiny stirring within me, resisting a vision of human life in which I already felt they were attempting to confine me. Every day I spent by that window at the back of the class took me a little further away from so-called societal values, while the wild world exerted an attraction on me like a magnet on a compass needle.

Only a few months after the end of the summer holidays, a seemingly banal event would give shape to that germ of rebellion. One fine morning I learned as I got to class that a trip to the swimming pool was planned. Somewhat timid by nature, I was already apprehensive. When we got to the pool itself I froze with horror. It was the first time I'd seen so much water, and never having swum in my life, I was filled with an instinctive fear. All the other children seemed perfectly at ease, while I was gritting my teeth. The instructor, a red-haired woman with a long, severe face, asked me to get into the water. I refused. Her face tightened, her voice hardened, she ordered me to jump in. I refused again. Then she walked heavily toward me like a military officer, took me by the hand, and hurled me violently into the pool. I swallowed great gulps of water, of course, and not knowing how to swim, I started to go under. Between two desperate gesticulations I saw my tormentor swimming in my direction. I panicked, certain that she was going to kill me. My survival instinct led me to do the impossible. I doggy-paddled to the middle of the pool and dived below the divider separating me from the larger pool, with a view to reaching the other side. Having reached the edge, I climbed the ladder and ran as fast as I could to seek refuge in the changing rooms. I put my pants and my T-shirt back on. Once she was back out of the water, the instructor looked for me everywhere. The sound of her footsteps on the damp tiles suggested to me that she was coming up the little corridor that runs between the stalls arranged on each side. I had locked myself in the third one on the left. She flung open the second door, which closed again just as violently. An infernal din that made me think she was smashing in each door in turn. Seized by panic, I started crawling from stall to stall, slipping through the spaces between wall and floor. Having reached the end of the row, I took advantage of a few seconds during which she was peering inside one of the stalls to cross to the other side and slip discreetly out of the exit. Once outside I went charging down the street, running straight ahead, my eyes blurry with tears and chlorine, until a familiar-looking man stopped and asked me to follow him, taking me by the hand. It was the bus driver. He had seen me coming out all by myself and had the presence of mind to follow me. Between hiccupping sobs I told him what was happening, and why I never wanted to go back to the pool. His voice and his words reassured me a little. Once my little adventure was over and the teacher had been told how my escape had ended, I found myself at the back of the bus, alone, being stared at by both teachers and classmates, like a dangerous wild animal that needed to be treated with care. After that incident, the decision was made to take me out of school. I would pursue my education at home thanks to the National Centre for Distance Education.

So I found myself alone in my room, isolated from the outside world, with no friends and no teachers. Luckily a big library was open to me, full of literary treasures—Nicolas Vanier, Jacques Cousteau, Dian Fossey, Jane Goodall—telling stories of nature and life in the wild. I also devoured all the books about plants and animals I could get my hands on, a mine of precious information that I tried to apply on my own personal scale, in my garden. An apple tree, a plum tree, a cherry tree, barberry hedges, cotoneasters, pyracanthas, a few rosebushes—there were all kinds of things around the family home to distract me from boredom. Tending to all that vegetation quickly became my main source of escape.

One morning, I discovered that some blackbirds had made their nests in the hedge opposite my bedroom. In my childish brain, that discovery produced an absolute command: I had to look after them. I started doing my rounds around the hedge like a parking lot attendant, shooing away the cats attracted by the scent of easy prey. At all times of day and night, as soon as adult surveillance relaxed, I would open my window and slip outside, discreet as a cat, in search of news of my little feathered family. From seeing me so often, they seemed to have gotten used to me. I gave them food, breadcrumbs, earthworms, or insects that I put on a little plate. The parent birds came and pecked at them and brought them to the fledglings. With each passing day I gained their trust a little more. Now I could actually go inside the hedge to watch the babies squawk, my face only six inches from theirs. When the moment finally came for them to leave the nest, it was the father who left first. The little ones jumped out behind him and fell to the ground. The mother bird brought up the rear. They all walked around the hedge. Sometimes they would come over to me. I felt as if they were trying to introduce themselves. My nine-year-old boy's heart hammered. It was my first contact with the wild world, and to immortalize it I took a picture of the fledglings and sent them to my distance school examiner, Madame Krieger.

Each time I went for a walk I would push my exploration of the surrounding area a little farther. Behind the hedge there was a fence beneath which a hole had been dug, presumably by foxes. I slipped through it without any difficulty, to discover the neighboring field and the promises of adventure that went with it. The first few times, at night, by the moon's faint light, the thirst for freedom was always tinged with fear, the burning instinct of the adventurer always reined in by the prudence of the good little boy. But the irresistible draw of nature soon tipped the balance toward life in the wild. And on that new playing field, all of my senses were awakened. Concentrating on my walk, I registered the topography and the character of the ground. Every evening, touch replaced vision, and my body learned the terrain until I could map its contours with my eyes closed. It was exactly the same memorizing process that the body uses when we get up in the dark and know exactly where the light switch is, except that in this case I was applying it in the middle of the countryside. The smells changed too. Nettles, for example, smelled much stronger at night. Even the earth didn't give off the same perfume. And when I sniffed the damp exhalations of the marsh of the Petit-Saint-Ouen, I knew that my jaunt would soon be over. If I pressed on a little farther, I would reach the forest ranger's house. And beyond that lay the forest, the unknown. The nightjars circled around my head, their flight producing a curious hum, harsh and monotonous. I wasn't afraid. I felt great.

Deep within me there was an instinct for freedom that made me escape as soon as the opportunity

Pine forest. I used to come here when a storm was raging. The pines acted as an effective windbreak, often producing a microclimate. It could add one or two degrees. The pine cones and the needles that had fallen on the ground made it easy for me to light fires.

presented itself. And one single rule seemed worthy of respect: that of nature. I never broke a branch; I wouldn't even touch dead trees. I made up increasingly sophisticated rituals, on the edge of the absurd, because I had an inexplicable sense that I witnessed more striking and more frequent events when I walked around the trees to the right. So I constructed my imaginary world, my spirituality, my relationship with nature, all well documented, well thought-out, and filled with a childish mysticism.

For some time, a fox had regularly slept under a leafy tree in our garden. One winter evening I decided to follow it across the fields. As it reached the forest ranger's house, I saw it carrying on along its route at a gentle trot. It was time to dive into the unknown. About a hundred yards farther off, on the edge of the forest, the cub revealed to me the entrance to its den. I had never ventured so far from my bedroom. The wind, still blowing in the same direction, carried all the scents in from the field. Suddenly the twilight thickened. The sound changed too. There were countless new sounds, because life was there, in the depths of the wood. I stepped inside a little way, ten yards, then ten more, just long enough to feel the little adrenaline shiver that mystery gives you, before turning on my heels. There was, in fact, nothing to fear. The animals know very well that the fields are the thing you should be wary of. The forest is fascinating, enchanting. I ventured a little farther in each evening, always cautiously, as if to avoid offending it. And one night I found myself face to face with a red deer. I'd often heard them braying at the end of the summer, but I'd never dared approach them. Their hoarse bellow at night was too intimidating for a little ten-year-old boy. And that unexpected encounter petrified me. That heavy body less than ten yards away from me, the ground shaking with each step he took—I was overwhelmed by the power emanating from the creature. My heartbeat must have been audible a long way off. Suddenly he turned toward me and started braying with that hoarse voice. Around him, the does started replying with a tone that was slightly less deep but just as loud. Each bray made my ribcage vibrate, like the low frequencies of a stereo channel. In the end the stag turned away. I did the same, to show him that I hadn't come just to see him. And we left each other like that, like two creatures that had met by chance while wandering at night. Slipping silently under my covers a few moments later, I realized that the stag had given me the finest lesson of my short life: animals meant me no harm. I already wanted to go back, but I had to be patient. The wild world doesn't open itself up to just anyone.

From then on, as soon as the house was asleep, I would open my bedroom window, slip behind the blackbird hedge, and cross the nightjar field to find the gloom of the big trees and the bustle of the animals. The foxes that were the first to lead me there revealed their burrowing neighbors, badgers. Above my head I discovered the various birds of the night. If there is one bone-chilling creature in the forest it's definitely the owl. A silent predator that isn't afraid of anything or anybody. Amid the constant murmur of the forest you can't hear it fly, and if you rouse its curiosity it will have no hesitation in coming right over to you. The first time I crossed paths with an owl I was still recovering from the infernal scenes in the film *Jurassic Park*. Without my noticing, the animal had settled on a branch about six feet away from me. All of a sudden, without warning, it made its *hoo-hoo* cry. I started backward, tripping over a log, landing with my feet in the air, my eyes wide and my backside in the mud. The night life of the forest is thrilling. Many animals get on with their daily tasks at night. But some of them never seem to rest. This was true of the squirrels that I saw strolling in my garden during the day and running in all directions at night. When did they find the time to sleep? The question obsessed me until I worked out what I was failing to understand. Flicking through a picture book about the world of the forest, I understood that the hyperactive little rodents that I observed at night weren't squirrels at all, but young dormice. I was misled by their tufty little tails.

All of those elements of my childhood were there as if to tell me that life in the wild awaited me somewhere, and that when I was able to shed the burden of human constraints the forest would be there to welcome me. I believed so firmly in that prophecy that I sometimes went to sleep with my fists clenched very tightly, praying for night to turn me into a fox so that in the early hours, when my bedroom window opened, I would be able to escape by trotting toward that woodland vastness that inspired my dreams. The reality was much less exciting. I lived almost entirely alone, without friends or classmates, without holidays or school trips, and apart from my nocturnal escapades I sat in my room studying by correspondence with teachers at the other end of France, or going on little bicycle rides around the garden. On my rare permitted outings, to go shopping, for example, I would sometimes talk to the various shopkeepers who quizzed me about this homeschooling business. I told them all that the situation suited me perfectly, because even if deep down I had a sense that something wasn't quite right, I had no way of comparing myself to other children.

The truth is that the life imposed upon me gradually turned into a form of mental torture. So much so that at the age of sixteen I made the decision to spend not only my nights but also my days in the forest. And my rebellion reached its peak on the day of the tests for the baccalaureate, the final school exam. I decided to scuttle the educational boat once and for all by throwing my registration letter into a cornfield. Over the previous few years I had discovered a passion for nature illustration, and wanted to start training as a draftsman. Except that the school wanted me to study "business practice and communication." I don't even know what those words mean. Finally, war weary, I agreed to sign up for a course of study for "apprentice sales staff," which included by way of consolation a photography correspondence course. My passion for wild fauna remained intact, and I intended to do something with it. I spent whole days and weeks in the forest, under the pretext of working on my photography course. Over the course of my forest outings, I became aware that the wild animals recognized my scent, my various postures. It took me a long time, but they welcomed me into their habitat until I was basically part of the scenery. When I got home I was told that what I was doing wasn't a job, it wasn't something I could make a living from. But money wasn't my priority.

My quest was for a certain emotional stability. Living in the present moment like the forest animals gave me my true place in the order of things. Animals showed me that the more I thought, the more I felt trapped by a sense of danger. The problems of my past, the uncertainty of my future, and my desire to hold on to the present were all slowly destroying me. But observing the nature around me and absorbing the wild world stirred my mind in a thousand ways and clarified my thoughts.

For several months I had not been aware of the time, the hours and days spent in the forest. My life was more intense, and filled with joy, wonder, and serenity. That didn't mean that I jettisoned all sense of reality, however. To keep from sinking into morbid destitution I did take some sports photographs for local newspapers, which allowed me to buy clothes and food. But nobody believed in me and I had no moral support. My parents tried to keep me at home by telling me that the "herd" would protect me and I wouldn't survive for long on my own. But the more they tried to hold me back, the more frayed the bonds between us became. And then one day they broke. The decision was made; I was going into the forest.

A fable by Aesop, later told by Jean de La Fontaine, gives quite a precise description of what I felt at that moment. The fable is called "The Wolf and the Dog," and this is the story it tells:

A wolf was all skin and bone
So well did the dogs keep watch.
The wolf met a mastiff as strong as it was handsome,
Fat, and shiny, which had lost its way.
The wolf would happily have torn it to bits;
But battle was called for
And the mastiff was big enough
To defend itself most boldly.
So the wolf approached it humbly,
Addressed the dog and complimented it
Upon its fatness, which it admired.
It's up to you, my fine fellow.
To be as fat as me, the dog replied.
Leave the woods and you will do well;
Your peers are miserable there.
Thin and mangy, poor wretches they are,
Destined to die of hunger.
For they have no elegant water jugs
And always face death by the sword.
Follow me: a better fate awaits you.
The wolf replied: What do I need to do?
Hardly anything, said the dog; chase people carrying
    sticks, and beggars;
Flatter the ones with houses, please their masters:

As the result of which your wages
Will be rich in every way:
Chicken bones, pigeon bones,
Not to mention occasional sticks.
The wolf was already imagining a happiness
That made it weep with tenderness.
As they walked on it saw the chafing on the dog's neck:
What's that, it said.—Nothing.—What? Nothing?—
   Hardly anything.
—But what?—The collar to which I am attached
May be the cause of what you see.
—Attached? the wolf said. So you can't run
Where you wish?—Not always; but what does that
   matter?
—It matters in that I wish nothing
Of all your meals,
At that price I would not wish a treasure.
Having said which our wolf ran away, and runs still.

    I interpret the moral of the story thus: it is better to be poor and free than rich and shackled.

2

MY EXPEDITION INTO the woodland realm began in April and I decided, where possible, to eat only locally grown fare, following an omnivorous but vegetarian-inclined diet. I cannot imagine living in a natural habitat and eating the wild animals that live there. My human values have not abandoned me, and I am sensitive about respecting others, even though I acknowledge that nature is overflowing with predators that have no choice but to kill in order to feed themselves and survive. To find food in the forest, I needed above all to create for myself a territory that would provide a concentration of food and shelter. So at first my ambition was to mimic the way in which squirrels look after themselves. With the money I had saved from my photographic work, I bought cans of food, drinking water, and the equipment that I thought I would need to survive in what we must honestly call a rather hostile environment. I hid everything at the foot of a tree, amid a lacework of roots that I thought I alone knew about, under a pile of branches and dead leaves. Unfortunately, a few days later, some wild boar discovered my hoard and reveled in it. All the cans were disemboweled by their razor-sharp trotters. My fortune was crushed, shattered, dissipated. Nothing survived the powerful trampling of the herd, which left behind it only a heap of debris, as if to say: "Well, where do you think you are?" I was shocked for a few minutes, and then I had to put things into perspective. Nature has funny ways of putting us in our place when necessary. From now on, to protect my scant possessions from the greedy and the curious, I would bury my little packages in old poachers' holes. Those cavities, dug about a foot and a half wide and six feet deep, were used in the past to trap foxes and badgers. I just had to remove the murderous snares at the bottom and cover them over with good solid wood to keep walkers from falling in.

This incident also made me realize that going to the store and bringing my supplies back into the depths of the forest in my fifty-liter backpack was frankly exhausting. And exhaustion, when you are living outdoors, is a factor that should not be ignored. In fact, for survival purposes, my most efficient strategy would be to eat as much as possible what I already had at my disposal. Bramble, silver birch, hornbeam, and bay leaves; nuts such as chestnuts, beechnuts, or hazelnuts; and also plantain, dandelions, sorrel, and a huge number of other plants that might not taste so good but are extremely rich in nutrition. From then on, I would only eat food from the outside world if everything else was in short supply. It became something to celebrate when I brought it out to eat; even a simple can of ravioli.

There was one other source of gastronomic delight: the food that hunters left at the foot of trees to fatten up the boar. So I got pumpkin, zucchini, tomatoes, and other fruit and vegetables, and bread too, very plain but bread nonetheless. It was by following the animals—boar, foxes, badgers—that I discovered this form of pilfering. They were the ones with experience, so they were also the ones who showed me the way, and with every passing day I came a little closer to them, I became a little wilder. Without being aware of it, I was performing a study in animal behavior (or ethology, to give it its scientific name) in order to become, very gradually, a guest of the forest. The boar, the red deer, and the foxes that I came across increasingly accepted me on their territory while at the same time keeping their distance. After a few months I felt as if I had melted into the most marvelous scenery imaginable, the world of the forest. It was then that I made

Pine cone battles. Squirrels are mischievous and territorial. They had no hesitation in throwing pine cones and anything else within reach at me to drive me away when I was sleeping at the foot of their tree.

the acquaintance of an enigmatic and fascinating creature, the one who would open my eyes to life in the wild.

One fine morning when I was plucking a few leaves to chew on by the edge of a path, a roe deer, the one that I would come to call Daguet (the name means "roebuck" in French), crossed my path and came to a standstill a few steps away from me. Very slowly, I crouched down. I was fascinated by his big, shiny black eyes. He straightened his head and pointed his ears in my direction. The hairs on his scut bristled. We stared at each other for a few minutes, which seemed to me to last for hours. He looked sideways as if inviting me to join him in discovering the forest. He turned slowly and elegantly away and plunged into the undergrowth. I had just been touched by something stronger than myself. I had felt the call of the forest. My knees trembled and my breathing was shallow. It was time for me to leave the world of human beings to live among the roe deer and learn to understand them.

3

I'M EATING FROM a bramble that provides a good supply of small leaves, slightly withered but very nourishing. I've been savoring this salad for three-quarters of an hour when I spot Daguet's little face emerging from the bushes in front of me. Rather than running away like a normal roe deer, Daguet chooses to stay and observe me. I realize that he must have been there for a while, because I didn't see him coming. After a few minutes I leave my bramble patch to go and have a rest, pretending not to have noticed that he's there. He watches me leave and the day continues. In the evening, I take advantage of the cool of sunset to eat a few yarrow leaves in the clearing. Once again I happen upon Daguet, who is following me everywhere as if it were perfectly normal. His curiosity surprises me; he seems to have decided to find out more about this newcomer who has invited himself into his home. And from one day to the next our relationship grows over the course of our encounters in our shared territory.

On one particular day I decide to try and walk behind him. With a cool north wind blowing through the still leafless canopy, Daguet is chewing the cud while lying at the foot of a tree. I approach him gently, picking the odd leaf here and there. I hide behind each tree in turn to avoid attracting attention. I resume the operation several times and he still doesn't move. I've probably developed an unusual talent for approaching stealthily, unless he's pretending not to see me. Just to be sure, I come out to the left of the tree that I've been sheltering behind, to appear within his eyeline so that he can't miss me, then I approach him slowly, half crouching. He regards me calmly. It's almost unbelievable. The rascal has been making fun of me from the very beginning, letting me advance from tree to tree like an idiot. When I'm about ten yards away Daguet gets to his feet and stretches. I stop. He considers me. And we stand like that for a good half hour. It's an absolutely magical moment. I feed on his mere presence. I have a sense of total communion with him and with all our surroundings. Daguet has made me a part of his environment, and I imagine I'm the first person to be granted such a privilege. My heart and soul are at peace. My brain is on hold. At that precise moment, the whole of my existence is governed by a single law: respect. After a few minutes, a first thought fills me: as long as we are not disturbed by other humans. It would be terrible if he associated me with them. Some Indigenous peoples say that when hunting deer you shouldn't think about them too much, in case they sense your thoughts and make their escape. That seems entirely reasonable to me. Thoughts become moods and moods become scents. So I force myself to have positive thoughts, in the hope of making that silent dialogue with Daguet last for as long as possible.

After a while my legs go numb, and I'm not sure what to do, when at last he starts moving forward. I walk slowly behind him from a distance of about ten yards, still crouching. His ears point backward, in my direction, alert for the slightest mistake. The dry leaves on the ground rustle under my weight and make him start a few times. He sets off at a trot and then stops again, turns around, and waits for me. I find that thrilling. I'm having a unique moment with a wild animal that is trying, in its own way, to tame me. I stand upright and imagine the effort he must be making to resist his instinctive fear of humans rather than racing off at the sight of this five-foot-seven mass standing in front of him. Suddenly the bark of another roe deer can be heard in the distance. Daguet reacts immediately to that bark and runs off toward it at such incredible speed that I find myself all on my own like a fool in the middle of the oak wood.

Daguet. He was the very first roe deer who trusted me. He was the one who opened the doors of the forest to me. This patch of forest was a large part of Daguet's territory. A ring road now runs through it.

Sharing the lives of roe deer involves giving up a number of things. Generally speaking you have to forget all about the human codes of life in society, like saying "goodbye" when you leave. You also have to give up on certain conventions, like eating at a fixed time or sleeping at night. With Daguet I discover the complexity of the nighttime life of the forest and try to become as much a part of it as I can. But I'm already getting exhausted. I would like to have the whole night to recover, but I wake up far too often and struggle to get back to sleep. The hooting owls, the screeching foxes, and particularly the boar make a terrible racket. They squeak and scream and grunt and run in all directions. Last year's boarlets playfully come and touch me with the tip of their snouts before immediately running off again. But the worst enemy of sleep is the cold. Several times I suffer from hypothermia. And each time it's the same. I go to sleep, I start dreaming, and all of a sudden I wake up feeling numb, feeling as if I'm going to be sick. After a few weeks, the lack of sleep starts making me hallucinate. I hear voices, see silhouettes, sometimes I even feel as if I'm flying. I'm completely wiped out. My nerves are shot, my shoulders heavy, and my head feels like it weighs a ton. Even worse, my eyesight is blurred. And I start asking myself serious questions about how my adventure is going to end.

The problem is that I never rest. During the day I look for my food and build little shelters to protect myself from the weather, which takes an insane amount of time. The problem with a shelter is that it quickly fills up with insects, so you have to rebuild it every day. One morning I decide to start all over again. If I want to survive I have to adopt a different strategy, a more efficient way of living. It is spring, and I still have two seasons to adapt before winter arrives, or else the expedition will stop right there. There must be something I've been missing, or something I've been doing wrong.

I find out the answers by observing Daguet. Roe deer rest for short cycles both during the day and at night: one or two hours depending on the weather. I decide to base the rhythm of my life on that of my fellow adventurer. When he gets up it's to ingest an impressive quantity of vegetation, then lie down, chew the cud (having only one stomach, I meditate instead), and sleep again. The rest of his time is reserved for games, for survival, for reproduction, or for territorial marking, depending on the season. Finally, it's by observing my roe deer friends that I learn that sleeping at night isn't compulsory, as long as you rest from time to time. To do that I crouch down, preferably in a dry place, with my right hand on my left knee and my left hand on my right knee and my head between my arms. After a while my mouth fills with saliva and that wakes me up. As a result my body doesn't have time to slip into hypothermia. And to compensate, like Daguet, I sleep during the day for about two hours at a time. That gives me time to eat, and more importantly to build up some stores of wood all over the forest, because it's vital to be able to make a fire anywhere and at any time of night without having to look for wood. And that's how I eventually work out that night in the forest is more important than day. The advantage of the night—animals understand this—is that you are no longer visible, and hence less in danger. You can relax your vigilance and walk around freely.

In the early morning, the sensations that I feel when seeing the sun rise over the meadow, making rainbows in the mist and the still frost-covered weeds, while lying beside my delightful roe deer friend, are irreplaceable. A new man is being born within me, and that new man has chosen the path to freedom. Daguet welcomes me into his intimate world, and as I become a part of his way of life I discover a deer brother who will soon become my real family.

4

NEVER AGAIN WILL I question the turn that my life took the day I decided to live in the forest; I chose the only possible direction to take, impelled by the same force that led me toward the forest realm at a very young age. I didn't want to live out my adventure naked, like Robinson Crusoe knocking stones against each other to make fire in defiance of all modern technology. Nonetheless, this strange expedition requires a certain rigor, because my woodland friends become nervous very quickly. I have to keep their trust, and not yield too often to the temptation of going back to the human world to rest and breathe for a few days. My determination is constant, in spite of the cold, the whims of the weather, or the hunger that holds me in its grip. The lives of my little friends take precedence over mine, and their willingness to continue the adventure with me will depend on my own state of mind. So I keep the modern world out of the forest as much as possible, taking in only what is necessary. First, some changes of clothes to keep out the cold: two pairs of canvas pants and a pair of jeans, alpaca wool underpants, linen or hemp T-shirts, virgin wool sweaters, and two knit seaman's caps. I abandoned cotton a long time ago, since it seemed to be impossible to dry. I store my clothes in sealed bags in a backpack to keep them from rotting, buried in a strategic corner of the forest. For cooking, I use only a small aluminum frying pan and a pot for boiling water. I also have a survival knife for cutting, hollowing, carving, peeling, and pruning. I've got a solar charger for my camera batteries as well as a lighter and my ID card, which I keep in a round metal case with a little mirror under the lid. A mirror is very useful, particularly when it comes to diagnosing an awkwardly located insect bite on your foot or your back.

    I know I live in the age of the fleece jacket and everything made out of plastic, in a society that's addicted to overconsumption of everything at all times, religiously devoted to waste and uselessness, a system that destroys the values and honor of even the most decent human beings, based on an economy that is constantly on the brink of collapse. So obviously I find it reassuring to know what to eat in the forest; how to make a fire in winter, in rain or wind; how to build a shelter; and everything else I need to survive in the wild.

But you have to be careful: total autonomy is a goal that you only reach after a very long transition. It's not something you can improvise. The greatest difficulty lies in making it through the winter, a tricky season during which food is in short supply. That means you have to learn to stock up. You begin by collecting plants in the spring. To dry them, after several failures (attacks by insects, rot, and other undesirable fungi), I develop an almost infallible technique, using mesh shopping bags hung from a branch during the day to take advantage of the sun, and Ziplocs to avoid the damp at night. Nettle, mint, oregano, dead nettle, meadowsweet, yarrow, angelica... Of course you also need to serve a full apprenticeship if you want to be certain that you can tell edible plants from poisonous ones, and have an idea of the energy value of each. Nobody normally picks angelica, for example. And for good reason, because it is almost indistinguishable from hemlock, the plant from which the Athenians derived the official poison that they used in executions. Socrates can vouch for its deadliness. The same is true of wild garlic, a plant that is delicious and rich in minerals, but one that can be easily confused with meadow saffron. The problem with meadow saffron is that you can eat it and then go to sleep like a baby. The toxic effects only set in after a number of days, once the sly perennial has attacked your liver, which

Gourmet. Unlike red deer, which "browse" large quantities of low-value grass, roe deer are precise in their selection of food, in search of certain tannins that exist in plants and which are necessary for their health.

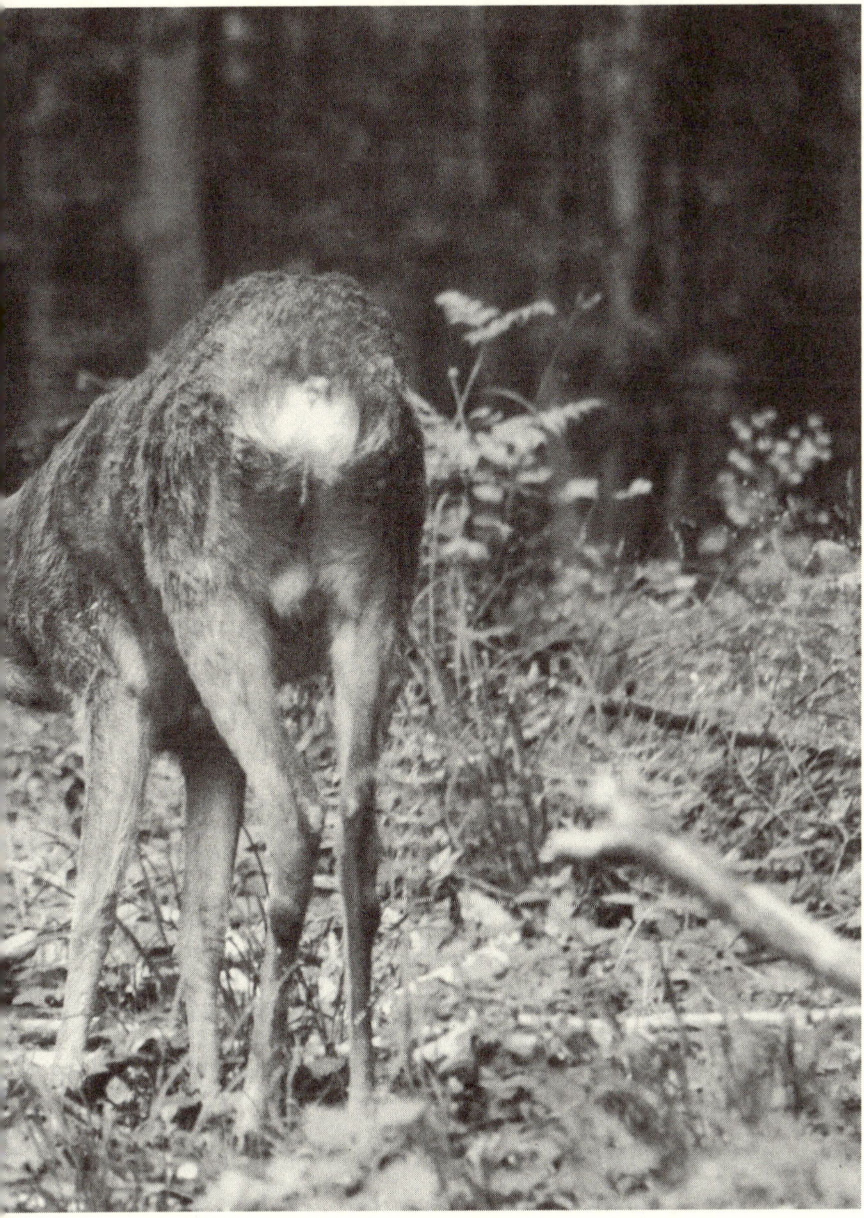

is bound in the end to fail. Care must be taken. The dock, for example, is a very flavorsome plant, and pleasant to eat, but in large quantities it causes very bad indigestion. Aside from minerals, you need to think about proteins. The arrival of autumn marks the start of the harvest of chestnuts, hazelnuts, acorns, and all the other shelled fruits necessary for a balanced diet without animal protein. Storing these foodstuffs is easier. Like a little squirrel, I keep them in a rocky cave or else in the hollow of a tree. Then there is the thorny issue of vitamins. The main source of these is in the fruits that are generally ripe between spring and summer. Except that keeping fruit for any length of time is unimaginable without a sterilization process that I don't have access to. The only solution consists of training my body to store vitamin C to get through the winter, just as animals do. The process may appear extreme. I would, however, test it out over many long years. In short, as long as you have rationed your food store and not had too many accidents along the way, and as long as you're reasonably physically resilient, you can expect to reach alimentary autonomy after a year or so.

In fact, my consumption of processed foods shrinks progressively as it is compensated for by foraging. I discover the willow herb with its little flowers and edible root, which used to be called "heal-all." You dig it out with a knife and eat it raw. There are also nettle roots, the little roots of the bramble, wild carrots. Frankly, at first it's repellent. There is nothing simple about moving from a gastronomic world in which everything is saturated with sugar and salt to a harsh and bitter diet. All of those plants and roots are good for your health, but you can say goodbye to the idea of delighting your taste buds. The red dead nettle, for example, a plant whose concentration of proteins and trace elements is essential for survival in the forest, well, it tastes like a spoonful of compost. Even more surprising, comfrey, another protein-rich plant, tastes faintly of fish. Luckily, it's not all bad. After a few months, when you've lost the sugary taste of cornflakes, certain natural foods like clover flowers or silver birch sap reveal that they have very pleasant sweet notes.

To get through the winter, you have to battle not only hunger but also cold. And in that struggle I prefer to use natural materials that have stood the test of time. Sheep's wool, first of all, to protect myself against both low temperatures and storms. Only wool allows you to stay warm even when you're wet. Moreover, I wear multiple layers of tops of different sizes and knits. The finest-mesh pullover with a dense weave is a good imitation of the layer of fur that roe deer have. A second medium-mesh pullover

Forest. In the morning, the warmth from the gentle rays of sunlight allows you to "dry" after a damp night. Then the dew settles on the vegetation lining the path; it makes the leaves tender and succulent.

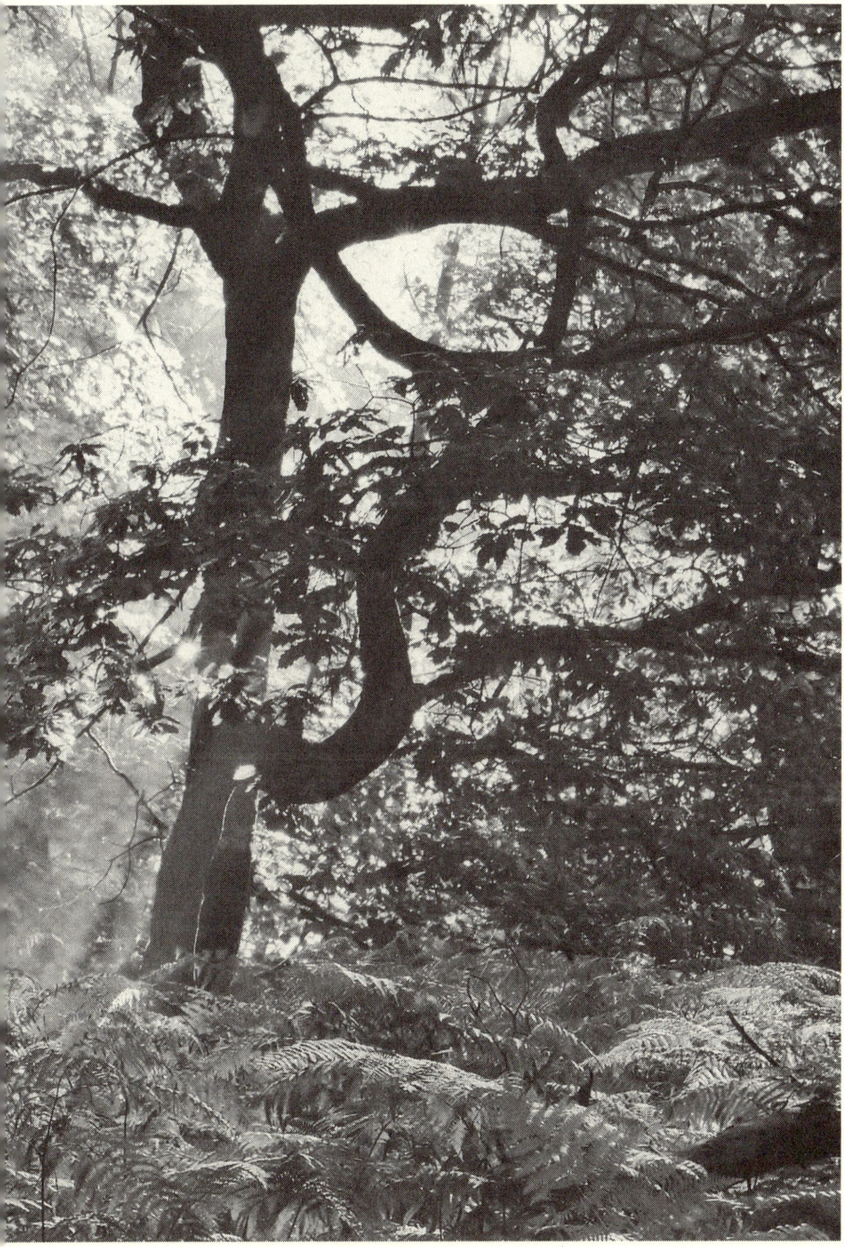

on top of the first retains the warmth but allows the air to circulate and keeps it from getting stale. The third pullover is made of coarse wool. It keeps out damp and frost. When it rains, this layer absorbs water without transmitting the moisture too quickly to the other layers. Then you just have to take that one off and wring it out to rid it of the accumulated water before putting it back on again; since the body is warmer than the temperature outside, the remaining moisture will evaporate naturally. I only wear a parka very rarely, because it keeps the perspiration inside, which produces an unpleasant sensation of penetrating cold and creates a higher risk of hypothermia. Under my pants, my underwear is made of sheep's wool—very effective—and so are my cap and gloves. My socks are made of alpaca wool. Only my shoes are made of synthetic material: Gore-Tex.

To live in harmony with roe deer, and to be able to walk behind them, I also cast off the swirling habit of thought, which acts like a parasite on my experiences. That's certainly the most difficult thing. But after a year I come to see the human world as ignorant in a way. Alone in the forest with the roe deer I don't think about anything; I don't define in words what I see, breathe, or hear. I am just happy to be here, with them, and to feel nature rather than to strip it bare. I speak very little in order to leave all the room to my intuition. I challenge myself to get to know Daguet by imitating him, observing him, and trying to understand him. He seems just as curious to find out about me, if not more so. Then I leave room for feelings. Taking this opportunity to "be" rather than to "do" or to "think." When I manage to do that I fall very quickly under the spell of these cheeky and playful little creatures, which have developed the skill and the habit of living at the expense of humans, often to the point of venturing into our orchards or vegetable gardens. In order to immortalize moments, I sometimes bring along, when possible, a camera with solar-rechargeable batteries. That means that I can slip a few into my pockets and change them regularly. Unfortunately they don't last long in the cold, and my little charger isn't much use in a forest where the light is faint.

Adaptation to the natural environment is a long process that demands patience. Your metabolism changes. Your mind changes. Your reflexes change. Everything changes, but slowly. I have to accept being malleable, accept that my body will adapt, and that takes time; I mustn't try to control it because that's not how things work. The forest is neither good nor bad—it just forces you to rethink yourself, constantly.

5

ROE DEER ARE ANIMALS with routines, and rather than spend my time looking for them in the undergrowth and pointlessly using up my energy, such a precious resource when you live outdoors, I sit down by the side of a path along which, as I know, a handsome deer that I call Arrow will take advantage of the peace of sunrise to nibble on some young shoots. The meadow is completely covered with frost, and the sun caresses my face, still frozen from the spring night. I feel its rays warming my body, which is almost pierced through with the ambient humidity now evaporating from my clothes. Territories take a long time to establish, and Arrow is on the alert. At regular intervals he lifts his head abruptly, turns around, and sniffs the air before returning to his main occupation of that moment: eating. A deer I call Six-Points, having sensed a potential rival on his territory, crosses the avenue in front of me, trots in my direction, pauses, thinks for a second, and then comes forward to pass me on my left. He goes on staring at me, neck elongated, eyes suspicious, as if to say: "Hang on—what are you doing here?" Then he continues on his way until he has reached his goal, which is none other than poor Arrow. I'm not yet exactly friends with Six-Points, but I've bumped into him on many occasions, even before setting off to live in the forest full-time. I know that he's territorial, and that he's a difficult character. I like to call him "Growler" because he barks at everything that moves. His companion, Star, a magnificent little doe with a slender body and mischievous eyes, breaks my heart every time I see her. She follows Six-Points from a few strides' distance and seems much less enthusiastic than her companion about the process of marking territory. I can tell by her slightly rounded flanks that she is going to have some little fawns this year, and I think about the names I might give them.

Six-Points recognizes Arrow, who is on the extreme edge of his territory. Like human beings, roe deer have a rather individualistic way of life and, during the phase of territorial marking, they like to quarrel a little. Unfortunately for the other bucks, territorial marking is an art at which Six-Points is a master. Once they are past the "band of brothers" stage, the youngest bucks often try to settle in a place that offers them both food and protection by virtue of their being the sole tenants. To accomplish this, the roebuck has to find a tract of woodland beyond his rivals' territory and set about defending it against intruders. Six-Points's and Arrow's territories are very close to each other, and overlap in places. Clearly our two neighbors will have to sort things out, and Six-Points is determined to get rid of this little upstart who's been nibbling away at his personal flower beds. Six-Points stands facing into the wind, regularly moistening his nostrils with his tongue. Arrow, in spite of his vigilance, doesn't suspect a thing and goes on eating. Suddenly, with a bark that splits the dawn, Six-Points charges at Arrow. With an incredible leap, Arrow starts running and barks as well. His run is chaotic, and in his panic he takes the wrong path, plunging farther into the territory of Six-Points, who stops breathlessly for a moment, probably outraged that such arrogance is even possible. He sets off again, barking at the top of his lungs, but in spite of his lack of experience Arrow isn't called Arrow for nothing. He leaps over a fallen tree trunk, veers to the right, hurtles through a little thicket, and disappears before the very eyes of Six-Points, who turns toward Star with a grunt of discontent, rubbing his head against all the surrounding vegetation to demonstrate even more clearly that this is Six-Points Land, and that no one can come in here without his permission.

Star still seems entirely uninterested in this activity. But her face doesn't tell the whole story, because I will learn later that does don't like other females visiting their territory either. Often bucks even create their territories in relation to the living areas defended by the does. A roebuck will always ensure that his territory crosses the area of activity of several does so that during the rutting season in July and August he has, how should I put it... options. When last year's fawns are still there, the doe will explain to them, sometimes clumsily, that it's time for them to live their lives on their own from now on. Still, many mothers offer their daughters territories close to their own.

Where possible, roe deer try to reconquer the same territory every year, but the logging business may have other ideas, chopping down whole areas of woodland and thus disturbing the cycle of territorial marking. (That's what happened to Courage, Chevy's half-brother, whose story I'll tell you a bit later.) In the spring, the roebuck leaves markers by scratching the soil with his front hoof, to impregnate the ground with the scent of his foot glands—what's known as "scraping." A few weeks later, to get rid of the velvet covering his antlers, he vigorously rubs them

Six-Points in the pines. Six-Points was the most territorial roe deer I came across. He barked so often that I called him "Growler."

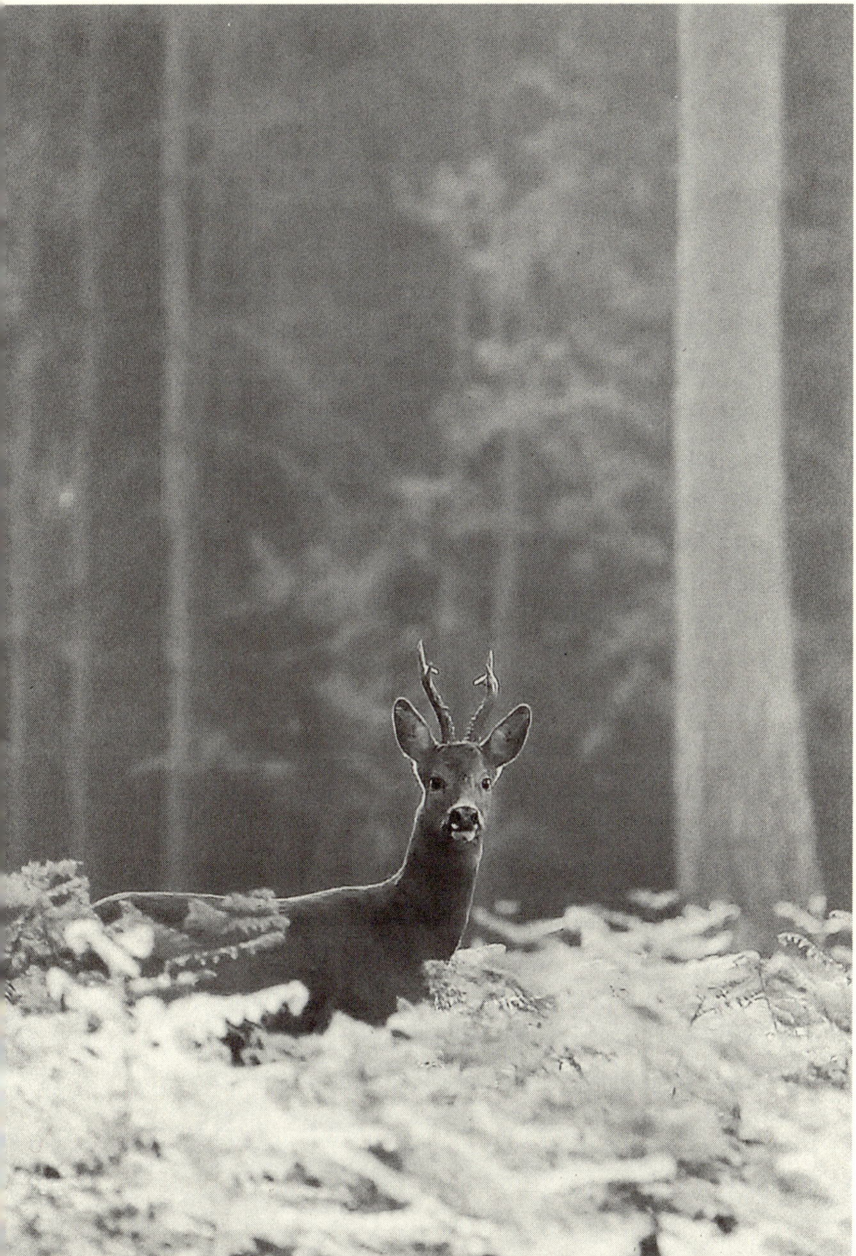

against the straight, supple twigs of young shrubs, then polishes and anoints them with a scented substance secreted by the gland on his forehead so that the other deer are aware of his presence. This marking technique is known as the "rub." Then, when pacing out his territory, sometimes with a surprising regularity, he rubs his muzzle against low vegetation to leave olfactory proof of his passage. The complete set of visual and olfactory markers allows the roe deer to demarcate his territory precisely.

The mist thickens and starts slightly covering the sun; I abandon Six-Points and Star to go in search of Daguet.

The Forêt de Bord is a forest of ten thousand acres located in the department of the Eure. Its horseshoe shape melds perfectly with the fourth bend in the Seine. If I travel from east to west, I pass through vegetation made up principally of pines and beech trees to reach a denser forest of oaks and wild cherries. I chose to base myself in the east, on a big overhanging rock called la Crutte, which dominates the whole of the Seine valley all the way to the Deux Amants. This place, beloved of hikers, takes its name from a Medieval poem that tells the tragic story of two lovers: Mathilde, daughter of the Baron de Canteloup, and the young Raoul de Bonnemare. To win Mathilde's hand, the baron obliges Raoul to climb a terribly steep rock face while carrying her in his arms. Arriving at the top, the boy dies of exhaustion. And out of sorrow Mathilde throws herself into the void. Consumed with remorse, Mathilde's father built a beautiful priory on the cursed summit, which still delights hikers today.

My "territory" covers about twelve hundred acres of forest. And I soon start finding my way around. There are the paths followed by the animals, which I know by heart, and then a few special tricks that I develop with experience. Olfactory points of reference, first of all, are essential, particularly at night. There are different smells if I walk toward the grain fields to the west, or if I walk toward the Seine. The oaks give off a scent of old wooden beams. Chestnuts, ferns, meadowsweet—all those smells help me find my bearings. If I approach a pond, for example, my nostrils catch the scent of rushes and mud. In addition my eyes have gotten used to the darkness. I don't yet have the eyesight of a cat, but my vision has already distinctly improved. And then there's touch. At night in the forest, you snooze, you go walking, and you eat. But how to spot the good plants? Plantain and dock, for example, look very similar, but I just have to touch the leaves to know which plant I'm dealing with: the ribs go in different directions. Obviously you don't acquire that level of knowledge after a weekend under the stars. It has taken me about two years to get there, and the forest still has plenty of secrets to reveal to me.

At this time of night, Daguet is bound to be in the spot where an ancient tree stands like the pillar of a cathedral in the middle of the young beeches. It's in a landscape bathed in light, where golden rays ripple in long cascades and strike the forest, that I meet up with my friend. He is standing upright; he spots me and goes on looking at me. He looks proud, my prince of the forest, in spite of his spring molt, which gives him a slightly seedy appearance.

In the spring, as the days lengthen, the roe deer lose their winter fur to make way for their magnificent summer pelt. Their livery, that elegant tawny fleece that demands to be shown off, contains all the shades of red that give the fur a silky, polished appearance, while the gorget—the paler area on the chest—the rump patch, and the underside take on a cream-colored tone. Conversely, the autumn molt passes almost unnoticed. Within a few days, the fine summer coat is replaced by the winter coat. The fur thickens, and the brush of the does, in the middle of the rump patch, lengthens and becomes more obvious. In the males, the hairs around the penis sheath also lengthen.

Daguet seems a little stressed and worried to me, as if something is keeping him from being himself.

I sit down on the ground, cross-legged, my left buttock on the heel of my right shoe, and with my right buttock in the air so that I can switch buttocks after half an hour and keep my legs from going numb. The precision might seem pointless, but it's very important: you should never sit directly on the ground, because if the soil is damp all the layers of clothing you wear will absorb water, and it will be difficult to get them dry during the day. This will be followed in the night by a very uncomfortable feeling of cold, which really does spoil the pleasure of being outdoors; more crucially, because of the ambient temperature, it could lead to chills or, worse, hypothermia.

Daguet stands and waits. Suddenly he looks straight ahead and I recognize the face of Fraidy, a fine buck at least six years old who has been here for a long time, since even before I decided to explore the forest. He's a very likable deer who, in spite of his age, his strong character, and his impressive build, is prone to run off if a pine cone falls to the ground a few feet away (much to the amusement of the squirrels). My young friend, facing Fraidy, lowers his head and presents his horny armor. He shakes his head to make more of an impression on his adversary and scrapes the ground with his front hoof. Fraidy pretends to ignore the "threat" represented by Daguet, and continues on his way as if the young buck didn't exist. In any case, he isn't interested in this patch of territory because he lives in the one opposite.

When two roe deer meet, they may sort out their differences by rubbing their heads against the trees and barking. At other times they resort to battle, head to head, but those battles are rare and the wounds are minor. After living with these animals for seven years, I never witnessed this kind of combat, which isn't to say that they don't fight. As with every species, some individuals are more aggressive than others. At first, the battles look more like a game. But things can sometimes get serious. Sometimes the game degenerates and an individual's aggressiveness can quickly mount due to a surge in testosterone. Territorial activity reaches a peak in May, and once the territorial perimeters have been established conflicts fade away, avoiding pointless demonstrations of strength.

In the background, behind Daguet, I notice another buck who is shyly coming forward. This is Brock, a very young and nervous buck who moves from territory to territory without being able to establish one for himself. He is among the less fortunate and more sensitive deer who, since they are unable to conquer a territory of their own, must seek refuge in little copses, thickets, and even hedges, which makes their lives uncomfortable, if not disastrous. These deer are often young animals, less than three years old, or else they are very old deer, over the age of ten. Some never manage to obtain a range, whatever their age. Wounded, sick, or too old, they can't compete and are liable to die, taking part in spite of themselves in the great circle of life and the self-regulation of the species. Other young deer each year, too weak or insufficiently combative to attract the attention of the older animals, are granted a second chance by their father, or by another older deer—a second year as "protégés." Later in the year, if something happens to their protector, they will temporarily assume his place and win the respect of their neighbors. They know the area, they have learned everything from their "master," and if necessary they can defend their territory against their adversaries, even those that are bigger and stronger than they are, at least until the following spring. As a general rule, all of the "homeless" deer, whether male or female, are effectively banished from the well-located forests and obliged to find precarious refuges, as well as poor-quality food, on open ground. Strangely, in the mountains and more particularly in the big coniferous forests of the Alps, I have observed that the roe deer in those situations do the opposite. They seek to live in the densest, darkest places, in the heart of the forests.

That's where they survive, ready to come out as soon as an area is reforested (naturally or artificially). They thus move from the edge of the forest to the interior, while the stronger males occupy the territories on the forest rim.

Brock, seeking friendship and comfort, comes slowly forward toward Daguet, who, seeing the weakness of his fellow, agrees to share a bit of territory with him. I have to leave my friend here and watch him move away with another new companion, because I'm concerned that this newcomer's jumpiness might break the trust that Daguet has granted me.

I realize that when my friend isn't with me, I'm quite lonely. So I decide to befriend some deer besides Daguet—Six-Points, Star, or Arrow—using the same technique; but it turns out it's not as easy as that. Just because Daguet trusts me and lets me walk behind him, it doesn't mean that the other deer who observe us will imitate him and trust me too. It's more complicated than that, because this "taming" work has to be repeated for each individual. Throughout the winter, the deer form groups that can include over a dozen individuals, and sometimes they regroup, like their red cousins, but that doesn't mean that they live in herds. Even in winter, when small groups form, if I have the trust of one deer I have to work with each of the other bucks and does separately in order to prove my good intentions, playing to the personality of each. And my roe deer do have different characters. I go back in search of Six-Points, but he has left with Star for the chalky slopes beyond my territory. The bushes that grow there are very dense, and it's hard for me to pass through them. So for now I abandon my attempt to go "farther" with them.

6

ONE EVENING I FIND DAGUET, and we stroll along together for a few hours. On this spring night, with the buds of the trees taking their time to open and produce succulent, sweet leaves, Daguet is hungry, and starts turning his nose up at the bramble leaves, which, even though they have the advantage of being there all year round, develop a bitter taste as the winter drags on. We walk toward the edge of the forest, to a typical Norman farmhouse with a magnificent vegetable garden. Carrots, potatoes, leeks, and beets grow here, near an orchard, under the envious gaze of the Normande cows that browse beneath the apple trees. Pretty flowers separate the furrows of vegetables, keeping harmful insects from destroying the crop. We cross a road, which isn't very busy at this time of night, but caution is still advised. Roe deer make big sacrifices to road traffic, since they constitute three-quarters of the ungulates struck at the edge of the road in France. In the spring, the increase in activity among the males is one of the causes of this. The bucks also scatter to find new territories and, in the autumn, roe deer are disturbed by human activities such as hunting or excursions into the forest. Daguet leaps a chest-high wall and then trots delightedly through the damp grass toward the vegetable garden. Here and there he plucks flowers covered with pretty pearls of dew. He lightly unearths the roots, he devours a beet and a few beans, then returns to the forest at dawn before the farmer wakes up. The owner of the farm, accompanied by his dog, can't miss noticing the results of this little nocturnal expedition into his garden. But it's not vandalism, it's hunger; you have to learn to share, that's life in the country, and at least it's not as bad as wild boar. I've only known Daguet for a few months, and the rogue's already leading me off the straight and narrow. I have to say that I'm feeling pretty ravenous too.

At this stage of the adventure, I'm still returning to civilization every now and again, two or three times a month, to regain my strength. The processed foods that I find in the family fridge are still just as appetizing as they were before, but I find them increasingly difficult to digest. Moving suddenly from my forest diet, made of bitter, harsh flavors, to the sweet-salt universe of industrialized food is a surprising experience. Fromage blanc—a kind of soft white cheese—has a startling whiff of fungus. Industrial bread has never been so hard to chew, and hard-boiled eggs revolt me. I grab a few cans to complement the emergency supply that I accumulated at the start of my adventure. I recharge my camera batteries. To my despair, my solar charger has proved to be completely useless in the low light of the forest. I also take a good hot shower. I sleep for a few hours in my childhood bed, and leave before daybreak. I avoid bumping into my parents, who disapprove of my new man-of-the-woods lifestyle and have no qualms about saying so. Do I wash my clothes? No. I don't want to bring the smells of the world of human beings into the forest. It would make my roe deer friends extremely nervous. Apart from that, I've noticed that in the forest, hygiene isn't a problem. I'll come back to that.

I'm still startled by the exactitude with which Daguet and the other deer choose their food. With his ultra-mobile lips and delicate, long tongue, Daguet easily snatches wood anemones, hyacinths, and several other plants that are supposed to be toxic to herbivores. He doesn't seem to be troubled by whatever substances they contain. It's because in his daily ration he seeks a precise quantity of tannins, which he needs for balanced nutrition. His salivary glands, more particularly the parotid glands, make proteins that can destroy the toxins contained in these tannins. He has learned this food science from the very first month of his life as a fawn. His mother took him to feeding grounds where, by imitation, he learned to taste these particular plants in very small quantities. Now, thanks to his selectiveness and his extremely keen sense of smell, he quickly recognizes the plants that give him what he needs and the ones that don't, without having to taste them. His liver, more highly developed in roe deer than in any other ruminant, inhibits the toxic substances secreted by plants to protect them from herbivores. However, he lacks a gallbladder, as a special process allows him to assimilate carbohydrates quickly, without them needing to be broken down by bile when they arrive in his stomach. Plants grown with fertilizer and replanted trees are more attractive to him than those grown naturally. The same is true of ornamental trees, new varieties of rosebush, ferns, or tobacco plants; in short, things that one is unlikely to come across in the forest. It's clear that my merry companions love sweet, salt, bitter tastes, and, as a rule, absolutely anything with a strong flavor. They are keen on woody and semiwoody plants with a high nutritional value. They can distinguish instantly between a plant bred in a greenhouse and another that has grown naturally. Brambles, ivy, heather, raspberries, haws, and all the young leaves of the

The scent of anemones. Highly poisonous to other herbivores, wood anemones are eaten in large quantities by roe deer in the spring. Because of their unique digestive systems, the toxin has no effect on them, aside from preventing certain illnesses.

springtime trees are of great nutritional interest to them, as long as the tree isn't too tall, because the small roe deer can't reach food that's too high up. Beyond four feet or so, the food will be eaten by the red deer, which are bigger than the roe. Tree trunks that were collar-cut the year before, and that have sprouted new shoots the following spring, are ideal. Much of the food that grows in the forest, such as brambles, oak leaves, and the leaves of the acacias, wild cherries, or wild plums, tastes bitter, harsh, or of nothing at all.

We spend whole days in the undergrowth, waiting patiently for sunset so that we can leave for the glade, the meadow, the field, or simply the edge of a path. You have to imagine the intense joy that we feel when we dare to venture out into open ground to eat plantain, wild docks, dandelions, and many other succulent plants, sweet or starchy, salty or spicy. With roe deer, you don't live *in* the forest but *of* the forest; it's a subtle but important difference. On the other hand, during the cold season, less food is available, and the bulk of their food comes from brambles. To adapt to the nutritional constraints of the forest, roe deer have had to change with evolution. Their first ancestors, which appeared 25 million years ago, had very highly developed canines in their upper jaws. With the gradual disappearance of large fruit trees due to the climate change at the time, roe deer evolved toward their current form during the Middle Pleistocene, 200,000 years ago, and the structure of their ankle bones suggests to paleontologists that they appeared long before red deer or fallow deer. Unlike other cervids, which need to consume a very large quantity of herbaceous vegetable food with a low nutritional value, roe deer have preferred to forage selectively, finding their food more easily on trees or bushes. That's why I call my companions gourmet gleaners, selecting their food for its high nutritional value and choosing the best they can find. If leaves, buds, berries, and the year's young shoots are part of their range of varied tastes, fruits are also highly appreciated. Without knowing it, my friends play an ecological role by dispersing certain seeds, like those of the sorb apple tree, which germinate in their digestive tracts. On the other hand, they eat grass only rarely, because it is not rich enough in nutrition for them to survive. As the species has evolved, the incisors in the upper jaw have been replaced by a little cushion of cartilage, a roll that bumps against the teeth of the lower jaw when the mouth is closed. They draw woody twigs deep into their mouths to chew them with their molars rather than sever them with their incisors as rodents do. A roe deer that lives in the forest, even an old one, will have incisors that are much less worn down than the roe deer of the plains, because there is more food of better quality in the forest, and the twigs tend to be more tender. A roe deer stomach, composed of the rumen, the reticulum, the omasum, and the abomasum, is so small (about five quarts) that Daguet must eat very regularly, ten to fifteen times a day. After each meal, when he is sated, he likes to chew the cud calmly under cover, or perhaps in the open if he feels safe. I can tell from his expression that this is a pure moment of relaxation for him. That isn't to say that he stops observing his surroundings, his ears detecting the slightest noise or his nostrils discerning the slightest scent. In order to digest, roe deer need calm, and intrusions (a herd of red deer, a group of boar, or some passing humans) have a direct influence on eating times. These untimely irruptions can put the deer in a state of extreme distress, and if this is repeated too often the deer become fearful, are startled by the slightest noise, and in some cases can find themselves in a real state of hysterics. Food must be taken regularly throughout the day, but also at night. With experience, deer learn to keep a low profile, and when they are bothered too frequently, for example at dawn or dusk, they can alter their daily routine to eat in the middle of the day so as not to be disturbed at an important moment.

Back in the woods, and after a good hour's rest, we pass through a recently planted part of the forest.

In a monotonous, rectilinear landscape we eat by gleaning the tender leaves of young plants. Oak, ash, and wild cherries, all important to forest management, seem to attract Daguet's special attention. It's budding time, and the buds themselves are a regular source of ecstasy. We're like kids in a candy store, faced with delicacies each tastier than the last. Sometimes he eats the end bud of the plant. Those terminal buds are no more appetizing than the lateral ones, but it's important to look ahead, because those young trees aren't going to be small all their lives, so they have to be preserved to ensure a perennial abundance of food. Roe deer are in a sense the gardeners of the forest, maintaining the vegetation. Their browsing does not lead to the death of the plants, but adapts the growth of the tree, which sometimes assumes a bushy shape with multiple bifurcations. For foresters, these trees have no value; they are economically "dead." But nature works differently, with each individual responding to stimuli and defending themselves as they can. Life always finds a way and you need to trust in it. The Corsican pines and spruces planted in the middle of the forest are of no interest to Daguet, at least not from a nutritional point of view. But they may be of use to us this winter in case of scarcity.

We gradually leave this patch of woodland and climb a little path lined with random growths of buckthorn and birches. After eating a good quantity of vegetation, we look for a place to chew the cud in peace. We are heading toward the territory of Harry, a very powerful roe deer. Like Six-Points, Harry becomes quite scary during the territorial marking period, and I'm a bit worried about my happy-go-lucky friend. I walk behind Daguet and the more I observe his gait, the more he seems to be going askew. He seems to be in a strange state, and looks a little agitated. Because he's making a lot of noise, grunting for no reason, even going so far as barking on Harry's territory, Harry's not going to be a long time in replying. I spot the outline of that impressive deer; he's big and muscular, with huge antlers. Daguet advances confidently, at a nonchalant pace, toward the strongest and most territorial roe deer in the area. He trips along gaily, and Harry looks intrigued. All of a sudden he barks very loudly in the direction of Daguet, who freezes for a moment and turns toward Harry with an idiotic expression, as if to say, "Have you lost your mind? You scared me there!" Harry charges furiously toward Daguet, who goes on acting strangely. He stops a few inches away from him. Disturbed and surprised, Harry recoils slightly and then charges again. Daguet takes a blow to the side, falls, and whines a little, but then gets up again as if nothing had happened. Caught off guard, the bigger, stronger deer is alarmed, moves away a little, and barks at the top of his voice. Daguet approaches me and hides just behind me. I'm not too happy about this, because if Harry charges again I don't want to be caught between the two of them. But in the end Harry leaves, barking, very disgruntled. He's bound to come back this evening to mark his territory again.

We set off for Daguet's home range again. Looking slightly distraught, he comes and stands against a tree on the edge of a clearing. He leans against the trunk and looks at me. In fact he has no choice: he has to wait for it to pass. Because, quite simply, Daguet is drunk! In the autumn, the plants concentrate large quantities of alkaloids, saponins, and polyphenols in their cells, as well as other substances that will enable them to protect their buds and resist the big winter frosts. They manufacture a kind of antifreeze, which, when ingested by roe deer, has the same effect as strong alcohol, hence the occasional amusing scenes of animals tottering down forest avenues. A few years ago, in the Eure, a roe deer living near a little town took up residence under a kitchen table in a hotel restaurant and refused to leave; it took ages to dislodge it. Since the quantity of these substances varies from one plant to another, it doesn't affect all roe deer, only the greediest ones.

7

IN THE EARLY MORNING I'm filled with an inexplicable sense of joy. Daguet is becoming more familiar with me, and even comes over to my feet to sniff the scent of my shoes. He observes my behavior, always remaining very vigilant. I notice that when he approaches he mostly looks at my hands, probably out of fear that they might grab him. But I press my arms against my body and present the palms of my hands so that he can smell them. That reassures him, and he can see that I'm not going to move. I don't even try and stroke him, and God knows it's tempting. We walk to the pine grove where Six-Points is master. I don't know if it's a provocation, but Daguet seems sure that he wants to go in there. It's very early, and still dark. The day is struggling to break through the ambient gloom when some little noises like whispers can be heard. Daguet, with his extraordinary sense of hearing, picks them up immediately and sets off, probably to discover where they're coming from. We move cautiously forward.

He stops regularly, sniffs the surrounding air, and seems intrigued. It isn't fear but curiosity. Suddenly a few yards away, I can just make out Star in the darkness. She's alone and lying down, and Six-Points isn't beside her. When she notices Daguet she sniffs in our direction, rises breathlessly to her feet, and struggles toward us, barking faintly. Daguet retreats with a series of little hops. I'm ready to follow him but I'm worried for Star, who doesn't seem to me to be in the best of shape. I let my friend leave so that I can stay and observe Star for a moment.

It's a very cold morning for June. Star has seen me and recognized my scent. Over the last few weeks I've gained some trust from Six-Points, but even more from Star, who seems intrigued by my presence. She's an experienced doe and, even though we haven't been through anything exceptional together, her curiosity goes beyond our encounters. I have deep respect for this intelligent little deer. She doesn't say anything to me, lies down again about ten yards away, and then stares at me for a few long minutes before resting her head to sleep for a while. At least that's what I think. I don't move, and that's the right thing to do, because a few moments later I see her gently opening her eyes, still staring in my direction. It was a trick to see if I would approach her, thinking she was asleep. When you play with roe deer, you must never imagine you're smarter than they are; you're bound to be wrong.

A few moments later, visibly weakened, she struggles to her feet, her whole body trembling, as if she's about to collapse like a house of cards. She takes a step forward and then stops. I pray with all my heart that there isn't something seriously wrong with her. I see a thin trickle of fluid emerging from her hindquarters. She utters some little groans and I see that she's making an incredible effort to contain her pain. I take a few steps to the side to gain a better view of her pale rump, when I realize that the greatest gift that life can give us is taking place in front of my eyes. She's giving birth! She's in pain not because she's ill, but because she's having contractions, and I'm witnessing the birth of some little fawns that are having trouble coming out. That must be why Six-Points isn't around. As a rule, female roe deer don't like males to be roaming around the territory when a pregnancy comes to term. Two trembling hooves that have pierced the amniotic sac dangle stiffly into the void. I'm so close to Star that I'm almost tempted to go and help her deliver them. But reason tells me not to go, and I allow her that moment of intimacy. I can almost feel her pain, and with each little groan that she utters I am aware of the immense effort the brave doe is making. First contraction, nothing. Second contraction, still nothing. She pushes again and the effort is intense. Minutes pass—another contraction, then another, when all of a sudden out comes the new fawn, falling to the ground with a noise proportionate to its weight: *bam*! There he is—welcome to the earth, little one!

    Deep within me I feel a joy as immense as if I had helped to bring this fawn into the world. I also feel pride for Star, who, alone with her pain, made it through this trial. I wait for a second fawn, but there isn't going to be anything more. There's only one; he's a little male, and I call him Chevy. Star takes a few moments to recover from her emotions, then turns to her fawn. Chevy's whole body is quivering. She licks him to dry him, but also to establish the bond that will unite them in the future. She finishes eating the placenta that is still stuck to him in places and which, if it happened to be discovered by a fox or another predator, could endanger both the newborn, who can't yet walk, and the mother, left very much weakened by this little tot—now ruffled by the rough licks of her tongue. After an hour, Chevy tries to stand up all by himself. The first attempt fails. The second go works, but he falls after a few seconds, then immediately gets up again and takes three steps before stumbling into the weeds. Exhausted by the effort of being born, the fawn collapses, huddled against his loving mother.

A little while later, Chevy gets up again, more confidently this time, makes his way toward one of the four teats, and starts pulling ravenously on it. His mother will nurse him for five months. Lying beside him, she also seems to want to go to sleep. She licks him all over one last time, runs her tongue affectionately over his muzzle, and then turns her head toward me. Clearly surprised, she stares at me for a long time. With all her efforts, she must have forgotten that I was there. I turn around very slowly and then, as delicately as I can, I go back to see Daguet, my heart light and my head still spinning from all the emotion. She watches me go. I know that Chevy will spend his first few weeks hidden in the undergrowth and then, once he's a little stronger, he will walk behind his mother. In the meantime, I have to leave him alone, because even though Star knows me well I don't know how she would react if my scent mixed with that of her little one. So I prefer not to take any risks, and to leave him in peace. I've already got Daguet, Arrow, and a few other acquaintances for company, and then, with Six-Points, I may also have the privilege of bumping into Chevy trotting behind his mother.

For a female roe deer, giving birth isn't really much fun. Births are staggered and in some cases several hours can pass between the arrival of the first fawn and that of the second. The intense efforts involved with giving birth weaken the mother, and if one of the young is in an unusual position she may not survive. That means three deaths all at once, because if the little fawns are not suckled by their mother they will die only a few hours later. Sadly such deaths occur frequently, because does are naturally predisposed to give birth to their young in different places. In that case the newborn may potentially fall victim to a roaming predator, or even die of cold if its mother does not come back very soon. The first six months are crucial for the fawns' survival. The mortality rate is higher during their first month of life, regardless of sex, and their deaths usually go unnoticed by humans. Does younger than two years old are not yet physically mature enough to have young. Weighing less than forty-five pounds, they very rarely come into heat, and so they reproduce little or not at all. Star has only one fawn likely because she is young and light, appearing to weigh under fifty pounds. Observing my different doe friends, I note that the number of fawns that a doe can carry is strongly linked to her weight. The lighter she is, the fewer the number of offspring she will have. I happen to know that a doe in a neighboring forest where food is abundant has had triplets, but her weight must be over sixty pounds. This phenomenon has to do with the self-regulation of the species in the absence of predators. The fluctuation of births is intrinsically linked to the availability of food supplies at the time of conception. Some females, like Magnolia, whom you will meet a bit later, do not have a very highly developed maternal instinct, and many of them lose their whole litter, while others, who are more devoted and have a dominant personality, manage to conquer a high-quality home range with a rich supply of food for themselves and their offspring. That leads to very rich milk for their sturdy young fawns. Since deer do not change, character traits persist, and each year, the same scene tends to repeat itself, which can shape the continuation of an entire line.

As with all other fawns, Chevy's first days on Earth are lived out in the undergrowth, where the doe knows that it is safe, and where it can develop its strength. It's also that first week that determines the maximum physical growth of fawns. Once past that critical phase, it will be able to follow its mother almost everywhere with great agility. And to defend her young, like most other does, Star demonstrates unflagging devotion. In fact, mothers have no hesitation in flicking vipers away, chasing off foxes, and even standing as an obstacle in a hunter's line of fire. In spite of this, fawns have a high rate of death due to natural predators, particularly in early summer, but also during the winter when the layer of snow hinders the movement of the young fawns when moving from place to place, making them more vulnerable than adults. Meanwhile, during that first week, when she sets off in search of food, Star puts Chevy in safety, "ordering" him with a little cry to lie there until she gets back. She can leave him alone for several hours. Luckily, Chevy's coat acts as an effective camouflage, a pattern of white patches on a brownish background. These markings will fade very quickly over the course of July, perhaps even from the first weeks after his birth. In August the initial pattern of patches will only be very faintly visible, making way by the end of September to a thick winter coat similar in every respect to that of the adults. His throat will also be decorated by a white patch known as a gorget.

My day continues beside Daguet, but I can't help thinking about that little fawn, so small and so frail, now living not far from me. The images keep running through my head. I'm sorry not to have had my camera with me at that moment, because I would have loved to immortalize those fine moments (this is the only time that I will ever witness a birth). Later I'll realize that I don't even have a photograph of Star from those days. My mind is so far away that I end up losing sight of Daguet, who was walking ahead of me and clearly didn't want to wait. A storm is rising. I don't think it's going to be a violent one, but I'd still like to get back under the pines that give shelter from the wind. I sit down under the trees. An hour later I spot Six-Points, who doesn't yet know that he's a father. I try to follow him and he joins in with the game to a certain extent, but it's always complicated with Six-Points. Even later, when we've spent years living close to each other, even though he is well aware that I wish him no harm, and even though he happily accepts my presence when I walk behind him, I still have a sense that his head has somehow understood but his body remains reticent. That gives him a strange gait—his front hooves are quite relaxed, in harmony with his head, while his stiff hindquarters seem to want to go faster and faster, as if trying to overtake the rest of his body. I put myself at a greater distance so as not to alarm him. In this kind of exercise you mustn't impose, just suggest. It's his choice. I talk to him, I tell him how much I'd like to pet him and share a moment of his life. I think the tone of my voice reassures him and helps him accept me. I let him finish marking his territory, then I move farther away and disappear.

For now I'm going to settle in for the night before it rains, prepare my "mattress" by breaking off some fir tree branches, and rest for a moment. That'll do me good after such an emotional day. It's summer, and I want to make the most of it.

8

IT'S WELL INTO SUMMER, and I'm honored by Daguet's growing trust in me. It's warm, the sky is deep blue, and the sun is blazing. The mornings are still damp, and to warm himself up a little Daguet decides to go and lie down in the tall weeds of what I call "the fox's clearing." It was here, at the age of fourteen, that I photographed the first doe of my life. A few weeks later I thought I might be able to see it again. But a fine black fox had taken up residence in a burrow not far away, and had probably put the doe off the idea of going for a stroll. It was also the end of spring, and if she was expecting young, she certainly wouldn't have wanted to risk venturing into this area. Daguet nibbles some grass, and while he does that I "borrow" some melons that the hunters have left at the foot of the young apple trees whose trunks are protected by wooden pickets and chicken wire. These "treats" aren't meant for me, but I'm sure the boar won't be angry at me for pilfering their offerings, and then I also figure that they're quite fat enough already.

My belly full of fruit, I lie down in the clearing. Daguet joins me and the strangest thing happens: he comes and presses himself against me, looking at me with a sated and trusting air. I feel his warm body against my leg. He curls up with his head on my knee and rests. I have an overwhelming desire to put my hand on his fur to stroke him, but I'm worried that he might not appreciate that, and that it would put him off getting close to me. A moment later he lifts his head slightly, yawns, looking at me, and then lowers it again and rests it against my thigh, near my hand. I take advantage of this to stroke his cheek a little with my thumb. He seems to like that. I withdraw my hand gently to put it on his back. I stroke him for a long time, observing his reactions. He relaxes and closes his eyes. Sometimes his muscles tremble slightly, but then you must remember that this is an animal who has no idea what a human caress is, so it's a completely normal reaction. I'm trembling a little too, because it's a first for me as well. The muscular tension eases as I stroke him and eventually he falls peacefully asleep. From time to time he groans a little, grunts, or twitches his hooves slightly. He is clearly dreaming. I know he's sleeping deeply, because I feel the weight of his body getting increasingly heavy against me. The roe deer is not an animal known for its liking of close contact. Nonetheless, when two individuals are fond of each other, it is not unknown for them to groom each other. They can repeat these demonstrations of affection at any time of the year, but especially during the mating season, when such gestures become more frequent since they are part of the courtship ritual. At any rate, my friend seems to enjoy my caresses, and I am delighted to provide them.

So we take advantage of this peaceful morning; the bees spin above our heads and gather pollen from the few flowers scattered around the meadow. Not a sound disturbs the fullness of the moment. I use the time to study the horizon for a while, because deep in the forest you can never see farther than twenty or thirty yards away. It feels good to "breathe." Suddenly, in the distance, I spot some walkers. They are walking in our direction, but I don't pay them any particular attention. They're on a hiking path, and we are hidden by the tall grass. A few moments later I become aware that they're cutting across the meadow where we are sitting, heading straight toward us while Daguet is still peacefully asleep. They are level with us now. A man and a woman in their fifties, walking at a steady pace, without a word, without a sound, stick in hand. Daguet is still

Daguet asleep. Though they appear nervous, roe deer are in fact peaceful animals that take time to enjoy life. One day I was sitting by a bramble bush along a path popular with walkers. Suddenly I heard a snore in the depths of the thicket. It was Daguet: he was sound asleep, untroubled by the people passing.

asleep. I am preparing to get abruptly to my feet, as soon as Daguet becomes aware of the suspicious scent or opens an eyelid at the sound of the people passing, but nothing happens, absolutely nothing. He's out for the count. The two walkers say hello as they pass, and I reply. They smile and then continue on their way. I can't believe it! On my lap I have a roe deer that I'm stroking—Daguet, who doesn't move so much as a hair, he feels so much at ease against me—and the walkers must have thought it was my dog. I'm blown away.

A quarter of an hour later, my sleeping beauty wakes like a flower. He studies the landscape for a moment, runs a tongue over his muzzle, sniffs the air, and gets to his feet. He stretches his whole body, snorts, and then licks his fur as if nothing had happened, and apparently for him nothing had. I imagine that he feels he can trust me, and that he's been able to relax a little, sleep without worrying about anything, set aside his vigilance by trusting a friend, and abandon for a few moments the heavy burden of staying alive.

It's an honor for me, my friend, to keep watch over you.

9

DAGUET AND I LEAVE the clearing to go deeper into the forest. While he eats some blackberries on the edge of the wood, I move away as discreetly as possible to keep him from following me, and edge in the direction of Six-Points's territory. To avoid any misunderstanding, I always try to make sure that Daguet and Six-Points don't bump into each other. At a bend in a path I come across Star, who is followed by Chevy, and it occurs to me that this would be a good opportunity to let this little fawn get to know me. Chevy was born three months ago; he's now been weaned and he will go on learning from his mother until the end of the winter. He's in great shape and that reassures me, because living in a hostile environment calls for a certain sturdiness. Many fawns don't make it through the first year. Anything can happen in the forest. Internal parasites, such as lungworm or liver fluke, and external parasites, such as sucking lice, nasal bot flies, deer keds, and, rarely, warble fly, or even just a very damp period of cold weather, can weaken the state of the young deer's health and sometimes lead to death. Of course, the discovery of these lifeless little bodies always fills me with sadness. That said, however, mortality has to be seen as a natural regulation of the species that preserves the balance of the woodland, if we allow nature to fulfill its work without ever intervening.

With Chevy, the few times that our paths have crossed, I never attempted to approach him. It's too dangerous for him, because he could still mistake my scent for his mother's, and she would probably abandon him. But now that he's getting older I think that befriending Chevy is going to be a lot of fun. His mother trusts me, his father knows me very well, and since he's a young animal with no preformed ideas about the world, he won't mind me approaching him. What wishful thinking! I move toward Star, who doesn't make a sound. Chevy is lying quite nearby, calm and serene. He observes everything, he's intrigued by everything, but just for fun, because he still—or at least this is what I imagine—takes all his cues from his mother. I approach very gently and sit down a few arm's lengths in front of him. He stares at me, ears pricked and pointed in my direction, furtively glancing at his mother to observe her reactions, but she still doesn't make a sound;

Portrait of Chevy. Roe deer are unguligrades: they walk on their nails, which are as sharp as a razor. Once Chevy, to give me a cuddle, climbed onto my shoes to reach my face. His hoof went right through my shoe and injured my foot.

she doesn't even look at us. With his big, hypersensitive ears turning independently in all directions, he reacts to the slightest suspicious or unfamiliar sound, immediately vigilant. With time he will learn to tell the difference between familiar and dangerous sounds. The noises of a tractor, for example, or a chain saw wailing as it cuts down trees, will be classed as "innocent," because they are part of his daily sound environment, while the crack of a twig when everything is silent will inevitably put him on maximum alert.

Chevy sniffs the air and seems to be startled, because he gets up quickly to join his mother. The hairs on his pale rump patch bristle with his growing alarm. In fact, the contraction of the subcutaneous muscles around the hairs on his rear form an alarm signal of immaculate whiteness, and allow a family to stay safe as a group; a pursuing predator will see a pretty white patch plunging into the forest until the deer turns off to the side and… the white patch is gone! An excellent diversion. At the same time the scent glands send pheromones into the air to warn the other deer moving around nearby of an imminent danger. I walk quite a long ways behind him, because he trots swiftly and goes skipping off in all directions. Every now and again Star turns to see where the fuss is coming from, looks at us, and then sets off again. Chevy presses against his mother's leg as if he is in mortal danger, whines faintly, and glances regularly at her as if to say: "Don't you see that big, strange thing that's been following us since a few moments ago?" Even if Star doesn't seem to pay much attention to his concerns (she knows I'm not dangerous), Chevy gives off such anxiety that he communicates some of it to his mother, who is now becoming a bit nervous. I notice that Chevy has an instinctive fear of humans and other animals, like boar and squirrels. Nothing will make him change his mind, not even his mother—or perhaps it will take some time before he works out that I'm harmless.

A moment later, when I'm walking alongside Star and not planning to go anywhere near Chevy (I'd lost sight of him, in fact), he sets off running at the speed of a bullet. Without thinking, Star runs after him, thinking perhaps that he's fleeing some kind of threat. I don't stop to think either and go after her. When we get close to Chevy, he runs off again at top speed. Star follows him again and I do the same. It's completely baffling. There's nothing, absolutely no danger of any kind. Everything is calm and peaceful. The little game resumes a few times in a row, and Star becomes anxious. The more we run, the more stressed Chevy becomes, the greater his mother's anxiety, and we have all become palpably nervous. Then I let him run some distance away in order to ease the tension. He stops, waits for his mother, and calms down. I let them both leave without pressing matters, because I don't want to exhaust him for no good reason or create a mental barrier that would later prevent him from living with me. I realize that fawns only put all their trust in their mothers for the first few weeks, and that their individualism and their free will increase as they grow. Now that he's a little older, Chevy isn't content with imitating his mother; he learns to listen and observe, guided by his own instinct. He sees that his mother trusts me, but he can't understand it for now, and it frightens him. He hasn't yet learned to decipher the different postures that I can adopt in front of him, because unlike his elders he has no experience of other humans, whether runners, walkers, hunters, or woodsmen, to act as points of comparison. His survival instinct takes the upper hand and, overcome with fear, he takes flight. So I abandon the idea of making friends with him for now, because he is too "wild." With time, perhaps he will accept me, as his father and mother already do. We'll see!

10

AUTUMN HAS SETTLED over the forest and adorned the leaves of the trees with a thousand colors, from pale yellow to dark red. When this season arrives, I always like to remember the old Native American legend of the Wyandotte, who give the deer the divine name of Dehenyanteh, which means "he for whom the rainbow has made a path of colors."

Envious of the Little Turtle, the guardian of the sky, the Deer wanted to leave the Great Island and, more than anything, wanted to have access to the big blue sky. To fulfill his ambition, he consulted the Thunder God, who advised him to climb into the sky using a rainbow. Then the Deer waited for the spring and, after the first rain sent by the Thunder God, he took the path traced by the rainbow. He quickly found himself in the sky, where he was free to run as he wished. At the same time, having met in council, the animals looked for the Deer. The Wolf searched the woods, while the Hawk studied the sky. It was then that they all saw the Deer gamboling with great agility. The animals decided to go to the sky via the bridge of all the colors. The Bear reproached the Deer for thinking only of himself and forgetting all the other animals on the Great Island. Defying his rebukes, the Deer provoked the Bear into a duel. The battle commenced straightaway. Swift as lightning, the Deer stabbed the Bear with his pointed antlers. The Bear was mortally injured and the blood flowed abundantly from his wounds. The blood flowed all the way to the Great Island, where the leaves of the trees were colored by the animal's blood. Since then, each year, when autumn returns, nature commemorates the battle of the Deer and the Bear, and the leaves of the trees turn red.

According to tradition, the beauties of autumn, when nature dies, are a source of nostalgia for the souls of the departed remembering their old terrestrial home. Even the gods return to live in the Great Island, because autumn is a time for the spirit. During this season the Pleiades, the most beautiful of the stars, leave their celestial home to come and live in the sky of the Great Island.

In the meantime, the equinox has passed, and as the season advances the nights grow longer until the winter solstice comes. In the cool morning I nibble on chestnuts that I grilled over a wood fire the previous evening. I have enough of them to eat when I want to, as snacks. You can't leave them too long, however, because there's a risk of them rotting, given the weeklong damp. I dried the last ones on a bed of embers that I'm going to go on feeding for several days. After that I'll seal them in an airtight bag to keep them for later.

Getting through the winter requires rigor. The most important thing is to come up with solutions to fight against the cold at any time of day or night, anywhere in the forest. I know only one way of doing that: keep little supplies of deadwood, made up of twigs, fir branches, tree bark, and pine cones, and store them around the place. As for food, I now have a good knowledge of the area. Even in the depths of winter you can find enough to live on: roots, tubers, wild carrots. To ensure a supply of protein I make stores of hazelnuts.

Sadly, even though I hope I'll be able to do without it one day, I still feel the need to stay in contact with the world of humans. Every now and again I go home, or rather to my parents' house, to stock up on calories and get warm again. But for several

Mist. Winter isn't the most difficult season. The body gets used to the cold. On the other hand the frequent rain in spring and autumn forced me to pay particular attention to my clothes. When they were wet, I wrung them out and then blew air into them so that the fibers would swell and become watertight again.

months now I've had a strange sensation when putting my feet on concrete floors. They're hard, cold, and perfectly flat. I'm not used to them anymore. I eat a bowl of fromage blanc with muesli and a lot of sugar. While I'm recharging my camera batteries, I'm assailed by smells: the smell of the fridge, the smell of bleach, of heating, of carpet, of clothes, clean or dirty, even the smell of the people who live in the house. Before setting off again I always slip a few bags of pasta into my bag, along with some cans of tuna and sardines. Last of all, I sometimes go to a store to buy the two items that are indispensable for my survival: resealable bags for storing food and matches to make fire.

I like to go walking at dawn and enjoy the sunrise when I can see it. But there's a frost this morning, and the clouds are piling up at the bottom of the valley. From the field where I'm standing, I can just make out the bell tower of the church in the village below. The grass is cool and the passing cows seem to enjoy this food, with its unvarying flavor. I lean against a barbed wire fence, on which some magnificent garden spiders have spun webs that are now pearled with dew. I feel good here, watching the world wake up. Young rabbits chase one another and then race against their mother. Three or four of them try to tip her over to get at the teats from which she probably stopped feeding them ages ago. A badger comes up the pebbly path, grunting and panting. I'm reassured to see him like this, because by nature badgers are gruff and apparently dissatisfied, but more so because the road at the bottom of the valley is particularly dangerous for them, and I always hope they'll make it back alive from their little outing. It's a shame to get flattened after a good night's hunting by a driver in a hurry to get to work. The chaffinches aren't really singing this morning; they're whistling the song of the coming rain. It may be the mood I'm in, but I find it oddly melancholy.

The fog thickens, and it's hard to make out the edge of the forest. I spot a black fox, a vixen that I know very well, having encountered her several times with Daguet. I call her Terylle; she's magnificent. Her chest is a sumptuous white that contrasts with her little grayish paws. Her brush, always aligned with her body, is majestically voluptuous. She's really a beautiful fox. She walks along the fence that lines the forest, stops for a moment, and seems to think. I don't move, because I don't want her to see me. I prefer to observe her in her natural state. She sniffs the air in all directions, lowers her head, and starts crossing the field, then freezes and looks at the cows. Given her size, they have nothing to fear, and neither do their calves. She approaches a first cow, which tries to give her a little kick with a hind hoof as she passes. Then she makes her way toward the next. I'm intrigued by her little game. One cow, lying down and drowsing, doesn't seem to pay any attention to Terylle, who approaches gently. She doesn't chase the fox away, as her attitude isn't threatening. Terylle sits down in front of the cow and observes it. The cow gives the fox a slightly stupid look and goes on chewing the cud with its eyes half-closed. Terylle takes a little step forward, then another, and quickly recoils. She starts again. One small step, then another, and a jump backward. She repeats this little game several times. Each time she carefully studies the reactions of the cow, which still isn't moving an inch. Then she approaches the swollen teats and starts licking the milk that is seeping from them, with no reaction from the cow. Terylle stops for a moment and darts a fearful look at the cow, still without the slightest reaction.

I'm dumbfounded. A vixen has just shown me what I should have thought of a long time ago: drinking milk! Sated, Terylle strides off into the mist. I slip in turn among the herd to try and find a cow that won't mind me approaching her, without getting kicked on the nose. I see one that might be agreeable. I squat down in front of her and start milking. Her udder is full to the brim, and the veins feeding it are enormous. It occurs to me that I'm going to bring her some relief. It will do us both good. What joy to feel the lukewarm milk flowing down my throat! It's fat and thick and naturally sweet, and I'm delighted by this moment spent in the company of the cows.

Drinking is one of the most intense pleasures when you live in a forest, because drinking water is never available in large quantities. The hardest thing isn't finding it, because the plants that I eat in the morning and the evening are covered with dew, and their leaves largely consist of water. I'm drinking and eating at the same time, you might say. And that's the reason roe deer can drink up to three quarts of water per day without going to a water source. But our consumer society has accustomed us to drinking a certain quantity of liquid by the glass or the bottle. So when you no longer have access to that sensation of having drunk, the feeling of dehydration can become distressing. To slake my thirst, there are two solutions: the first, after rain, is to use a sock to filter the water that has accumulated in a witch's well—those little natural cavities formed in trees when they split into two or three trunks, which are often found in beech woods. Once it's been filtered, I just have to put it in my billy can and boil it on a little wood fire. The second solution is to go one and a half miles west of my territory. There's a little reservoir station there, called Wolf Valley, not very secure, with an outside tap, mostly used by inspectors to check the water's potability. It's unofficially free to use, behind a fence damaged by the woods and the weather. I just have to slip underneath to get to it and fill my two water bottles with cold water. Well, now I've discovered a third way of slaking my thirst. And it's with a bellyful of milk that I set off in search of Daguet, to continue this day that has begun so well.

By this stage of the story, you're probably wondering how I address issues of hygiene. Well, first of all, I have one considerable advantage: I barely grow a beard. Regular washing of my feet, armpits, and genitals is quite enough. But if I struggle to find things to drink, what trick do I use to wash myself? Well, right in the middle of the forest there's a remarkable tree called the Four Brothers. Four magnificent beeches, 130 feet high, which probably sprouted from a fallen tree, and which have grown perfectly symmetrically, like quadruplets, forming at their center a big cauldron that acts as a perfect collecting point for rainwater. That store of water is pretty much enough for me to wash in. And you're probably wondering what I look like? For the first few months, the insects wouldn't leave me in peace: I was bitten everywhere. But over time the skin hardens and thickens, and resistance to the cold improves. The result is that my skin is in great condition. As for my dental hygiene, it's no longer a problem because I no longer eat sugar. I run my index finger over my teeth with a mixture of water and ash, and the job's done. Obviously this little concoction doesn't taste like drugstore toothpaste, but compared to the flavors of my diet since the start of this adventure, there's nothing really shocking about that.

II

ONE ENDLESS AUTUMN NIGHT, I've been walking with Star for a few hours. She's on her own; she has probably left Chevy somewhere in the beech forest with Six-Points and Daguet, who have formed a winter friendship, and in whose company I have spent the last three days. In the morning it's cold, and the undergrowth is covered with a layer of thick mist. The morning silence isn't troubled by a breath of wind. In the plantation currently under development, the brambles have been crushed by tractors, and we struggle to find a place where food hasn't been replaced by mud. The ground is slippery everywhere, and several times I nearly fall into the ruts left by the wheels. It's been raining constantly for several days, causing the ponds to overflow and soak the ground. It's harder and harder to keep going without sinking into the ground with every step.

We continue our walk into the pine forest where it's less damp, and that's where we spend the afternoon. Star eats some chanterelles, and I take the rest and put them in the bottom of my billy can. My plan is to cook them over a wood fire this evening. I'm soaked, I'm cold, and a good hot meal with soup made from old nettles and bramble leaves with mushrooms will do me a world of good. The little fire will also dry my clothes. Star moves along a steep path at the bottom of which a woodcutting path separates the pine wood from the oak forest. I hold back a little, because I know her habits, and in particular, I know that she's so cautious that it will take her several hours of reflection before she crosses the road, so I wait behind and pick mushrooms.

Then all of a sudden something strange vibrates under my feet. I don't know what it is; I've never felt anything like it. An earthquake in Normandy? Impossible! All of a sudden a gunshot rips through the silence of the forest. I immediately look around for Star. Panicking, she is climbing the ridge of the narrow valley that overlooks the forest path to try to assess the situation and work out where the noise came from. The ground under my feet goes on vibrating more and more intensely, when I see about twenty red deer, stags and does, charging toward me in a disorderly gallop. I manage to hide behind a tree and narrowly dodge a collision with a running doe. At last the crazed herd disappears into the distance. In one brief and dizzying moment a

Jimmy. Jimmy was a fabulous friend; he weighed over two hundred pounds. Trapped together during a battue, we bonded. Gobette, his companion, had had one foot torn off by a bullet and almost all of her boarlets had been killed. After that, whenever he saw hunters, Jimmy had no hesitation in charging at them.

second rifle shot rings out and a bullet grazes Star. She starts running again, dashes past me, barking to signal the imminent danger to the others: *Baaah!... Baaah!... Bah, bah, bah!* She runs with all her might. My blood freezes, and I drop my billy can and run after her through the pine wood. I struggle to follow her, because the trees are densely packed together, and there are so many branches on the ground that it is hard to run while also looking ahead. Finally, a few seconds later, she slows down. I see her tottering slightly. I run breathlessly over to her and try to gauge the seriousness of her wound, without being able to find it. In the distance I hear four blasts on a hunting horn—the signal for roe deer. The hunting hounds, recognizable by the bells around their necks and the loud rattle they make, spread terror through the undergrowth. They charge toward us. Star sets off again, leaping as best she can. A few hundred yards farther on, she takes refuge in an area where blackthorn bushes form a dense thicket with hazels and brambles, an almost impenetrable fortress. I can't get in there, but I do see Star. The hounds arrive and, seeing my stance and aggressive posture, they continue on their way without stopping. A moment later, the hunters show up, shouting loudly, accompanied by more dogs on leashes. I leave my backpack by the entrance to the path along which Star fled. Since it's drenched in my scent, it will put off the pursuing hounds. I hide in a thicket nearby. They pass, my ruse works, and I know they won't be coming back right away. Out of prudence, I stay hidden for another hour or so, long enough for the battue to move away for good. I'm extremely worried about my friend.

As soon as possible, as evening approaches, I go back to see her. My poor Star... She's lying a few yards away from me, fatally wounded in the chest. She's trembling, and I still can't get into her hiding place. I talk to her, reminding her of the good times we have had together.

"Thanks, my little Star, for everything you brought me, your knowledge, your friendship, your respect, your love."

"..."

I try to make my voice sound reassuring but I'm suffering in the depths of my soul. I know that in that part of her body the wound is too serious for me to attempt an intervention. She looks at me affectionately and then raises her head slightly. A few rays of sunlight struggle to cross the sky, and the scents in the upper air don't reach her nostrils. A few birds fly through the soft air. My eyes fill with tears. And I'm filled with a form of hatred, because I'm aware that she will never know all the pleasures, all the joys that I had imagined for her. The life gradually slips from her body. She looks at me, uttering little sobbing cries, before resting her head on the ground. Star struggles to breathe and starts to fade away in the still, gray light. Lying on the damp, frozen autumn ground.

"Oh, forgive me, Star, I wasn't able to protect you. I wasn't strong enough. Forgive me."

"..."

"I promise I'll look after Chevy. He's only five months old. I'll take care of him so that he grows up, gets big and strong, and has his own territory. A fine territory. I promise you, my friend. I promise."

Her sadness is there, perceptible in her surroundings. The grass doesn't stir, no new light plays in the thickening mist, no particular scent imbues the cold air, and yet a great weariness lies upon the forest. She is tired, she is in pain; all around her desolation spreads like a toxic miasma. The clouds are still forming low in the sky, reddish against the pale November air. My friend closes her eyes... The sun has just set. My Star has gone out, but she will shine forever in my heart and, I hope, up there in the sky of the Great Island. She lived her life fighting the intense heat of summer, the darkness of the long winter nights, and all the events that she confronted with the same strength and courage. Let those who walk in the forest, and whose eyes have met those of a deer, think for a moment about her life, shattered by a bullet on an autumn day that had begun so well. Life in the wild is like that, and in this natural world that I love so much, at once so lovely and so cruel and to which the woods bear witness, I say to myself that if the trees could weep, rivers of tears would flow in our forests.

I stay there, by my friend's lifeless corpse, for several long minutes. I have to move poor Star out of her thicket. I know the hunters will come in search of her. They know they hit her; they will go looking for her with bloodhounds and follow her trail until they find her corpse. I take my friend in my arms to bury her far from the site of the battue, in a place where no one is likely to find her. The weight I am carrying is too heavy for me, and it's exhausting. My strength is failing me, but I don't want my friend to end up in a freezer and then on a human's plate. She deserves better than that. Her name was Star. I hold her tightly and redouble my efforts. Once I've reached my destination, I break the ground with the survival knife that I carry with me at all times, and then continue digging by hand, but the ground is too hard. I can't break through the layer of clay and flint to make a deep enough hole. I set Star in the shallow trench I've made and then camouflage her body with two palisades of fir tree branches bound together with linen twine, then bring them together to make a kind of little roof, a discreet grave. I cover the whole thing over with soil, moss, and bracken, hoping that the rotting smell of the body doesn't attract a stray dog over the next few days.

It's raining, I'm drenched, I'm shivering, but I want to join Six-Points, Daguet, and poor Chevy, now orphaned by his mother. I search all night and find them at last in the early morning. They fled too when the hunt began, and I'm happy to find them alive. They're there, safe and sound. Daguet and Chevy are lying down. Six-Points, standing upright, lifts his head. I don't know if he can smell my emotion or the scent of Star's blood on my clothes, but he comes toward me, frightened and trembling, sniffs me for a few seconds, and runs off barking. I am overcome with emotion and I weep. I'm afraid I've lost another friend. Maybe he'll think I killed his companion? He will have gone in search of her, but I know he will never find her, because Star is no more. Daguet and Chevy don't seem troubled by my presence, nor even by the pestilent smell that I must certainly be giving off by now. With this ceaseless rain the blood on my clothes won't dry, and the backpack containing my change of clothes is buried more than half a mile away. I'd like to go there, but I can't abandon Daguet and Chevy. Reason demands that I should go and look for that backpack, but I can't bring myself to leave.

A few hours later, Six-Points is back. He comes over to me, looks at me for a long time, sniffs my clothes as he walks around me, and then licks my bloodied trousers. It's then that I realize that he's understood. I don't know how, but the whole of his attitude shows me that he knows now. Then my sadness mingles with a feeling of joy. He isn't angry with me, and our friendship hasn't been affected. We spend the morning together with the sorrow and gloom that I'm sure I must be involuntarily communicating to the group, then I make up my mind to go and find my bag after all. It's stupid to keep dirty clothes on, and in any case it won't change anything. I wash my clothes with the rain that's still falling a little. I put on clean, dry clothes, then light a little fire to heat up something to eat and dry my old clothes.

I didn't imagine that the time would come when I would take such pleasure in eating food from a heated can. When you haven't had any food for a long time and the hunger becomes too insistent, your response to taste sensations is surprising. All flavors are heightened. Salt, sugar, pepper—all of those tastes explode in your mouth like a firework.

Six-Points and Chevy join me. The still-smoking embers have left a charred log, and they hurry to eat it. It's a good source of carbon, so scarce in nature that they seem just as satisfied as I am. Six-Points greedily lowers his head over the can, but there's nothing left in it but some sauce for him to lick.

The three of us spend the rest of the afternoon together. Six-Points seems still to be looking for his companion, and Chevy utters little squeaking sobs that make my heart ache every time. I don't know how, but Six-Points manages to find Star's trail. He takes the same route as we did the previous day when the hunt arrived, then recovers our tracks and finds the grave that I built for Star. He paces around it with Chevy, who recognizes his mother's scent. He makes little whispering sounds, no doubt hoping that his mother will reply to him. I'm sorry to see that, and overwhelmed. I'm filled with guilt: I wasn't able to protect her.

After a few hours we set off again without looking back. I have a feeling that a page of our story has been turned, and I can't accept it. As the days follow on from one another, Six-Points and his life force teach me that you need to move on. You have to remember the best of those who you have known without regrets. There are so many daily deaths in nature that you would spend your whole time weeping if you stopped each time someone was lost. Life goes on. Now Six-Points will take Chevy under his wing. The little one will spend winter and spring with his father, even more of a presence in his life than he had been before that cursed day.

12

AFTER THE TERRIBLE TRIAL of losing Star, I can't come to terms with the idea that this is how things will be. In spite of a long meditation on my vision of life, the reality on the ground forces me to accept the loss of the creatures dearest in my eyes, and my heart is hardened by harmful emotions. How can I accept the death of my friends without doing anything about it? Anger rumbles in the depths of my soul. My friends and I regularly experience battues during the winter season, and I realize that I have the same feelings and the same fears as my companions. Since mid-November I've been living in a kind of perpetual fear that a van might appear on a forest path. A forestry barrier creaking and breaking the morning silence at some unexpected hour immediately awakens my instinct for survival. People shouting or dogs barking in the distance immediately make me think of that sword of Damocles. Every day from autumn onward, I pray that we won't be caught up in tragedy again. However much I might try and remind myself that fear doesn't prevent dangerous things happening, my feelings are still too powerful, and I can't rid myself of the burden that weighs down on me until the start of spring, the end of the hunting season. Living in the heart of the lives of the roe deer, I notice that in spite of a supposed "controlled cynegetic management," in the newfangled hunting jargon, my friends are still misunderstood and very much disdained. Listed like trees (above twenty per hundred hectares—about 250 acres—they have to be culled), then hunted on the grounds of species regulation and trapped in the forest behind fences to limit possible "destruction" to cultivated fields, they have now become an "accident-creating factor" along the countless roads that run through their territories. Seeing them in these terms—as we wish to see them, rather than as they are—is too simplistic, too unrealistic, and, let's admit it, inhumane.

Whatever territory they live in—mountains or valleys or vast open plains—roe deer conquer different microhabitats, such as plantations, gardens, orchards, and fields, responding to the constraints of our civilization. The roe deer is an extremely intelligent animal with unique qualities, and it adapts to everything, or almost everything. The proof is that it has developed the ability to live near humans where other wild animals faced with similar conditions have declined and sometimes even disappeared. The uniqueness of its social life, which is both individualistic and herdlike; the talents that it develops in order to take advantage of its environment and optimize its territory; the nature of its population, which adapts to changes to its habitat thanks to a mode of reproduction unique to cervids—all of these features make roe deer unusually ecologically adaptable. However, our desire to control populations, along with galloping urbanization, put these animals in a state of constant panic. There is the risk of being seen, crossing roads, lacking food, lacking shelter, and, of course, dying. This anxiety-inducing environment leads them to make compromises between all these dangers and ways in which they might otherwise benefit. Our economic development, contemporary demographics, hunting, and forestry deeply alter the behavior of my friends and cause them to live in a landscape of fear.

After several battues we go elsewhere for a few days to seek refuge, and we don't return to our home range until the dead of night. Roe deer become anxious, fearful, and stressed during the hunting season. The most seasoned of them, such as Daguet or Six-Points, start observing the behavior of humans along the forest paths to see whether or not there is any danger. In fact, because runners or hikers stop coming into the forest on hunting days, their absence becomes a reliable indication of the presence of danger. To an extent, present-day hunts artificialize the behavior of roe deer. My friends move less during the winter season; they learn by heart every square foot of their territory and make refuges for themselves in well situated thickets, so that they can hide there in the event of a battue. But wild populations can't be controlled, because in the words of the philosopher Francis Bacon, "We cannot command nature except by obeying her." And to do that we have to see the deer as they are and make these marvelous animals responsible for their own management.

When you live like a roe deer, the hunt feels a bit like a tornado. You don't know where it's going to go or how much damage it's going to cause, and there is nothing you can do to prevent it in advance. For all those reasons I decide to teach my friends some tricks to recognize and avoid the battues before they begin. To start these lessons, I choose Six-Points.

In the life of a deer, there are days when you're the leader. In the winter, groups form, without the appointment of a leader as such. Nonetheless, a management committee is established according to the characters of each individual. By a sort of consensus, an individual then becomes "the boss." A point of reference in a way, who has the necessary knowledge and experience. And that knowledge is beyond dispute, because it will be placed at the service of all the deer in the group. The deer that inherits this responsibility is generally the most experienced at protecting the group, and the most likely to fill their stomachs, because he knows the best feeding areas.

The deer that constitute a group are at the same time deeply autonomous and very dependent on each other, and each one fills their role in an individual fashion. Life becomes more instinctive, and has a direct connection with nature. Information is exchanged between one deer and another, but the main preoccupation is to stay alive and maintain one's own equilibrium. There are no inferiors, and no slaves. Each deer is a complete individual, one who makes choices, and the sum total of those individual choices ensures the cohesion of the group.

While I'm sharing a moment with Six-Points, Arrow, and Velvet, a young buck with whom I'm just becoming acquainted, four vans driving at low speed pass in front of us, along a logging path. At this hour of the morning, it can't be a simple woodcutting operation. A battue is underway. It appears that today I'm the leader, and that's fine with me.

My three companions are resting and ruminating in the undergrowth. Then I decide to take everyone to the patch of pines so that every whisper I make is heeded, and the smell of my body is not too diluted by the wind. I know from experience that deer are sensitive to our moods, and more particularly to the scent of our moods. In fact, when we are aggressive or stressed, the scent of our bodies is rather acidic, like that of an onion, while a happy or peaceful mood will give off sweet, subtle aromas like those of a gourmet patisserie. Posture also plays a large part. If I turn in a circle, scratching the ground while panting and looking at the horizon on all sides, that conveys unease more clearly than if I sit down cross-legged and yawning or plucking leaves. The fawns learn to detect all of that with their mother or their elders from a very young age. All I have to do is make sure they understand what I have to say to them.

I don't have much time before the battue begins. I notice that the hunters have left their vehicles and their weapons unsupervised by the spot at the top of a hill where hunts used to meet when they were done on horseback. While the men take up posts at regular intervals along the paths for the battue, I lead Six-Points near one of the vans so that he can sniff the smells of the powder and the "death" of other animals that have fallen in previous hunts. Along the

Chevy and Fern. Crossing a path is always a delicate matter. You mustn't be seen or scented by a predator. Sound and smell cues help to sense the general atmosphere of a forest. But take care: a calm forest isn't a forest that's free from danger.

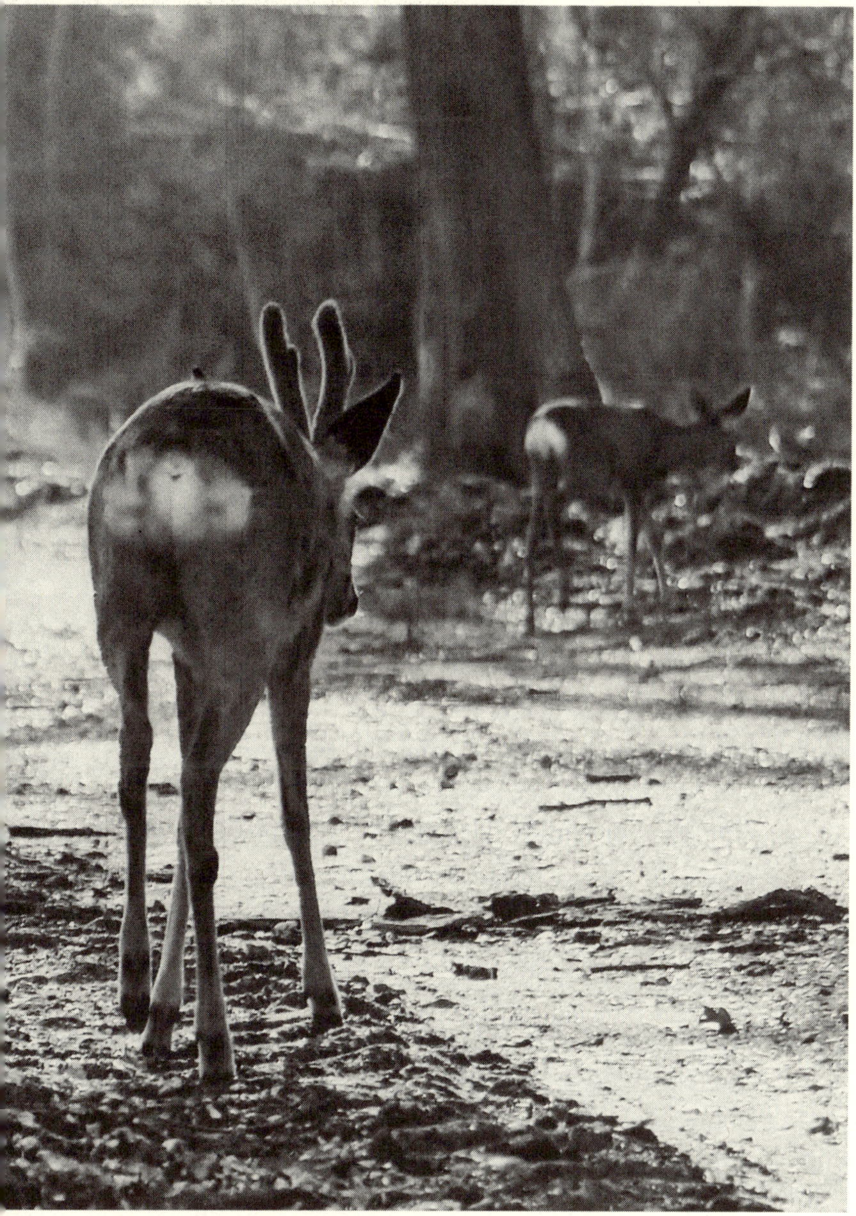

way I lose Velvet and Arrow, who, I understand, are very frightened. I make Six-Points smell the scent of a Teflon-coated jacket hanging on the wing mirror of a 4×4 and try to communicate my anxiety and my fear. The scent of my stress-induced perspiration is enough to convey the sense of danger. I want to make him associate this smell with hunting. Then we pass by an elevated tree stand, which I climb up and down several times, uttering regular little cries, as the young deer do to call their mother when they are worried. I want him to grasp the fact that a human might be above his head, and that it's worrying. In fact, deer don't always think of looking into the air when walking; scents don't come down all the way to their nostrils, and they can be shot without even being aware that they're being hunted. I return to the clutch of pine trees off to the side, about twenty yards down the path. Through the faded bracken I show him the men posted at the edge of the forest, sitting on their little folding stools with their rifles. Six-Points is pressing against me and I feel his heart beating very hard against my shoulder. He looks at me and sniffs me, and uneasily observes this strange procedure going on in front of our eyes. The hairs on his rump are erect, which tells me that he's aware of the danger.

A quarter of an hour later, the battue begins, and we are still standing in front of the marksmen.

Since the vegetation is very tall, we have the advantage of seeing without being seen. A boar scurries about thirty yards to our right. He's going down into a little valley. A first shot rings out, then a second. I bark faintly, imitating the danger signal. We set off quickly through the brambles to get up the hill to safety. The shouts of the hunters make our heartbeats race a bit more. Six-Points starts moving away from me; he wants to flee. Then I bark twice in his direction, which in roe deer language means: *stay in a group*. He stops quickly and decides to trust me. At last I can reveal the key to my hunt-saboteur plan. I run off to an area of the forest that, in theory at least, the hunters are not allowed to enter. He follows me and it fills me with joy. There's nothing to fear here, and I show by my scent that I feel much better, that I feel at ease. I sit down and relax. We stay in safety for a moment and wait for it to pass. I'm surprised by the trust that Six-Points places in me. He has barely listened to his own instincts, deciding to put his faith in everything that I've suggested. I'm lucky to have a friend like him.

A few hours later, we hear the hunters moving off in the distance. The hunting horns sound the end of the chase and we spend a calm afternoon. At nightfall, my day as leader comes to an end. Six-Points will find his family. We look for the "survivors," hoping that my friends are still alive. Today two roe deer were killed, along with eight boar and five red stags. That fills me with deep sadness. I hope that Six-Points has understood my message, and that next time he will imitate the survival plan that I taught him.

A few weeks later, when a battue takes us by surprise, I realize happily that Six-Points understood very clearly. He understood the vans, he sensed the dangerous atmosphere of the barking dogs, the smell of gunpowder, and all of those elements that darken a day. To my amazement, I notice that he's leading Chevy, Arrow, Daguet, and others into the hunting-free zone that I showed him. I knew that Six-Points was intelligent and brave, but I never imagined that he would have the ability to pass his knowledge on to the other deer. Today, the hunters failed to hit a single roe deer, and I'm proud of the fact.

13

THIS PARTICULAR WINTER I only leave my forest three times. Chiefly because there is no longer anything to be gained from my visits to civilization. Walking three miles for a bowl of fromage blanc with a handful of muesli makes no sense. When you're trying to optimize your chances of survival, you can't afford the luxury of wasting energy, even if the idea of spending a few hours in the warmth is always seductive. Besides, I no longer need to stock up on food as frequently as I did at the start of my adventure. I know how to manage my stores of firewood and nuts, and I'm no longer worried about shortages. Now, since the first cold spells, my metabolism has slowed down to adapt to these three months of scarcity. I move less, I eat less, and my stores of processed food have become almost pointless. Finally, under the ceaseless assault of the cold and damp, my rechargeable batteries have given up the ghost, pouring their toxic contents into the camera. So I've drawn a line under my activity as a photographer. There is one remaining reason I still go back and forth between the forest and the world of human beings: to restock on matches. You can't spend the winter without fire; you would risk dying of cold.

Luckily spring has arrived! Nature wakes up and all the living creatures in the forest are filled with a kind of joy. With the first rising sap, the first opening bud, an invisible presence enters us. Everyone is happy to come back to life. The birds sing differently, the sounds of the forest are more open. Varied species come together. It's as if the whole of nature is saying "hello" to itself. I go for a walk in the middle of the forest where Daguet usually sleeps. Along the way I collect sap from several silver birches. Some time ago I used a gimlet to dig a little hole in these trees half an inch deep, about eight inches from the ground. In that I placed a little straw that allows the sap to flow into a water bottle tied just below it. If the tree is big and generous I can fill a good quart in a single night. The juice is deliciously sweet for anyone who has lost the habit of consuming the enormous quantities of sugar that you find in supermarket food. A quart of this juice gives me an incredible boost for the day, and all the essential minerals that I have so cruelly lacked during the winter. I also like to lick the sap that runs down the trunks of the pine trees. It provides a bit more sugar, and if you mix it with the silver birch sap it has an astonishing flavor, with a springlike freshness. Having said that, you've got to work quickly, because as soon as the first leaves appear at the top of the tree the sap stops flowing.

I continue on my morning rounds, and at last I come across Daguet, who is clearly very embarrassed, because Chevy, now one year old, is marking his first territory and doesn't seem to have understood the rules of the game. For a few weeks Fern, Daguet's little sister, who was born shortly after Chevy, goes for a walk on Daguet's territory, which is just an annex to their mother's. That means that Fern is protected by her big brother. Except that Chevy has clearly fallen in love with the young lady, and is invading poor Daguet's territory. He's already been thrown out several times, but Chevy is so besotted that he keeps coming back. And sometimes it's even Fern who draws him into her home range, which is Daguet's territory. It all seems very complicated, and Chevy and Fern's romantic future seems to be compromised. That's without taking Daguet's big heart into account, though: seeing that there is no point in keeping Chevy outside his territory, he finally lets him woo his sister while also protecting him against potential competitors.

I am contemplating this scene of daily life when all of a sudden Chevy, intrigued by my presence, approaches slowly, sniffs me, and walks around me in a circle. I turn on my axis to go on observing him without craning my neck. For some time he has agreed to let me walk behind him, but only at a distance of about twenty yards. It occurs to me that the time may have come to take things further. Perhaps it's the right day for him. Perhaps he's ready. Three-quarters of an hour has passed and Chevy has started nibbling at the carpet of ferns around me. He stares at me for several minutes at a time with his big black shining eyes. Roe deer don't use their eyesight as much as their cousins the red deer to notice movement, but his slightly protuberant eyes as well as his long, flexible neck give him an excellent panoramic view of his environment. The structure of his eye consists almost entirely of rods, cells that send the brain black-and-white images, and a few scattered cones, which play a part in chromatic vision. That's why Chevy sees shades closer to gray more easily than color itself. It's that anatomical peculiarity that gives him sharper vision at dusk, and allows him to detect movements more quickly.

A pheasant passes elegantly about ten yards away. Chevy, apparently startled, moves away from the bird and comes closer to me. He looks at me for a long time without moving, sniffs the air around him, lowers his head slightly to pick up my scent, and understands that the distance between us is really very small. Having said that, he is intelligent and bound to notice that in spite of my proximity I haven't attacked him. Out of caution, he moves a little way away with a very confident gait, a way of walking that I call the "firm hoof." It's a step typical of roe deer, which, when they are curious and move closer to something or else farther away from it, makes them look proud and almost noble, with their slender bodies and their incredibly graceful, slow-motion movements; they appear to be stamping the ground. The front hoof rises to the shoulder, then stretches out fully before planting itself confidently on the soil. I take advantage of the moment to get to my feet. Chevy turns again to look at Daguet, shakes his head, and presents his antlers to invite him to fight. He seems strong and invincible with his two little antlers, which, without tines, look like the horns of a goat. He scrapes the ground with his front hoof in a cloud of dust. Daguet prepares for the game and, just as Chevy lowers his head, barks so loudly at the little buck that he jumps back and runs about twenty yards away before coming back, quivering. I burst out laughing and they both look at me. They're like two kids in a playground. Chevy is well aware that Daguet is stronger than he is, and that he doesn't need to engage in this kind of jousting. He also knows that the only way to win territory is by cunning, but he enjoys playing so much that he forgets the harsh reality of life as a roe deer. He nonchalantly turns toward Fern, who has been equally jittery. I walk a little ways behind them, leaving Daguet to his activities. I move toward Chevy and try to walk less than five yards behind him; he makes a little jump to get away from me. Fern lies down and Chevy goes on marking his territory. The game goes on, and then he wants to cross the forest path, which at this time of day is used by horse riders, cyclists, and runners. I follow him. He gives me a sideways look but continues on his way. After a few minutes' reflection, he crosses the path. I run after him. Having reached the other side, he seems intrigued by my stubbornness in following him. He runs a little, climbs the steep path into the recently logged beech forest, and hides behind a freshly felled pile of wood to eat some accessible leaves. I walk over to eat some leaves opposite him. The unease fades, making way for playfulness. Chevy knows that I live in the forest now, and he can tell the difference between me and all the other humans who visit. Like the other roe deer, he only recognizes me, my unique smell, and if another human tries to approach him he runs off without further ado. It's as if he's sending me a message: "I want to find out about you; you can follow me, but be gentle because I'm still a bit fearful." Message received. I walk ten yards behind him.

The sound of the leaves on the ground no longer seems to disturb him, but we're joined by a buck that I don't know very well, a two-year-old. He comes from an area higher up the hill, which I call "the slopes." The newcomer observes us from a distance, clearly not wanting to come any closer, and sniffs us a bit, still from far away. He is muscular and seems suspicious. I'll call him Sus. Chevy observes him while coming closer to me, walking around me at a good distance to hide and also to ensure that I'm between him and Sus. I immediately note Chevy's bravery, but I can't intervene. It's their business. Sus finally comes over to get further acquainted. After a few minutes he tries to chase Chevy away, but my presence gets in the way. In spite of his slightly nervous approach, Sus is determined to chase Chevy, who is still hiding behind me. At last, weary of the fight, Sus gives up and moves away.

I spend the afternoon with Chevy, aware that the encounter with Sus has brought us closer, and something tells me that a great friendship is about to form between us. I observe him from very close up, studying him and taking in this magical moment.

Sus in full flight. His uncanny intelligence and his knowledge of the terrain allowed Sus to escape hunters and stay alive on more than one occasion.

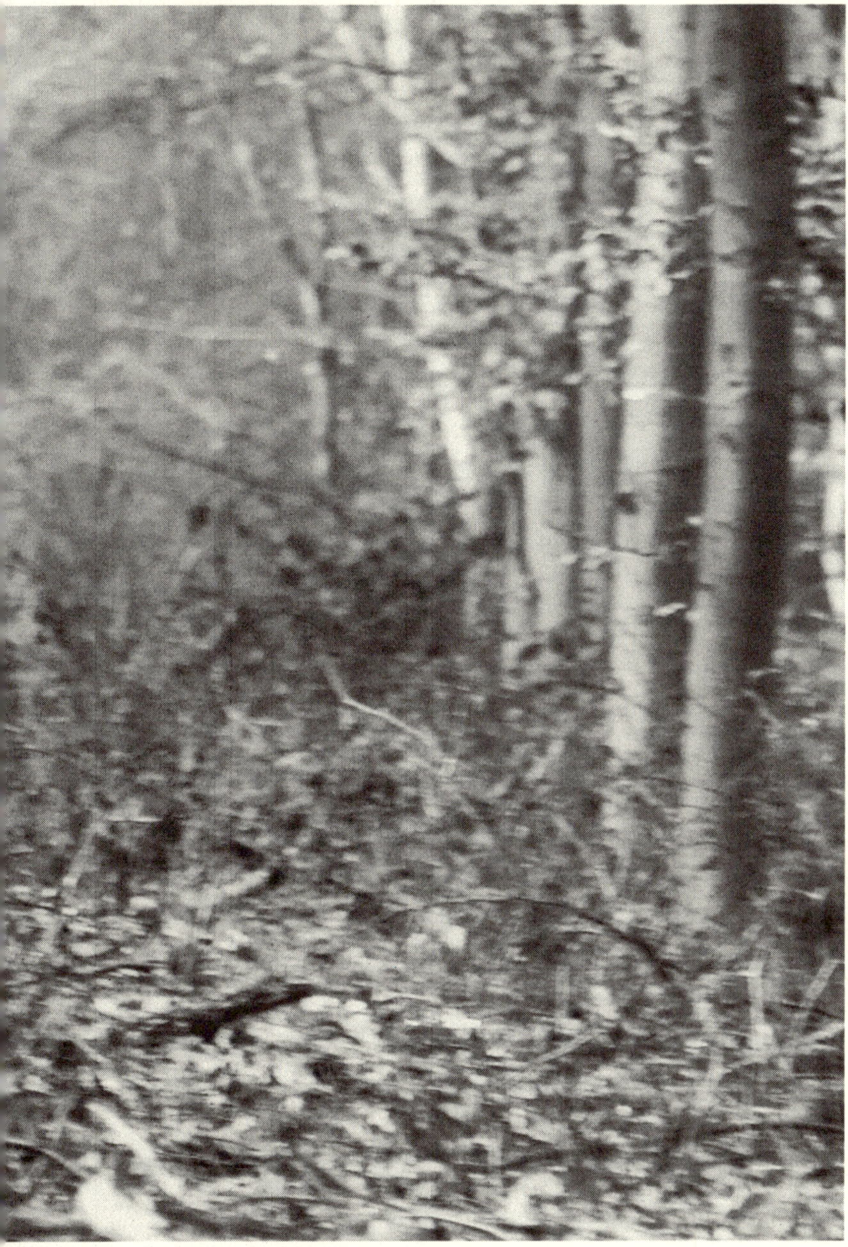

I placed myself upwind of him so that he could more easily sniff my scent, which he seems to like. You have to understand that Chevy moves in a universe saturated with scents. His slightly wrinkled nostrils, hairless and damp, allow him to distinguish all the aromas carried on the wind. By definition, damp air carries smells better than dry air. That's why today, in this dry April weather, Chevy constantly licks his nostrils to increase the humidity of his breathing. Sometimes he raises his muzzle a little to get a clearer definition of the different layers of air. Scent is how he can distinguish a human who visits the forest honestly and innocently from an individual who enters his territory slyly and furtively. A roe deer downwind of a walker will always know that he is there.

Chevy continues his little territory-marking stroll. Every now and then he scrapes the ground with his front hoof, takes a few steps, urinates, and rubs his antlers against an eagle fern and then a young poplar, finishing with an old shrub. Bear in mind that roe deer have a number of scent glands that play an essential part in their daily life. The gland between the "toes" of each hoof, the interdigital gland, secretes a substance that is deposited on the ground. It allows the members of a family or a group to follow each other, even when the forest terrain is dense. On each back hoof, level with the ankle, a small glandular zone concealed by slightly longer hairs called the tarsal gland secretes a scent that roe deer leave by brushing against low vegetation as they move. Every animal, and hence every human being, is a unique cocktail of scents, an alchemy of secretions that pass through the pores of the skin when they sweat. This olfactory print allows the roe deer to locate in their memory an animal or a human that they have bumped into before, and therefore recognize. And it is in this way that I manage to become part of their universe. My clothes, my equipment, my sweat, my urine, are impregnated with my scent. That scent is mixed with pollen and dust, and the sap of the plants that I break or crush when walking, which makes the information the deer receive more complex but allows them to grasp my position and know which direction I am traveling in.

Now that Sus has passed through, Chevy leaves his mark with another glandular area on his forehead. It all asserts his presence. On everything from ferns to shrubs to dead branches, Chevy marks his passage and his territory with this substance, which to me smells a bit like apples. It's also what allows bucks like Sus or females like Fern to show that they have passed along this way. Then he scratches the base of his antlers with his front hoof and presses the hoof down very hard to make a clear print, as if to sign his work. The size of this gland increases between May and September, when the territorial activity is at its most intense. Deer rub their heads on trees whose diameter is no greater than the space between the trees, and only rarely does this affect the growth of stands. Still, if the foresters are crazy enough to replant standard deciduous trees on bare ground after a logging operation without putting protection around them, well… you make your choices!

I stay with Chevy for a few days to learn his territory and the paths he takes. Very gradually, he allows me a degree of intimacy that I haven't achieved with the other deer. It's almost as if we'd always known each other. We think about the same things at the same time. Wherever I go and he goes, we bump into each other without planning to. As if fate were forcing us to get to know each other. One evening, when I've left him with Fern, while I'm collecting my little harvest of birch sap, I catch him following me, licking every trunk behind me that leaves a thin trickle of sap running along the bark. Fern, more fearful but never very far from her lover, is a long way from saying "hello" to me but is highly interested in my activities, and Chevy, as if demonstrating bravado to his Juliet, sets himself challenges like letting me walk behind him without being frightened, eating from the same blackberry bush as me, or approaching my shoes to sniff at them. I'm impressed by the behavior, because until now no roe deer has ever shown such interest in me or been so quick to let me approach.

In a few weeks we move from a state of fear to a progressive trust before ending up with complete and total friendship. Now Chevy makes me a part of his life. I can play with him, walk beside him, eat blackberries side by side with him, and all kinds of other things. Sometimes I even feel that there are fewer barriers between Chevy and me than there are between Chevy and Fern. He makes me feel a bit like a roe deer. Fully integrated. I'm at ease with him. He doesn't judge me, and even gives me the impression that he understands me. We are blood brothers. An inseparable trio forms and we spend an incredible April, full of joy, friendship, and mutual discoveries.

14

EVER STRONGER BONDS of friendship form between me and Chevy, and our curiosity about each other brings us closer every day. Chevy observes me and learns from me at incredible speed. He takes in all my movements and my scents, to the point where we can communicate more easily with each other. I learn little whispers or grunts that I didn't hear with Daguet or Six-Points. And one remarkable thing, he listens to me sing and talk to him. He even seems to associate my words with my actions. When we cross a forest path and I say to him, "Careful, now, because there are humans," he associates my unease, my scent, and my general posture with the situation of the moment and the imminence of danger, even though he hasn't understood the actual words that I've said. When I crouch down behind him and say quietly, "All right, Chevy?" he stops and looks at me tenderly with his head to one side, licking his muzzle. He has a sparkle in his eye and he seems to be replying, "Sure, fine! And you?" I realize the extent to which roe deer communicate with one another. By paying attention, I've noted that they communicate more by sound than sight, because they can be very noisy about it. They yelp to ask questions, to challenge one another to a game, or simply out of curiosity. A series of barks accompanied by marked little jumps indicates danger to all the other bucks and does in the vicinity. Fawns with their mothers make little whispering noises so as not to get lost when they move around or when they get bored. If they're frightened, they utter a louder little cry, a kind of sharp and rhythmic squawk, not unlike the cry of the tree creeper. The purpose of those sounds is to make their mother come running, even though it might be dangerous. During the rutting season, in July and August, a buck's breathing develops a very striking whistle. He grunts and sometimes groans to himself. A doe in heat makes different cries, little whistling sounds, slightly hoarse and plaintive. Pursued by a rutting male she utters a more ringing yelp, a little cry from the heart that is difficult to describe.

 Chevy allows me to understand the mentality of roe deer, and I very soon learn to imitate their language. Those complex codes with precise intervals of sound are not easy to pick up. I never call a

Chevy at night. Nighttime arouses the senses, of smell and hearing but also of touch; I became keenly aware of the feel of the plants that I needed to recognize by moonlight.

roe deer friend in the same way every day, because you have to take into consideration the influence of temperature, wind, rain, and, even more difficult to sense, atmospheric pressure. To this we might add honesty toward roe deer. It's not about barking stupidly and selfishly to attract your friends, but about knowing what you want to say, do, or make them understand when they reply. They don't appreciate false alarms and I don't want to let them down. At the same time, it's hard to find grumpy roe deer, because happiness seems to be their natural state. Nor is it a matter of giving orders to Chevy, because I don't want to reduce him to the rank of a domestic animal. He wouldn't obey me in any case; he's as stubborn as a billy goat. In this story, after all, I'm the companion animal, and I'm the one walking behind the wild animals, not the other way around. Sometimes I wish they listened to me, because roe deer are so adventurous when they strike out for new territories that they sometimes throw caution to the winds. They're not oblivious, but they're reckless. For his own safety I've already tried to dissuade Chevy from going to places that are too dangerous, like sports grounds, the edges of roads, or tracks across the clearing in the middle of the afternoon. But even blocking his path doesn't put him off, and then I ask myself: who am I to stop him from doing anything? We will both agree that the best thing about freedom and life in the wild is never to be given constraints or orders even if there is danger everywhere. Living is dangerous in itself, so why keep him from living? There are already plenty of obstacles in nature.

Speaking of natural barriers, there's one that Chevy hadn't imagined for a second, and that's Sus. He seems to have his eye on Fern, who doesn't seem to be rejecting the handsome fellow's advances. Chevy and Sus are very different characters. One is affectionate, a little childish, slim and cunning, and very tender. The other is more brutal, mature and macho, hefty and direct. Sus has also established his territory directly beside the one belonging to Daguet, who, remember, protects Chevy. It risks being a long and complicated story for my friends. Fern, since she's the one who has to decide which of the two suitors is most deserving of her, has chosen to alternate between them. One day Chevy, one day Sus, and as it turns out, the two Don Juans agree on one point: the situation is not sustainable. This late spring coexistence is tense, and Fern finally decides to isolate herself for the summer. At the same time Sus abandons his territory. It's too risky to live alongside Daguet, who can be very off-putting, and even more so with a barking, groaning neighbor like Six-Points. Chevy is opportunistically taking over Sus's territory, which is now vacant, and seems already to have found his feet. I discover him to be surprisingly intelligent and cunning. Here he is, the owner of fifty acres of territory for which he hasn't had to fight once. Half of it is protected by Daguet, and the other half left unoccupied by its former owner. Worth taking risks from time to time!

A few days later Chevy surprises me again. I'm walking behind him and Fern in a patch of beech trees. They're eating a few leaves here and there, particularly wood anemones. My friends consume this plant, a member of the ranunculus family, in large quantities, because it contains a tannin that lets the roe deer purge themselves of enteritis, an illness not unlike our own gastroenteritis but generally fatal for roe deer. The plant grows in the gloom of damp undergrowth, and not all roe deer have access to it because of the nature of their territories, particularly the ones that live in coniferous forests with acidic soil. Chevy and Fern, their stomachs full, look for a calm, serene place where they can chew the cud in peace. Fern lies down against a little pile of recently cut logs. Chevy looks around him, and nowhere seems to suit. He ventures over to a little slope, and I follow him as simply as a child. Having arrived a few yards behind him, I crouch down. It's then that he decides to turn around to come and see me. He stops just in front of me, studies me, and sniffs. He grooms himself a little and looks furtively around. After a few minutes he takes a step forward, shivers slightly, and looks at me. I don't recognize this posture, and haven't seen it in any other roe deer. He lifts his head and then lowers it to the ground to sniff the different scents he finds there. He steps forward gently, walks around me, and goes on sniffing at me, his unease overcome by his curiosity. He comes over to my face and starts licking it. I can feel his hot, sweet little tongue passionately caressing my skin. I can feel his warm and rhythmic breathing, while my heart is beating fast. It's the first time that a roe deer has shown me such affection. A great happiness, a joy, fullness, pride— no word can describe what I feel at that moment. Thousands of emotions run trembling down my spinal column. With these little strokes of his tongue Chevy is washing and "tasting" me so that he can remember my unique scent, which will seal our friendship forever. His tongue passes over my eyes, my ears, my nose, and then he examines my lips. He very delicately takes off my hat, sniffs my hair, plays with it a little, and runs his head under the collar of my sweater to reach my neck. Then it's over and the grooming is complete. A few moments later, while

I stroke his chest, Chevy looks at me, clearly satisfied with this exchange, then lies down right at my feet. Still crouching, I sit cross-legged to ensure that my legs don't go numb. Something unique is happening between us, and from the spark in his eye I know that our relationship is one of trust, respect, and goodwill, the key terms in a successful friendship between a roe deer and a man.

15

ON A FINE AFTERNOON in early summer, Chevy and I are walking in a grove where a magnificent birch tree spreads its light, supple branches. Chevy lies down at the end of the trunk of a big tree felled by the last winter storm. We look at each other for a moment. I really wonder what might have led him to want to befriend me more than any other roe deer before him. Does he sense the huge pleasure I get from living with him, drawn into this unusual adventure that is teaching me a bit more about myself every day, changing my perception of my weaknesses, my strengths, and even my desires? Does he want to learn more about me, just as I want to learn more about him? The treetops dance slightly in a warm south wind, and a shadow with a hint of green passes over his face and vanishes again. I lie down on the ground, with my back on a bed of ferns, and contemplate the translucent tangle of emerald foliage. We stay there for a long time, lying under the sun-dappled trees, taking advantage of this magical, enchanted moment to abandon ourselves entirely to nature, and letting the weight of the constraints of life in the wild slip from us. Absolutely nothing can describe that joy or the peace that enters me then. We spend the afternoon enjoying the time passing gently until sunset.

We get up, still drowsy from our luxurious repose, a little dazed by the calm that reigns around us. We walk together through the copse in the wood. I push aside the ferns that are absorbing the freshness of the evening and allow myself to be filled by the warm smells that have accumulated during the day. Now cool, now lukewarm and humid, the air impregnated with the honeyed aroma of the grasses, both coarse and tender, makes my head spin. At this time of day when you're never really sure if it's day or night, the blue tits, the robins, the chaffinches, and all the other birds gradually fall silent to make way for the deep silence of night. All the sounds fade into the scented coolness of the shadow that falls around me. The whole forest has woken up, and yet not a sound disturbs this serenity. We walk and make our way into different layers of the forest while night continues to fall. Some nightjars flit nervously over the clearing that we're passing through, leaving their daytime retreat to go in search of insects, breaking the monotony of the moors with their very particular call, like the purring of a cat.

 A few moments later, we pause in the middle of the oak wood where a male tawny owl is hooting loudly. A female joins in with these calls in a duet that makes the darkness ring, and another couple responds in the distance. Once it's pitch dark, a barn owl, its wings beating silently, creates a faint draft above my head. The full moon casts its pale light on the undergrowth, my shadow appearing on it like a ghost. The forest's aspect shifts, its features alter. My senses are on alert tonight, each step carrying me farther into a cathedral of trees. I feel the roots moving under my feet. I hear the trunks creak like rigging when a zephyr stirs the canopy. The trees are communicating with one another. Am I the subject of their conversation? Everything encourages reveries in this magical and mysterious universe.

 Chevy brings me back to reality when, with a series of little whispers, he lets me know that we need to get a move on if we're to get wherever he wants to go. If I don't respond, he comes over, lowers his head, stretches his neck as if to sniff my shoes, and snorts before setting off again at a trot for several yards. Later on, during a brief pause, I doze near Chevy, and while I'm sleeping a shrew, the world's smallest mammal, slips into my pant leg to take advantage of my body warmth for a while. I seem to be running a guesthouse for small mammals! There are two ways of being woken up in that situation: with a squeak and a swift getaway, or sometimes with a little bite by way of thanks.

A moment later we climb a little path that leads to a thinly wooded platform. From up there, under a crystal sky, I contemplate the stars. The tops of the fir trees that line the glade form a pretty dark-brown frame that makes the starry sky seem even brighter. Chevy looks at me and raises his head slightly, just as a shooting star passes overhead. I make a wish—I hope it will come true—that we can be friends for life and nothing will ever part us. *I will look after you and protect you with all my might*, I tell him, *I know that we will have our best times together, and that nothing and no one will ever take them away from us.*

Dawn approaches, and the faintly orange light sharpens the outlines of the forest, still cool and damp. We reach the exposed clay slopes to take advantage of the sun that is shyly appearing over the neighboring hill. The mists of the Seine and the Eure mingle and evaporate as the sun's first rays settle on the surface of the lakes and ponds below. In the distance I hear the roosters crowing to announce the start of a fine day, while the village church at the bottom of the valley rings out its first chime. A black

Two neighbors. Rummage and Mimi were badgers that I encountered regularly. For them, I was one of the forest dwellers and did not represent a threat.

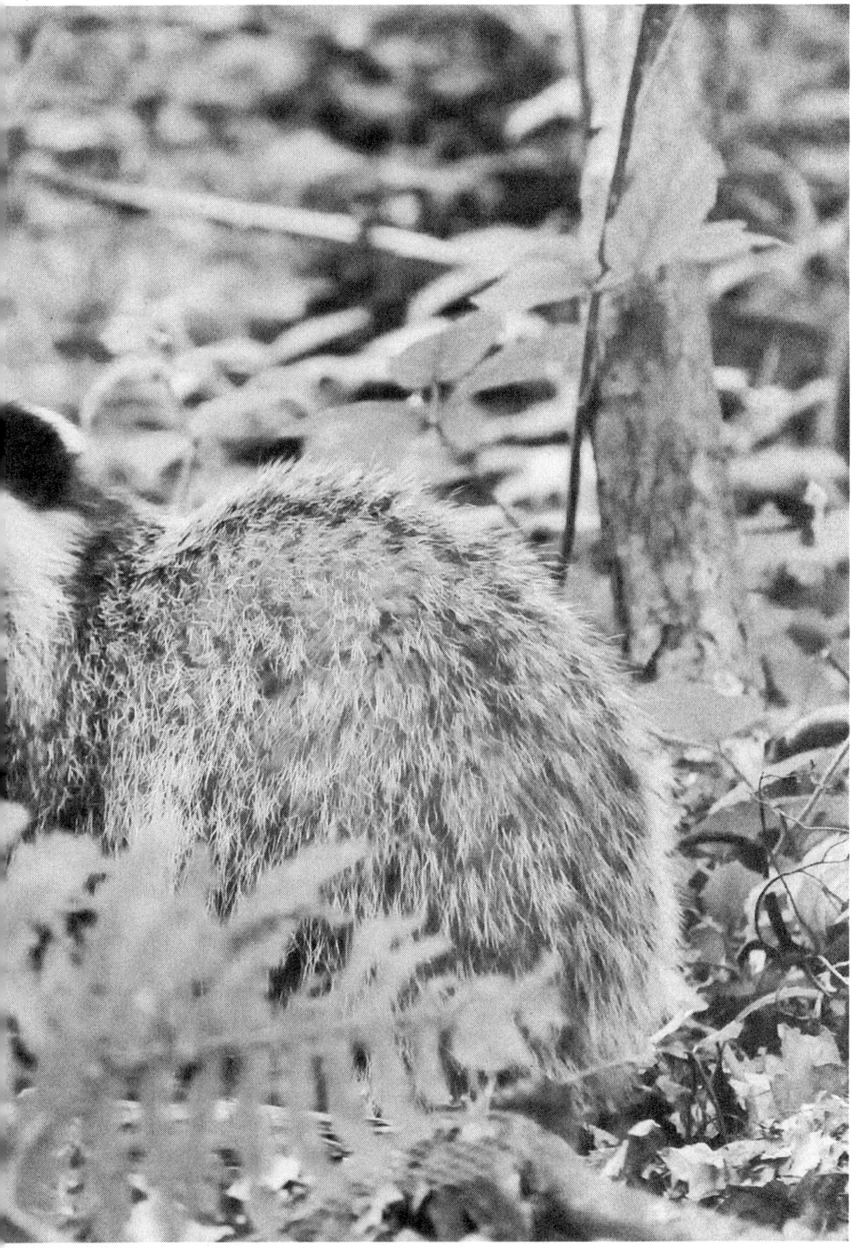

fox returns from what seems to have been a good night's hunting. The last boar cross the meadows and the dew-drenched fields to reach the depths of the forest before humanity awakens. In the summer the days are long...

16

THE ATMOSPHERE BACK HOME has suddenly become horribly oppressive. I'm clearly no longer welcome. So to avoid getting in anyone's way I only go there if absolutely necessary, always at night, and I'm as quick as possible. A brief wash, a bowl of fromage blanc wolfed down very swiftly, I nick some matches if I find any, and go again without leaving any traces. Everything in the house makes me nervous. The smells assault my senses now, the clicking of the various electrical devices irritates me; I'm even bothered by the light. I don't think I can bear the world of humans any more. I feel so much better in the woods.

Thanks to Daguet, Six-Points, Chevy, and all the others, I can sleep outside now, without a sleeping bag, without a shelter, and without heating. They have taught me to live, eat, and sleep in brief cycles, which makes life—or survival—possible without too much physical suffering. It's impossible to build a shack or make a fire each time you stop, before abandoning it after only a few hours, and the idea of setting up a base camp is pointless. That doesn't stop me from making a palisade with some bits of wood and string to shield myself against the wind, or building a little makeshift shelter in case of a big storm. But it does take time and energy. If I do engage in that kind of work, it's only because I'm soaked, because I want to dry the various layers of my clothes, and because the temperature has become unbearable. Leaving aside the fact that at this stage of my adventure nobody, absolutely nobody, is concerned with my life in this forest, I'm now afraid of attracting the attention of human beings, and it would be unwise to leave evidence that I've passed through. My routes within the undergrowth follow the paths of boar and deer, where I can hide easily. I'm as cautious and persnickety as the roe deer when it comes to crossing a forest path by day, because my worst nightmare is to be spotted by the forest ranger, even if he doesn't appear on the terrain very often. So I opt for this motto: "To live happily, live hidden."

Surviving outside isn't an impossible task. The essential thing is to have good equipment and be organized. You need to know how to save your energy, control your heartbeat with slow breathing, adapt your pace in the coldest days of winter,

Fern in the mist. Mist is a valuable ally. Scents travel through the air thanks to the microdroplets contained in the high humidity. It means that roe deer can sense a human presence even before they can see it.

because perspiration becomes your worst enemy. I don't have the option of migrating south in autumn like the geese do, their flight forming a V for "voyage," inviting us to dream of far-off lands. I can't live in slow motion like dormice, marmots, or hedgehogs, which are lucky enough to be able to sleep while winter and its storms rage outside. I have to get by on my own with what I have on hand and wait for it to pass, with two major challenges: staying warm and finding enough to eat. Sleeping for a long time either by day or by night is potentially lethal, particularly in winter. Lying down, your cardiac rhythm diminishes, and in half an hour, you will feel the effects of the cold. In a few hours, your feet and hands grow cold and numb and then, progressively, you're in a state of hypothermia. Insulating yourself against the ground is therefore of huge importance, so like the roe deer I scrape the ground with my foot to get rid of the layer of fallen vegetation. Even though the earth is cold, it's a warmer and drier carpet than rotting leaves. I lay down some branches from firs or other coniferous trees that allow me to insulate myself from the ground and retain my bodily warmth. Thanks to my sweaters I'm able to sleep for several hours depending on the temperature, but when it gets really cold the hours to sleep are very short, and sleeping has to be done by day. I take advantage of the late-morning rays of sunlight, the warmest ones, to sleep a little. I often wake up feeling groggy and a bit numb, but still happy to have taken advantage of that moment of peace. Sometimes I don't sleep at all. I just snooze for a few minutes, sitting cross-legged under a few bundles of twigs to protect myself against the wind, and then I set off again.

Where food is concerned it's exactly the same principle because I'm not going to discover a pantry. Depending on the intensity of the seasons, if the autumn and winter don't provide enough food, I'm forced to move when the deer do, which is completely incompatible with the idea of a base camp. But that doesn't bother me at all; I find it easier to adapt to the terrain and become a nomad. When the winter is drawn out and food supplies are scarce, the deer are forced to go and feed from cultivated fields. They might be winter crops like canola or root crops, or equally weeds. Except that since winter is the time when farmers spray their fields with crop-protection products, the deer only adopt that strategy as a last resort. Once the shoots in the fields have reached a height of about four inches, the roe deer move on to something else. In the spring, these plants will continue to grow, and the trauma dealt to them will disappear in a few weeks.

For older bucks like Six-Points and Velvet, the older forests with their fruit trees, oaks, or chestnuts are a godsend, and when the spring vegetation grows back and the abundance of food returns, they set off back to the woods to defend last year's territory. As for the does, they can remain for several extra weeks in the fields where they found refuge with their fawns, and if they feel safe, if they aren't troubled too often by passing humans, they can even spend the whole summer there. So a doe without a partner can leave in search of a buck that already has a territory to persuade him to follow her and bring him to the mating zone of her choice. It should be noted that roe deer have very little effect on agricultural yields (less than five percent). On the other hand, farm machinery causes terrible damage to roe deer, particularly to fawns, which can be accidentally crushed. Fields of alfalfa or grass meadows are particularly attractive to young deer, because they establish their resting areas there, and the damage from machines can nearly halve the annual growth of a population.

Roe deer are very attached to their territory and display great intelligence when it comes to not being noticed. They have an incredible memory, and it's greater when they are on their own terrain. With a strong kinesthetic sense (an awareness of their own body and its relationship to their surroundings), they know their environment by heart. They can run and leap at tremendous speed along their usual paths without looking at obstacles on the ground or even needing to think about them. This muscle memory that we know to a lesser extent, because it's how we can find the light switch at night or avoid bumping into the foot of the bed, is an enormous help to roe deer, particularly when they are being pursued by a predator. Besides, since he has no mirror to admire his antlers, the buck must remember their position, their shape, and their length, because once they have been stripped of the velvet that covers them, they lose all tactile sensitivity.

I also observe that Chevy and many other roe deer are capable of memorizing the best feeding areas, as well as the position of the trees that give them the best quantities of foliage and fruits. This behavior tends to demonstrate that they remember experiences that they have had in the course of previous seasons, sometimes over a period of more than six years, depending on the variety of timber species, and explains certain psychological disturbances when there is regular logging on their territory. The human behavior changes due to the clock shifts in spring and autumn for daylight saving time can disturb deer for a few days, or even a few weeks. When deer are most active, as the reader knows by now, they lead a crepuscular life; if they regularly cross a road at 7:30 PM and the traffic is light at that time, when the clock changes it will be 6:30 and the traffic will be heavier. This is an accident-creating factor for roe deer, even if some, more observant than others, very quickly change their schedules so as not to be by the roadside when the traffic is bad. Unfortunately this isn't true of all wild animals, and too many die on the roads.

17

IT'S SPRING; a light wind from the southwest, warm and humid, carries to me the delicate perfume of wood anemones, pilewort, and other flowers of the undergrowth. I let the warm rays of sunlight stroke my face as if to convince me that the long and difficult winter season is over. In the treetops, the birds parade and chirrup in chorus. It's the season of love. All the songs come together in the canopy to form a single great symphony, the sound of happiness.

Down below, the roe deer and I are preparing our territories, nibbling a few seasonal specialties along the way. Courage, Chevy's half-brother, is a very young buck born of the union of Six-Points and Dew, his new partner. Rather gentle by nature, Courage tries to prolong his winter friendships with his companions. His sister, Lila, has an adjacent territory given to her by Dew, her mother. That will help her avoid the amorous advances of the neighboring males. Every day, Courage marks his territory a little more, refining his markers and defending them vigorously against the other bucks that are roaming around. Weeks pass and he manages to conquer a little parcel of just over twelve acres, which isn't bad for a buck his age.

One morning, in the distance, a noise breaks the fullness of the woodland kingdom. Courage and I decide to go and see where those unfamiliar snaps, wails, and shrieks are coming from. An invader has entered the wild fortress. This area of forest, planted about forty years ago, consists of Scots pines, amid which some beautiful old birches, beeches, and oaks have survived. In its depths we discover an impressive machine, a kind of tractor mounted on eight enormous toothed wheels, and with a mechanical arm. At the end of this arm are chain saws and a huge iron jaw. The machine encircles the tree, grabs it, cuts it from the base, lifts it effortlessly, strips its trunk from base to tip, then severs the head of the tree and cuts it into long pieces to form a pile of logs before moving on to the next tree. The destruction is so swift and the noise so intense that I imagine I can hear the trees crying. Courage, terrified by the presence of this beast on his territory, runs off, barking. For three days the young buck refuses to mark his territory. Three days during which this mechanical monster finishes its work.

Once calm has returned, we go back to that area to take stock of the changes. The machine has devastated everything. In place of the haven of peace and quiet, burgeoning with food, where squirrels, dormice, and birds had built their nests, we discover the silence of a bleak plain. The feller buncher has razed everything to the ground. Only one rotten tree trunk has been spared in the name of biodiversity. A little label will be fastened to it some months later.

Maurice Barrès, in *The Great Pity of the Churches of France*, writes:

> *Do you know this kind of anguish, this protest that forms within the depths of our being... every time we see a spring sullied, a landscape degraded, a forest cleared or simply a fine tree felled without replacement? What we feel then... is something other than merely the loss of a material asset. We feel invincibly that for our full expansion we need vegetation, freedom, life, happy animals, untapped springs, rivers that do not run down pipes, forests without metal wires, timeless spaces. We love woods, fountains, vast horizons for the services that they give us and for more mysterious reasons. A pine wood burning on the hills of Provence is a church being blown up. A little ravine in the Alps, a bare flank of the Pyrenees,*

stretches of desert in the Champagne, limestone plateaus, moorlands, the scrubland of the central plateau correspond in our minds to those village squares where our steeples are crumbling.

I observe Courage, who I have never seen so nervous. He looks from right to left and then from left to right at what was once his territory; he sniffs the air, filled now with a smell of burnt oil. He takes a step forward, hesitates for a long time, and then gives in. Despondent, he is filled with terrible anxiety. I see by his desperate expression that with his territory destroyed, his shelters no longer exist, food will now be difficult to find, and he will no longer be able to participate in the mating season.

Courage finds himself without protection in the territory of his competitors. No doe is going to want a male without a territory, who can't give her a peaceful place of refuge. Unable to recreate a new domain in such a short time, then chased from territory to territory by the other bucks, Courage spends the summer in a thicket measuring fifty square feet. The lack of food in any quantity or variety is beginning to destroy him physically and psychologically. His miserable existence, the terrible conditions in which he lives lead him to take risks that put his life in danger. He is exhausted and thin, he's losing his fur, parasites are invading his body, and I'm worried that he will fall ill. He cries, groans, and waits for the autumn, a season when winter friendships are reborn. I've never seen a roe deer in such a poor state of health.

The foresters' lack of consideration for the forest and its inhabitants concerns me deeply. A forest is above all a community of trees that welcomes other vegetable and animal communities. When the woodland balance is disturbed, all of those communities are weakened. The forest reflects life as a whole: complex, mysterious, changing. It gives its inhabitants resources, protection, shade, comfort, beauty, and, most importantly, it is its own biological ecosystem. I am able to live with the roe deer and the other wild animals not because I'm applying scientific knowledge, but because I've discovered their secrets, understanding one of the most magnificent works of nature: the forest. We don't learn a language by translating word for word. We learn it thanks to the subtlety of its idiom, the way of life of the inhabitants of the country who speak it, without comparing it with what we know of our own language. I have the good fortune to live with wild animals because I don't translate nature, I speak it.

The present mode of forest management is not adapted to nature, because the damage caused by clear-cut logging is turning into a real catastrophe for roe deer, which are very attached to their

Destruction. Chevy during the logging of his home range.

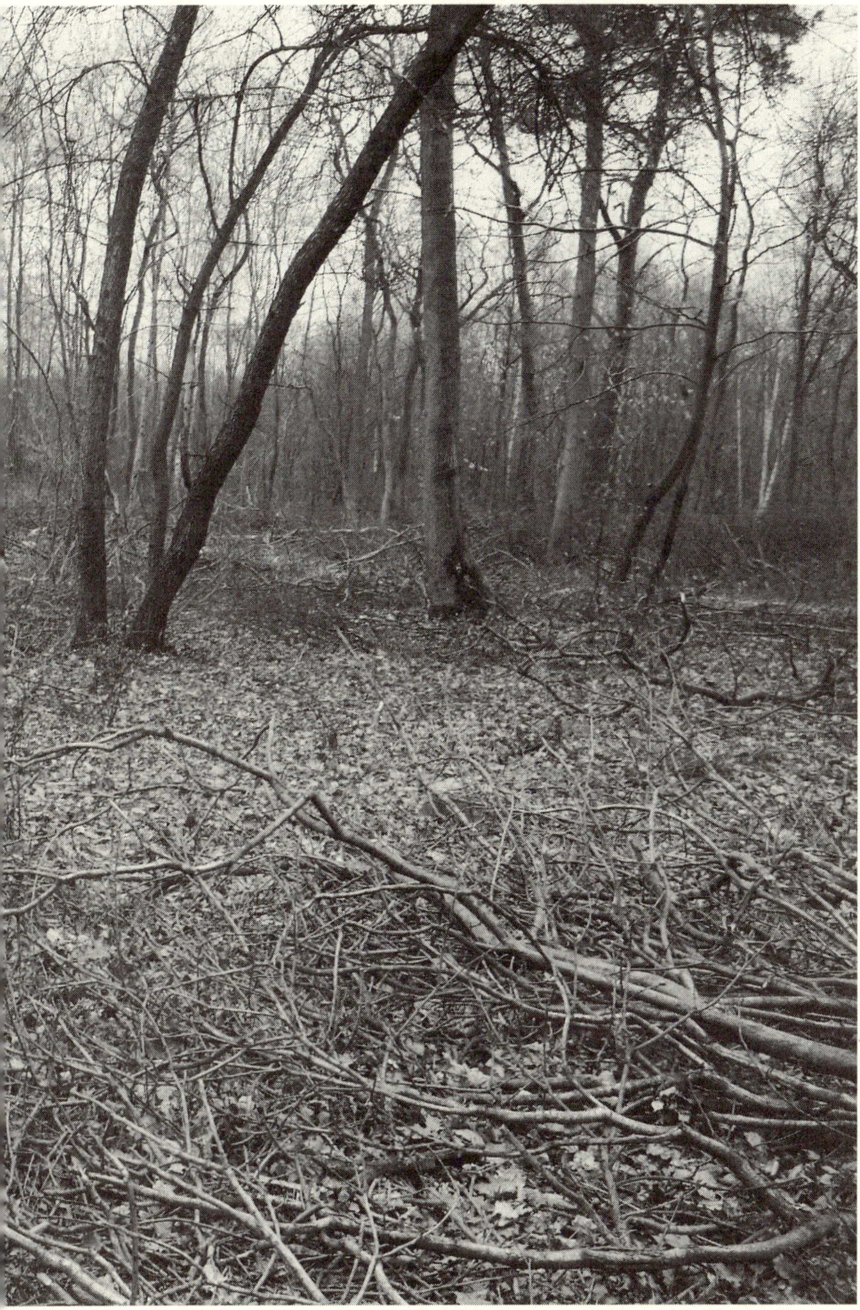

territory. Game and forestry management needs to adapt to natural laws. Humans have created artificial conditions of forest life for my companions by planting forests the way one might plant peas. The valleys, the clearings, the terrains that people see as being "of poor quality" give my forest friends the irregularities that they seek in the landscape. Today the logging industry, with its mechanical felling practices, its industrial rhythm, and its methods of reforestation in monotonous tracts covering hundreds of thousands of acres, leads to an imbalance among cervids, forcing them to wander through cultivated fields, orchards, and young plantations.

We are witnessing a massive exodus of deer populations from forest environments. Before the mechanization of logging in the 1990s, the plains of northern France were home to very few roe deer. Today, they live in groups of five to ten individuals in copses during the day, waiting for dusk and dawn to go and forage in the fields. In the vineyards, on the western coast, no roe deer used to come eat the leaves in cultivated areas. They were a rare presence in orchards or gardens. Today the forest no longer offers them the variety, the quality, or the quantity of the food that they need, and it offers them even less protection. Roe deer are more at home in the undergrowth and at the edge of the forest than they are in the depths of the woods, but humans, with their constant need for urbanization, are colonizing the valleys and eating into their environment. If forests grow naturally, let us look at the artificial clearings that we are making at the heart of them.

There is no point in putting huge pressure on deer populations in order to control them, because they are already under attack from the natural predation of foxes and buzzards, which eat young fawns; in some regions, it is lynxes and wolves who take over, not to mention illnesses and, more often than we imagine, stray dogs. However, there is a numerical balance between deaths and births, so that the number of roe deer remains more or less constant in a given place. One of the solutions to correct our poor management would be to preserve the most territorial adults while limiting the density of roe deer to the capacity that the environment can accommodate. Then the principle of self-regulation of the species will settle gently, generation after generation, because animals are not suicidal, and they don't eat more food than nature can offer. Animals should be allowed to eat in peace throughout the day with thickets arranged across the forest to avoid areas with too high a concentration of wild animals. Forests of deciduous trees with few conifers should be planted to encourage vegetation on the ground. Clearings should be created near bramble patches, with berry-growing bushes planted in the undergrowth so that the deer can find sloes, haws, blueberries, and other fruits. Those clearings and forest edges should be welcoming, and the grasses so beloved of roe deer should be allowed to grow to full maturity, and timber varieties should be maintained to produce forest fruits.

Each layer of a forest's development has its animals. Hares, partridges, voles, buzzards, and hawks live on the plains. The warren welcomes rabbits, foxes, and badgers. The edge of the forest hosts deer, weasels, and martens. The more the forest grows and the denser it gets, the more we plunge into its heart, the more we will see larger animals. We should see the trees of the forests as a bond with the other animals that live on the planet. Foresters should return to more humane types of logging, respect natural cycles, and give something more interesting and tastier to the other animals that also live off this habitat, so that they are less interested in the trees that we want to use. Nature is not a financial deposit; it's an asset shared by all animals, humans included.

Let us remember:

> *If civilization and culture enter a country by killing the first giant of the forest, they in turn will disappear when the ax has finished its work and the last tree has been felled.*

18

ONE NIGHT, when everything is calm, I decide to go home. What I want most of all is a hot shower. I don't know why, but I've had a kind of premonition. There are no stars tonight. A light wind blows in the tops of the Scots pines, which give off a fresh scent of resin. I walk along a little path that leads down toward the forestry building in the valley, on the edge of the forest. I cross a slope where foxes and badgers have dug their earths. I come across Valloux, an old roe deer friend, with his partner, Noelle, who are playing by jumping into huge shell holes from the Second World War. They both live along an electric line that has recently been built. A huge clearing about a hundred yards wide and several miles long now passes through their territory. The ponds have dried up and several hundred acres of beech trees have disappeared. Just think, this was once all forest...

I continue on my way until I reach the undergrowth. I find myself on a small paved forest road. I walk over the cattle guards recently installed to stop the animals leaving the forest, a device that becomes part of an enclosure system set up along the full length of the forest. The red deer won't be browsing in the meadows in the autumn anymore. It's been a while since I left the forest. I'm used to the sounds, the smells, and sensations of this environment, to which I have adapted completely. As I reach the edge of the forest, the wind changes, the smells are no longer the same, the air is less humid. I catch a scent of grass. The wind is stronger than in the forest and passes through all my layers of sweaters, making me shiver. I continue on my way across the plain while the forest calls to me. It's like leaving a girlfriend on the station platform and feeling, as the train pulls away, that you will never see her again.

I walk on the pavement, along the dimly lit street. The gate in front of the house is double locked, so I climb over it. Reaching the front door, I put my key in the lock, and something sticks; I can't open it. I decide to try the little garage door and then pass through a second door that allows me inside the house. I go to the fridge: it's empty. I look in the different food cupboards, and they're empty too. Some are even locked. I will later learn that the food had been hidden. I leave with tears in my eyes. I know it's the last time I'll be coming to this house.

I walk at a jog, without turning around, to get back as quickly as possible to the ones that I now think of as my real family: the roe deer.

As soon as I reach the forest I look for Chevy, my precious friend, but can't find him. I spend the whole morning looking for him without success. The hours pass, and a wave of depression hits me. I absolutely need to tell him of my pain. I walk back and forth along his usual routes without seeing him. I take a little break in the clearing—I haven't eaten anything, and nothing would have stayed down anyway. In the early afternoon, physically and emotionally exhausted, I set off for another part of the forest where he and I are in the habit of relaxing. It's then that I spot his silhouette. He is there, upright, proud. He studies me. I run to him, full tilt, and hug him. With both hands around his neck I start weeping on his shoulder. He stands motionless for several minutes. I feel his heart beating against my cheek, and he rests his muzzle on my shoulder. The warmth of his body does me good. He bristles his fur as if shivering, then starts licking my face. I'm so happy to see him, to be his friend. I'm convinced that he senses my dismay.

Roe deer have the ability to feel emotions, to tell the difference between good and evil, or between those who wish them well and those who wish to do them harm. I'm disgusted by my own species, which savagely kills my friends, destroys their environment, and lacks respect for the forest, and wounded by the attitude of those around me. I decide from that moment to spend as long as possible in complete autonomy, living off the forest without returning to the inhuman human world, which I definitely don't understand. Chevy is the most intelligent roe deer that I know; he doesn't judge me, he's sensitive to my distress, he always comes to my aid when I need him. There's something "human" about his behavior, in the noble sense of the term. He's more than a friend, he's a brother, and although I don't want to succumb to anthropomorphism, I've found a nonhuman person that I hold in incredible esteem.

19

TIME PASSES AND CHEVY develops a magnificent set of antlers. They grow quickly, and my friend starts finding their tips itchy. Sometimes when he comes to me to be stroked he takes advantage of the moment to rub them against my arm, my leg, or my backpack. Other times it's against Fern. When he does that he rubs his head against her fur and then, clumsily, against her face. Fern recoils a little; she doesn't like it, but in the end she lets him do it because she realizes that it eases the itch.

    The growth of antlers has nothing in common with cow's horns, which have a living bony core, which explains why they grow all the time. In roe deer, the bone is covered by a kind of skin called "velvet." That velvet is run through with large numbers of blood vessels that supply the nutrition necessary for the growth of the bone. As they begin to grow, the antlers are extremely sensitive; that sensitivity fades a little with time but only disappears completely when they have finished growing. During the first six months in the life of a male fawn, the bony pedicles form, to be replaced in February by little horns, which will be followed by the first antlers the following year. They finish growing before April. What is incredible is that the growth of the antlers is regulated by a hormone, the production of which is stimulated by sunlight. The velvet appears in winter, while the male hormone levels are very low. In the spring, the hormone, when secreted again, halts the growth. The antlers solidify and the velvet atrophies. The roe deer has only to get rid of it by rubbing his head.

Beneath the velvet, the antlers are white, but the tree sap on which the deer rubs them gives them a honeyed or brownish color. A roe deer that rubs its antlers against a beech tree will give them a light color, while a deer that rubs them against a conifer will turn them almost black. The antlers will at first be covered with little protuberant bumps, which have the same effect on the trees' bark as a parmesan grater. Within a short time those "pearlings" are smoothed. Needless to say, the foresters take a dim view of roe deer at that point, because by trying to shed the velvet they damage the trees intended for logging. But the percentage of trees affected remains extremely low, and if they are not cut within the year

Chevy. I never take a photograph of an animal with whom I haven't bonded in some way, because I want their eyes to express the friendship we share.

they will be used the year after. By May, all antlers should have been stripped of velvet, and the oldest bucks will have gotten rid of it by March. The velvet that falls to the ground doesn't take long to turn white, and rodents eat it for the calcium.

When Chevy encounters another buck he presents his antlers, shakes his head, and sometimes engages in head-to-head combat. The antlers can't really be seen as a weapon, since they are rarely used for self-defense; flight is more prudent. A roe deer can run at speeds approaching forty miles an hour, while their predators seldom get much above fifteen. More than anything, the antlers represent a beautiful ornament that it is considered stylish to wear in the spring to subdue your rivals before the eyes of a pretty doe.

The growth of the antlers stops with the loss of the velvet. Then, in the autumn, the natural weakening of the cells of the coronet (the junction between the antlers and the skull) leads to their loss. They fall off all by themselves when the deer runs or rubs itself against a tree. It's worth noting that the age of the individual has no influence over the length of the antlers. A deer like Six-Points has a very large territory, and it's easy for him to find rich and varied sources of food. That's why he has such big antlers.

We continue our territory-marking path and set off in search of different rubbing spots. We come across Fraidy, who doesn't have very impressive headgear. His antlers look stunted. They are still covered with velvet, but something has gone wrong in the course of their growth. Antlers grow very quickly, and when they aren't yet solidified they can undergo all kinds of traumas and accidents. This is the case with Fraidy this year. His left antler, damaged by a bramble bush when it was still growing, is now covered with a pile of unattractive skin that complicates his life. Luckily, this malformation will be shed in the autumn like any other antler, and the next set will not bear a scar of the incident. However, in some more serious cases resulting from an illness, a bullet wound, an abrasion, or something else, it can really become disastrous, because the cycle of antler growth is controlled by a very fragile hormonal balance. An ill-timed wound can have serious consequences for their growth, affecting the marking cycle and ultimately compromising the deer's social life.

20

IN MIDSUMMER, I bump into Fern, spread out on the ground in a path of ferns. The heat is intense, and she is relaxing in the sunlight. I can't help comparing her to the starlets tanning themselves on the beaches of the Mediterranean. At last she gets up and makes straight for Chevy's territory. I keep following her as best I can, because she walks quite quickly. She slips among some brambles, sniffs the different layers of air to work out where Chevy has gotten to, and then continues her quest. She finds him, and her attitude changes completely. Her gait is both slower and more determined. She stops in front of Chevy, who still looks at her quite affectionately. He approaches, and the lady pretends to ignore him. He tries a little embrace, without success, walks around her, and then slides his muzzle under the tuft on Fern's rear, making her shiver. She gives a little jump, shakes her head, looks at him, and gallops a few yards. Chevy follows her, and she stops abruptly. He comes up behind her at full speed, arches his back to avoid colliding with her, and starts putting his front feet on Fern's back. She sets off again at a gallop, and the game seems to arouse the two lovebirds.

Fern is in heat, and attracts Chevy with the secretion of her scent glands, along with a language made up of peculiar cries. The preliminaries consist in checking the physical strength of the buck, and thus naturally selecting the strongest genes to make good sturdy little fawns. Roe deer are quite polygamous, but Chevy and Fern, like Six-Points with Star, depart from the rule, not by becoming monogamous but by privileging each other in their territory. So Fern rejects the advances of other males and generally avoids gallivanting in other territories.

Chevy and Fern's little amorous game consists of long and passionate pursuits that end up in a circular run around a tree, a log, or a rock. The game lasts until the two lovebirds finally form a little path of beaten earth around the tree, called "the witch's ring," on which Chevy whinnies, groans, and even barks to warn competitors who, equally aroused by this little dance, might imagine that they can join in. They shouldn't even think about it!

Make no mistake, at this stage it's the doe who calls the shots and decides where coupling will take place. If the poor amorous buck gives up or collapses with exhaustion, she will find another one and bring him back to the same mating spot. This isn't the case with Chevy, who redoubles his efforts to make sure such a thing doesn't happen. A moment later, Fern is ready to receive Chevy. She stops running around the tree, and Chevy takes advantage of the fact to mount her several times, obviously with a certain pleasure, until the frolic is at an end. With a bit of luck, Fern will lead him into the same game tomorrow, the day after, and all the days that follow, and that can go on until the end of August, even though the period of estrus only lasts two or three days.

In Europe, the fertilization of does takes place from the middle of July until the end of August, during the rutting season. As soon as it is fertilized, the egg begins to divide and goes on "floating" in the womb for about six weeks before developing very slowly until December. Then this little collection of cells is implanted in the uterine wall. This process, called "delayed implantation," does not exist in any other cervid, and occurs only in a few mammals, including badgers, martens, weasels, and stoats. The fetuses grow rapidly until the birth of the fawns, nine to ten months after fertilization. Though there are forty weeks of gestation, the growth from embryo to fawn needs only twenty, and since nature knows what it's doing, a doe that goes unfertilized in the summer can be fertilized in a secondary rut that takes place between November and December. In that case, the implantation is not deferred and the birth occurs as normal in the late spring. When the time comes, Fern will probably give birth to one or two fawns that will stay with her until the following spring.

A few days later I come across Magnolia, who is playing the same game as Fern. She is one hundred percent polygamous, and so are her partners, like Bobo, Fraidy, Harry, and many others. Magnolia has led the dance for several seasons without ever producing offspring. She attracts the bucks, seduces them, and brings her suitors to the mating spot at a rapid pace until... they've exhausted. The poor things always give up in the end. And if by chance she happens upon a more persistent deer than the average, at the moment of mating she disappears! This time too I expect the same drama to play out. Having said that, there's something that intrigues me. The territories have been established, Magnolia is in heat, and three fine bucks are lying a few yards away from each other, which is far from usual. Magnolia brings along her first suitor, Harry. A few hours pass. Harry is about to give up. That's when I see Bobo trotting toward Magnolia. Harry leaves

Magnolia. A real seductress with a flashing eye. More doe than mother, she finally gave birth to Haw, who met a tragic fate.

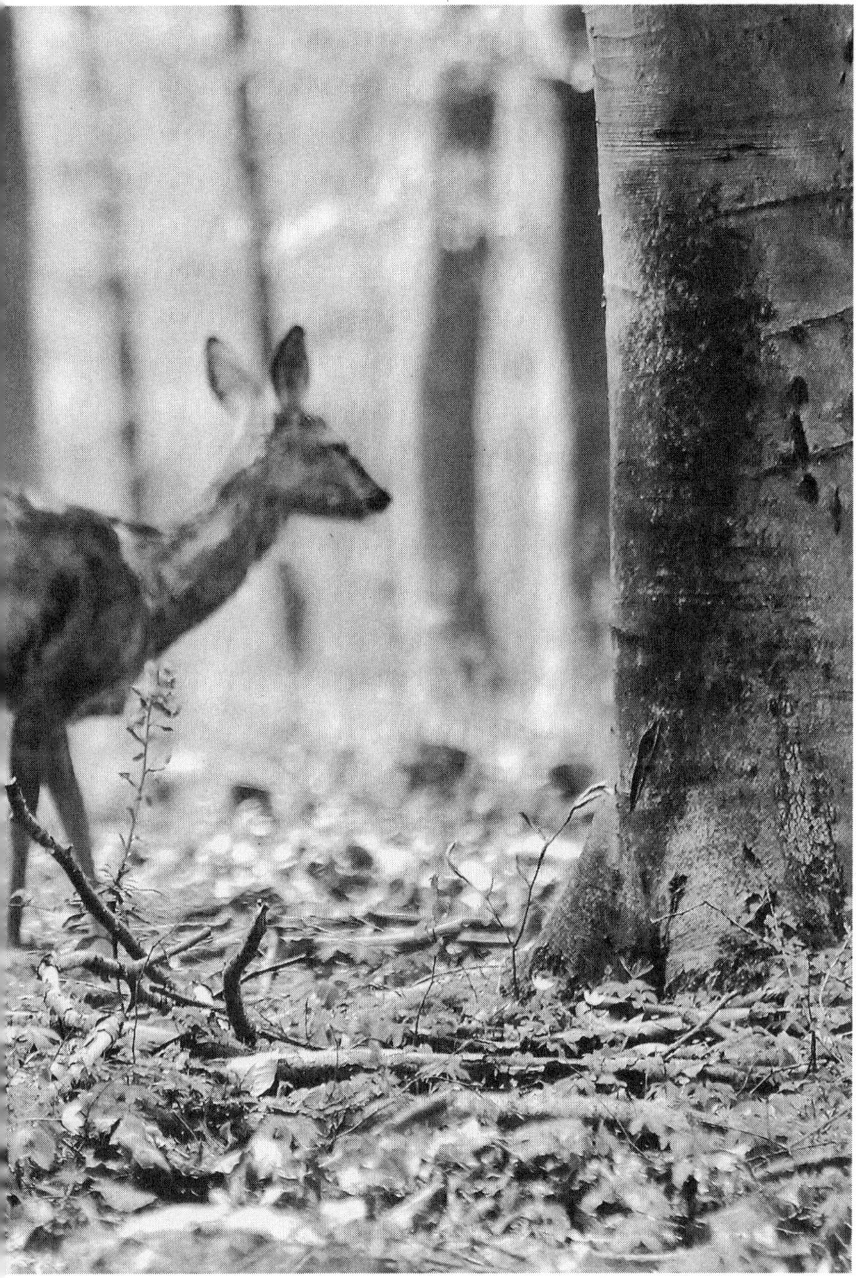

the witch's circle and Bobo hurries toward Magnolia. Harry goes off and lies down next to Fraidy without any conflict. Magnolia clearly hasn't noticed the funny business and goes on circling the little tree trunk. A short while later—here we go again—Bobo leaves the circle and Fraidy replaces him. I smile at this scene from a French farce. I can see that Magnolia is starting to get tired, and that she no longer knows how to escape this situation. She doesn't have the strength to run off to abandon her suitor. Then she gives up, stops, puts herself in the coupling position—head lowered, belly contracted, and body rigid. Fraidy starts his frolic and mounts her several times, then Bobo gets into position, mounts her as well, and then it's Harry's turn. All three of them go again several times, and they seem satisfied with their pact. Magnolia didn't choose this little merry-go-round, or to have fawns next year. After all these years, I'm still surprised by the adaptability of roe deer, capable of going against the most basic rules of nature when it suits their purposes.

21

SINCE THE END of the summer, Terylle, the little vixen, has been defining her territory, which is enormous given that it occupies nearly three square miles. She and her partner, whom I have called Vulpes, defend it to keep out intruders. It's the third year that she's been with the same partner. Sometimes I see them hunting together, but most of the time she's on her own, preferring to hunt alone. Once her territory has been defined and protected, she turns an old rabbit warren into her little home, but Vulpes isn't allowed in. Winter is the mating season for foxes. In the relative nocturnal calm of the forest, I can hear my two lovers shrieking, singing, wailing in the distance. A few hours later I bump into Terylle, who looks chipper; the concert given by Vulpes has clearly charmed her. For a few days they don't part; they play together, exhausting themselves in breathless games of chase without taking into account either their surroundings or any potential dangers. Lovers, in short!

The lovely vixen. Terylle was the companion of Vulpes, a fine black fox with whom she had cubs. I lived with her for a while, but I think that life with foxes is less exciting than life with roe deer. Foxes aren't very interested in other animals and don't try to interact with them.

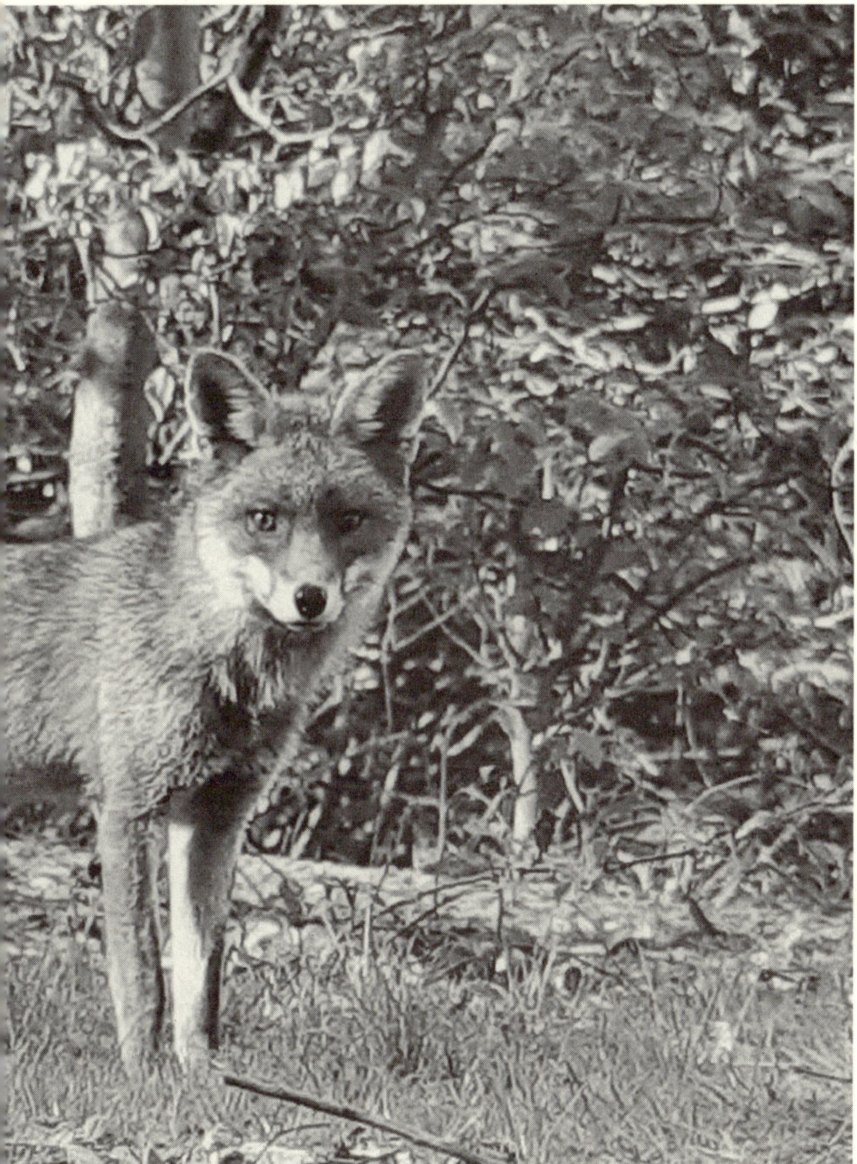

April comes. I know that Terylle has given birth in her den. Before, she pulled out some white hairs on her belly in order to reveal her teats and allow her little ones access to them. And now, after a fifty-two-day gestation, the little cubs have been born. I can't see them, but I can hear them. As the cubs need maternal warmth, Terylle has to stay with them for two weeks. During that time she depends entirely on Vulpes, who brings her an impressive amount of food. The fox seems less skilled at housekeeping, because a pile of organic detritus accumulates at the entrance to the den. Once four weeks have passed, only two cubs have survived natural selection. It's their first outing from the mouth of the den. Now that their mother's milk reserves are exhausted, solid food (field mice, shrews, beetles, etc.) will be their only source of nourishment. Terylle, now very thin, goes off hunting while the two little ones play. They are boisterous, frisky, and very curious. When she comes back, she brings food, sometimes burying some for later, and then deals with her two offspring. She licks them constantly, because the cleaner their fur the better insulated they are from the cold. Sometimes I lie and watch them with Chevy, who is also curious about all the comings and goings. They are fearless, and come and play at our feet. Their eyes are deep blue, and their faces turn red at the same time as their little muzzles lengthen.

Six months have passed, and I now regularly come across the cubs walking alone in the forest. They are weaned and already look like adults. The little male has been chased from the territory by his parents; his sister left of her own accord shortly before. Magnolia, the skittish doe, has had a fawn that I've called Haw. She is a little female, overflowing with spirit and curiosity. I can't tell who the father is; her mother had so many suitors. Magnolia lives quite far from Terylle and doesn't have anything to fear from Vulpes either. So I watch Haw growing up like lots of fawns before her.

One morning, when Haw is less than three months old, I hear her crying in the distance. Her voice is plaintive. She is running frantically in all directions. I approach her and see a magnificent fox in hunting posture. He's a male. I recognize him: it's one of Terylle's cubs. He has clearly established his territory not far from his parents, and he's attacking one of my friends. I look around for Magnolia, who is supposed to defend her child, but she's not there. I get closer, telling myself that my presence will drive the predator away, but I'm quite wrong. The young fox knows me very well, and remains concentrated on his first idea: having Haw for dinner.

For the first time I'm confronted with the dilemma of life and death. Do I save Haw from the jaws of a predator, or accept the law of nature in all its cruelty? After all these years, is my place still that of a mere spectator, or have I become an agent within the woodland kingdom? As I come forward, I realize that Haw is seriously wounded in the throat and the back legs. She calls her mother, who doesn't come. What on earth is going on? Magnolia should be running to help her! The young fox jumps on Haw, bites her belly, and clutches her neck to bring her down. My young friend won't be getting up again. I can still chase away the predator that has seriously wounded its prey. But to what end? To see Haw die of her wounds in front of me? I can't do anything; I arrived too late. And I have to accept it. Overwhelmed, I choose to leave, to avoid witnessing something that's unbearable to me.

 I don't understand why Magnolia isn't there. Does are devoted mothers, and I'm surprised by this behavior. When I find her at last, she's groaning and making little whispering sounds to call her daughter. She obviously lost her trail. Magnolia's a very young doe, inexperienced and clumsy. She's also been suffering for some time from a sort of allergic rhinitis, which must affect her sense of smell. She sniffles all the time, and her nose seems to be blocked. Haw is her only daughter, and I notice the distress in her eyes. Making little cries and groans, I invite her to follow me to the scene of the tragedy. Once we get there, I can see her grief. She understands that her daughter is dead. She looks around, finds the fox, and runs after him, but it's already too late. It will take Magnolia several weeks to recover from her ordeal.

22

FERN IS WALKING in a grove, nibbling at the ferns and a few scattered reeds, then she makes her way toward the clearing that offers her ample quantities of small plants. A replantation a few yards away particularly attracts her attention. The logged section has allowed the first colonizing trees to regenerate, like birches, hazelnuts, ashes, whitethorns, and other woody or semiwoody species. My friend takes advantage of natural coppicing, which provides an incredible variety of young twigs, some of them filled with tender leaves and succulent buds. But Fern doesn't just want to eat; she's also looking for a place where she can hide her fawns, because I can tell from her rounded flanks that she is expecting little ones. In some very precise spots she leaves marks to define her home range, which she will defend as best she can. It's here that she will give birth and bring up her young. Chevy and Fern have quite a sizable range, about a hundred acres in total, in which all their activities are played out. The other bucks and does are "tolerated" there. This range guarantees them a supply of food, shelters, and some calm and well-located places where they can rest in peace, all crisscrossed by a formidable network of paths. Chevy, for his part, marks his territory with great rigor and defends it jealously. It's a kind of district within their home range, which of course overlaps with Fern's zone of activity.

In early May, Fern gives birth in the middle of a meadow. She has only one daughter, whom I call Pollen. I leave them in peace for the first few weeks; in any case I'm kept busy during the day by marking territory with Chevy. One afternoon, my best friend joins Fern and her daughter. I walk behind them without a care in the world. Fern is at the front, followed by Chevy and then by her daughter. We pass along a logging track where there's a plantation of Scots pines, and the air feels milder. Conifers actually have the advantage of conserving heat. The sun warms us, and we look for a suitable place to rest.

All of a sudden I'm paralyzed by an unpleasant hissing sound. The noise comes from the ground—a snake. I nearly walked on it, and it doesn't seem too pleased. It's in defensive position, its head slightly raised, and it's not moving. I stand completely motionless, as the roe deer have taught me, my leg

The lovers. Chevy giving Fern a kiss.

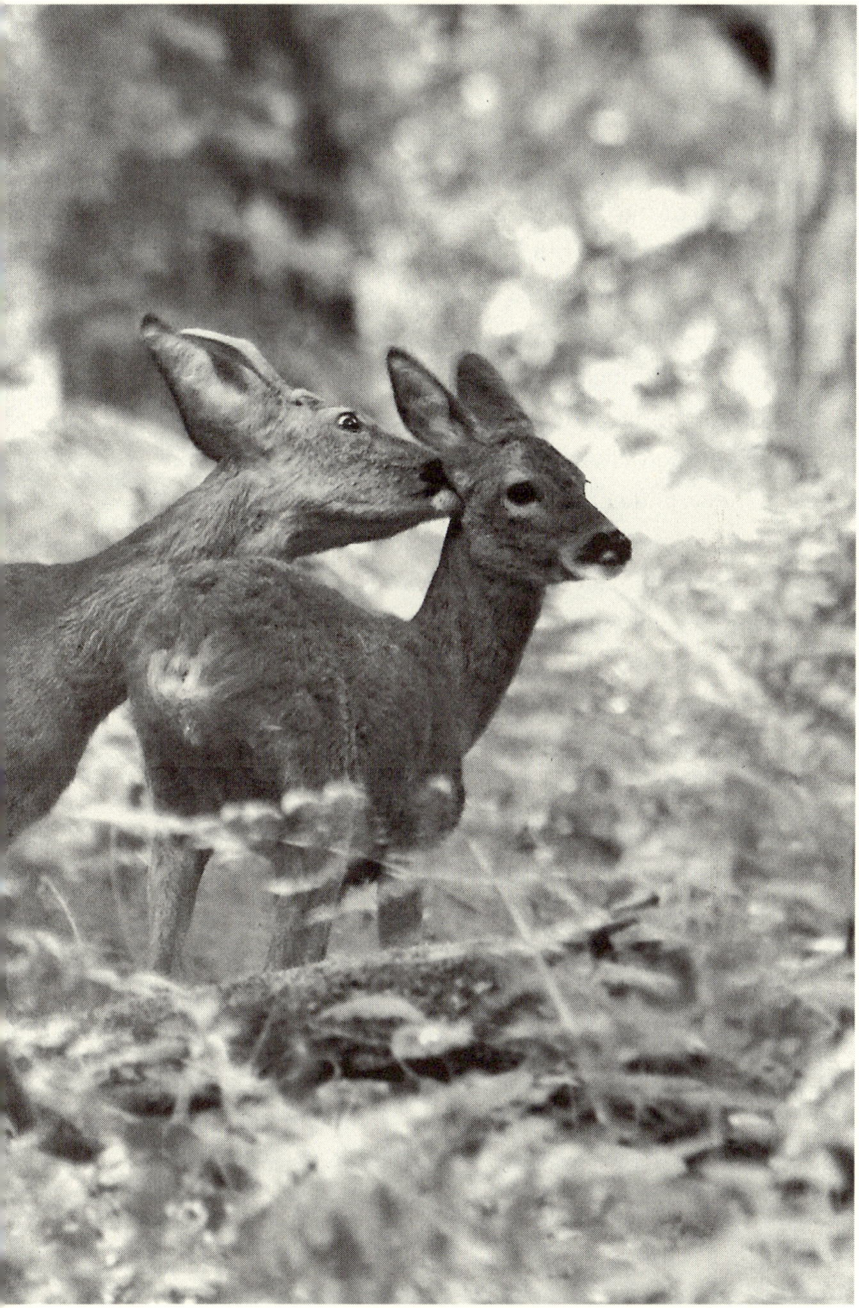

raised, frozen in the moment. The snake isn't calming down and I see my friends moving away. I try to groan like a fawn to call to them and tell them of my distress, but neither Pollen nor Chevy pay attention, and Fern seems a bit too far away to hear me. Luckily she turns around for a moment. Pollen has stopped as well. They both look at me. I go on groaning with my best imitation of the cry of a frightened fawn. Fern retraces her steps, passes by Chevy, and comes toward me. Seeing the snake, she lowers her head. She keeps on coming slowly forward, cautiously, raising her hooves very high. Now she is level with the reptile, which probably hasn't noticed her arrival. She walks behind it, raises her front hoof, and violently strikes the snake, which starts to flee. Fern pursues it and goes on striking it, aiming at its head. The poor creature is hurled around in all directions like a scrap of rubber tire. It must be dead by now, but Fern goes on stamping and stamping until she's sure she's finished it off. Then she comes back to see Pollen, gives her a few affectionate licks, and resumes her place at the head of the procession. I was in luck. Chevy, his curiosity aroused, comes and looks at the lifeless snake, sniffs it, turning back toward Fern from time to time, looking at me for approval. I don't think he's ever seen his partner act so violently, but Fern, like all other does, hates snakes, even more when the little ones are around. I'm glad she took this initiative, even if the snake was more frightened than me, and would have left of its own accord after a moment. I'm alive and relieved; thank you, Fern.

Chevy and Fern go on living their lives with their daughter. One fine morning, toward the end of spring, an unexpected thing happens. An unexpected thing by the name of Magalie. This magnificent and experienced doe is Sus's sister. I don't know why, but she has left her area of activity above the forest to come into our sector. I notice that Magalie has huge flanks, a sign that she too is pregnant. Since Fern has already given birth, and her territory is already marked, I imagine that Magalie will go back to her own territory to give birth. Sadly, that's not the case. Magalie is very territorial, and even if her sweet face makes my heart thump, I have to admit that she has a terrible personality. While I'm spending the morning with Fern and Pollen along a forest track, Magalie approaches. Fern doesn't say anything. Magalie comes forward a little more, sniffs me, and then makes her way toward Fern. Chevy's girlfriend, who is very sociable, tries to give Magalie a few licks. Suddenly Magalie starts barking and running resolutely at Fern. Fern stops, stands her ground, and tries to repel her, but Magalie, who is stronger than she is, manages to make her run off. After this long battle, I'm left alone with Pollen and we wait for Fern to return, but it's Magalie who comes back. Pollen, frightened, is breathing in fits and starts and hides her head between her two front hooves. She's petrified. Magalie doesn't seem aggressive, and pays no attention to Pollen. We wait for a long time and then hear Fern calling us, or rather calling her daughter. Running in a straight line, Pollen plunges into a nearby patch of forest to join her mother while Magalie watches us moving away. Fern, expelled from her territory, will not return. Magalie gives birth in high grass, also to a single fawn, a little female that I call Clara.

Months pass. Clara and Pollen become friends. Magalie is more curious about me than she was before, a rare thing among does. In general it's easier for me to unblock psychological obstacles in males, because they have a higher level of testosterone. That hormone gives them a bit more self-confidence, and makes them feel stronger. With females it takes me twice as long, because they're more watchful; they tend to be protective, guided by their maternal instinct, even when they have no young. They're more analytical, and more inclined to be fearful. But Magalie isn't at all like this, and she isn't like her brother Sus either. She approaches

Magalie. She thought of me as a trusted friend. She even made me the official nurse to her fawns Sloe and Hope.

easily, observes and understands quickly, and we soon establish a rapport.

Magalie spends the autumn with Fern, Chevy, me, and some other deer who join us: Pond, Bobo, Magnolia, Courage, and Sus. With Pollen and Clara we form a fine little group of eleven individuals, and take advantage of our winter friendships to have adventures and explore new parts of the forest. Even though roe deer are home-loving creatures, we cover about three miles a day in search of new territory. We play along the various fringes of the forest, running, jumping, and hurtling along the big hills just behind the forest ranger's house. We negotiate the barbed wire fence of a meadow full of lush grass and enjoy a few moments of pure happiness.

While my friends chew the cud, I rest among them. Courage gets up to nibble some leaves. All of a sudden, right in the middle of the meadow, he takes a few jumps and stops. He starts again, leaping more than three feet into the air. What's gotten into him? Nothing. He's playing. He dances, imagining that he's a big buck; he has a standoff with a twig sticking out of the field and performs the most incredible pirouettes. He is filled with a happy madness, the joy of life. Under the amused gaze of his fellow deer, he calms down a little before starting all over again. He throws himself into the air and wiggles his hindquarters at the same time; he kicks into the void, falls back to the ground, and arches his back. The game goes on: he spins around, points his antlers at some imaginary deer, and runs around like crazy before resuming his capers. After a brief moment of rest he leaps into the air again, turns around, and then lands on the ground with his legs splayed. Intrigued by everything and amused by trifles, he goes on playing like that for several minutes before finally coming back to lie down near Magalie as if nothing had happened.

We return to the interior of the forest; Pond has a cheeky expression on her face, and even though she's used to seeing me she regularly puts me to the test. In the late afternoon, when she's lying down and everything is calm, she suddenly sets off at a run, stopping to observe the others' reaction, but particularly mine. She is trying to exert a kind of authority over the group, but it doesn't work, because roe deer don't have leaders. Besides, since she's a little crazy, no one trusts her. Sometimes she breaks the serene atmosphere of the group. She becomes overexcited and spends her time teasing the others. I confess that she occasionally gets on my nerves. At any rate, she's cute, and her strong personality promises great things for the future.

Amid the group, I didn't notice winter passing, and spring is already on the way, but it's still cold. It's drizzling, and an icy wind penetrates all the layers of my clothes. The few years that I have spent in the forest are starting to do me harm. Because of my drastically reduced diet, I become physically exhausted more quickly than before. Since I'm in good company, and trusted by my roe deer friends, I decide to doze for a few minutes. I take shelter from the wind behind a big tree. The rain comes down in pelts, but I ignore it. In fact a band of low pressure is on the way and the temperature is about to plummet. I start dozing off and sink quickly into a deep sleep. My body temperature drops.

When I wake up I don't know where or who I am. To make matters worse, all my limbs are paralyzed. I can't get up. Chevy comes to see me and starts licking my face as he usually does after his nap. His little hot tongue running over my face wakes me a little and drags me from my torpor. It's then that I become aware of where I am. I see the big shining eyes of my friend, with his little nose pressed against mine. I try to get up, but I'm fixed to the ground. My legs are heavy, and I feel as if my commands to them are going unanswered. With one final effort, I cling to a branch and try to stand up. My heart pounds in my chest, my head is heavy, the landscape is spinning around me, and my whole body is numb. I throw up. I try to take a few steps to warm up and take a candle out of my pocket, which I manage to light after striking several matches. I put it on a handful of dead leaves that struggles to catch, adding some little twigs that I always carry in my backpack for emergencies. The flames start rising and I begin to lose my chill. I put on a little log, making cuts in it with my knife so that the fire doesn't go out. There we go; I'm getting my spirit back. Chevy and the others approach the fire, which I go on feeding, and then we spend the evening together.

I'm angry with myself for being so careless. It could have cost me my life. That little scare was like an electric shock. It isn't the first time that has happened to me, but it has never lasted as long. I would rather live a short, full life with my friends the roe deer than a life that is long and dull. But if I want to save them from the destruction of this world that is losing its mind, I know I have to stay alive, to tell their story and make the wider public aware of the reality of life in the wild.

23

IN ORDER TO UNDERSTAND roe deer, you have to understand their history, which is sometimes tragically bound up with our own. In prehistoric times, hunting was a pillar of the survival and continued existence of humankind. At first it was played out in big areas of grassland, but the climate change of the time and the rapid growth of trees altered the nature of prey. Red deer, boar, wolves, and roe deer took advantage of these huge changes. The growth of animal populations sped up and humans hunted, not only to provide themselves with food, clothes, and tools, but also to defend their nascent agriculture. This new activity, of course, influenced the behavior of animals and gradually transformed the forest into a refuge for them. Still, archaeological research finds very little evidence of the presence of roe deer on human menus. Perhaps roe deer didn't damage crops enough for them to take an interest. Perhaps the intelligence of these animals, their solitary lifestyles, and their ability to escape danger made them in a way inaccessible. We don't know.

Until the high Middle Ages, European kings organized hunts that were supposed to protect harvests from damage caused by wild animals, with peasants acting as beaters. The hunting of red deer was common practice, while some historians say the hunting of roe deer is purely a twentieth-century invention. Then kings and lords turned hunting into a "leisure activity" and ceased to protect the peasants from the repeated incursions of animals into their fields. A law of 1396 went so far as to ban peasants from hunting, even though the game was damaging their land. Hunting, the chief mission of which was to get rid of wild animals, moved away from the interests of the farmers to become a selfish pleasure of slaughter. Francis I of France, known as the father of hunters, protected the animals against agricultural interests. As a result a split arose between the king and the people over the simple pleasure of hunting.

If this passion of kings had the advantage of preserving Europe's finest forests, it deeply altered their appearance. Paths were traced within them to make it easier to get around in the mountains. Star-shaped roads were created, going off in several directions from a central point. In 1763, a very precise map called "The King's Hunts" was published, to identify the countless trails that ran through the forest ranges and provide orientation. This gave rise to modern cartography, until it became what it is today. Forests became so important that they were granted certain privileges of protection. New forests were even planted. In my own part of France, Norman noblemen regulated and sometimes even banned agriculture in certain places so that the forests could grow and their fauna thrive. Forests were no longer useful to human beings as a source of wood or foodstuffs, but only for the leisure of the hunt.

One of the first privileges abolished by the French Revolution in 1789 was the exclusive right to hunt. The social order was broken, and with it the lives of thousands of wild animals, roe deer included. Until then, only kings and nobles had been allowed to hunt, and roe deer were left out, if not completely ignored. From the nineteenth century onward, roe deer were given the status of "small game," and were not subject to restrictions. Hunting became democratic, and in less than a century the roe deer disappeared almost entirely from our landscapes. The twentieth century and its two great wars also led to the deaths of many wild animals. It wasn't until 1979, when the so-called hunting plan, a series of restrictions on hunting seasons, was made law in France, that roe deer were able to breathe a little. The species reproduced and began to stabilize. Except that the postwar reforestation—those monotonous tracts of woodland planted in straight lines—the development of winter crops, the practice of scattering grain for wild animals in forests, and all the measures taken at the time to industrialize the country totally destabilized the roe deer biotope. The industrialization and mechanization of the rural world are increasingly making wild fauna incompatible with the viability of agriculture and forestry. Roe deer have not changed since the arrival of humans on Earth. On the other hand, the cultural modifications of the last few centuries, and particularly the last few decades, have changed the lives of woodland creatures.

Not so long ago, the forest provided just as much food as our fields do now. Neolithic humans essentially lived on acorns. In the Middle Ages, acorns were a fruit consumed by the people, in the form of pancakes or bread. They were also used in the distillation of alcohol or as a substitute for coffee. It was the arrival of the potato that marked the end of acorn consumption. Other nuts and fruits such as chestnuts, hazelnuts, walnuts, hawthorns, sloes, wild pears, wild cherries, and sorb apples were among the popular foodstuffs. In the Alps, the stone pine, a conifer that produces large seeds, was used

Scarcity. Forestry has reduced the amount of available food, and sometimes forced us into cultivated fields or gardens in search of roots and tubers.

by country people who stored them for the winter, and the undergrowth of those forests was just as rich, if not more so, than many forest trees. Strawberries, raspberries, blackberries, and lingonberries were widely consumed. The mushrooms of French forests were famous even in Rome. Ferns were used in former times to stuff mattresses. The beech tree leaves used to stuff palliasses were poetically known as "plumes de bois," or "woodland feathers." Scattered rushes were used as floor coverings. Since the dawn of time the forest has provided us with resins, lacquers, gums, latex, fruit, and wood. This cultural connection that binds us to the forest allows us to "regulate," without really noticing, the quantity of food available in the same forest. With the help of natural predation, we are also involved in the regulation of animal populations. It's also thanks to this cultural connection that I have been able to keep this adventure going for so long. The problem lies in the fact that we have moved on from gathering nuts and berries to an intensive and destructive system of arboriculture whose sole purpose—at the expense of all the little plants that constituted the greatness and richness of our forests—is profit.

Today, when a roe deer nibbles the terminal bud of a young sapling intended for sale at some point in the more or less distant future, this "mutilated" sapling, in the eyes of the forester and the logging industry, is unviable for commercial exploitation. For this industrial park—still called a "forest"—to regenerate, investment is made in protective measures such as fences, for example, but these are expensive procedures. And those fences, often erected in clearings or clear-cut tracts of woodland, lead to a loss of territory and a significant lack of food for the roe deer, which are obliged to move to other areas of forest where they will continue to eat, leading to the erection of still more expensive fences. There are also individual protections for the young plants. They take the form of plastic sleeves or little nets, and allow fauna to circulate freely, but these protections are often more expensive than the saplings themselves and do not solve the problem of feeding roe deer.

 The forest as it has been colonized by modern humans leaves no room for the other species that also live off it. However, it's easy to learn to share, and I'd even say, "learn to give in order to receive." If I plant a willow tree of no financial value next to a beech or a spruce, it's the willow that the roe deer will eat, because it's tastier. If I leave bramble patches growing in the "unexploited" areas of forests, I create a refuge and a protection, which will mean that the roe deer don't need to go off to see how they might fare better elsewhere. If I leave the grass in the clearings unmown, the roe deer are less likely to go to the edge of the road to eat it, and so on. The forest should be considered not as an industrial development, but as a resource that provides interest of which we can make unlimited use. In our "fields of trees," roe deer won't stop eating just because we want them to. They interact with the forest. They don't exploit it; they maintain it. They live off it, and have no interest in wasting this vital natural resource. There's no point in trying to achieve the ideal density of animals for the wood industry to be preserved from all these wild beasts. There is no need to foster a balance between forest and game—it has never been and can't be done, because it is unstable and has varied since the dawn of time. It depends on climate, weather conditions, food supply, predation, and many other factors. In our own century, modern industry introduces quotas and overproduces for a demand that is unpredictable. This way of working cannot operate in the context of the forest, or in any natural habitat.

Applying a maximum density of twenty roe deer per hundred hectares has no meaning for animals that live very far away from our mercantile rules. It isn't good enough to establish a balance between nature and industry in a world already greatly troubled by climate change. The annual counts represent only an evolutionary average, not an absolute guide. No balance can exist when you force a natural environment to become a financial deposit. It's up to the forestry industry to follow natural laws, without which balance is broken. It needs to allow the formation of thickets in the forest and create sanctuaries, practice coppicing, leave natural clearings, encourage natural seeding, reduce the pressure from hunting, and allow roe deer to self-regulate. No, humans are not useful in this process, they do not replace predators, and they need to know their place.

If animals are suffering from the industrialization of the forest, do walkers and hikers and all the other users of the forest realize the extent of the damage this is causing to the natural environment? One day it will be too late to react. It's time to accept our responsibilities. There's no point in going to the other end of the world to film endangered jungles. The ones near us are equally biologically important, and they too are busy dying.

A little thought for the forest:

Human,
I am the flame of your hearth in the winter night
And, at the height of summer, the cool shade on your roof

I am the bed you sleep on, the frame of your house
The table on which you put your bread, the mast
for your ship
I am the handle of your hoe, the door of your shack
I am the wood of your cradle and of your coffin
The material of your work and the frame of your
universe
Hear my prayer: do not destroy me...

24

CLARA IS GROWING UP, and Magalie tries to show her in different ways that it's time for her to go and live her life on her own, elsewhere. But Clara doesn't really seem inclined to get it. Magalie, however, has prepared an adjacent territory for her on which she'll be able to live in safety. Clara couldn't care less; the young doe doesn't want to grow up and prefers to stay near her mother. Magalie waits for another few days, but time is pressing, because more fawns are on the way. And then, seeing that her daughter doesn't react, she finally expels her from her territory as she did with Fern last year. Clara settles in the adjacent territory, where she will go on seeing her mother, who continues to protect her.

A few weeks later, Magalie calves in the same place where she gave birth to Clara. I call the little ones Liberty and Charlie. Magalie introduced me to Clara when she was almost weaned, and it was only then that I started walking behind her. This time, she introduces me to her young after only two months. I'm flattered. Her posture suggests that she is proud to let me meet them. I think she's holding me in greater esteem because I'm not trying to see her children at all costs, and she likes the way I let her have some rest.

The year passes quietly and then, the following spring, starts over again. The young roe deer are politely invited to leave their mother to go and make their lives elsewhere. Since Liberty is the little female, she claims a territory adjacent to Magalie's. Clara has been able to use her territory for two years in a row. Charlie isn't allowed a favor of this kind, because he's a male. He has to set off in search of a territory, or find a roebuck to act as mentor, friend, or father. He chooses Courage as his tutor. That makes sense, because they spent the winter together, they're bosom buddies, and Courage seems to be in love with Magalie.

When the logging industry puts intense pressure on roe deer territory, the size of their spaces declines, and young deer can no longer settle outside of the place where they were born. They adapt to the situation by avoiding all confrontation with their neighbors; they maintain an overly close relationship with their mother, and end up settling in their mother's territory. This "philopatric" behavior creates groups

Magalie and Sloe. Magalie taught Sloe how to recognize plants. In this part of the forest it was easy to find the plant called yellow archangel, which female roe deer like because it's rich in nutrition. Sloe would need it when she had little ones of her own.

of roe deer that expand via couplings with brothers and sisters from the previous year, or indeed with any close relative. This leads to an increase in affection and lower levels of aggression, but also a great reduction in the size of the home range.

Spring passes quickly, and the summer that follows is equally fine. Courage manages to court Magalie, who is happy to accept the advances of this young suitor. Together, they will have two fawns, a male that I call Hope and a terribly cute female that I call Sloe. This year, Magalie doesn't wait. As soon as the birth markings have disappeared, she introduces me to her two lovely fawns, each of which weighs a good three pounds as far as I can tell. I take great pleasure in following them on their walks, and one day I understand that Magalie, when she's tired, is giving me her little ones to look after. As a general rule, does don't go more than two hundred yards from their offspring. But Magalie is an efficient mother. Exhausted after the delivery, she has recruited me as an official nurse to her kids, and while she is off going about her day-to-day business, feeding in the long grass, I'm left with two very unruly little fawns. Since mom isn't there, they only obey my barks very rarely. They run in all directions, bumping into each other. Hope tries to knock his sister over by putting all his weight on her. Sometimes she collapses, bringing her brother down with her with an indescribable racket.

Luckily Magalie has to come back ten times a day to suckle them. She can't store her reserves, and has to pass on to Sloe and Hope the vital energy and the nutrition that she extracts from nature, hence the importance of preserving the quality, the variety, and the quantity of the food sources in the forest. Quite simply, it's about the survival of the fawns. Rainfall is important, particularly at the end of spring. And it's water that defines the quality and availability of food. The more water there is, the more food, the richer the milk will be, and the better the health of the young. Sloe and her brother grow quickly and put on weight, about five ounces a day for each of them. So Magalie has to produce quality milk in great quantities every day, to ensure that her two fawns can grow by their combined ten ounces. Bearing in mind that Magalie only weighs about fifty-five pounds, this is an exceptional achievement. It represents the most important maternal investment known among ungulates. Unfortunately, in spite of this complete devotion, the does that live in an area of woodland exploited by people, where trees are regularly clear-cut, can no longer supply either the quantity or the quality of milk necessary for their young fawns. Food such as yellow archangel or nettles becomes scarce. This leads to a high mortality rate in the first three months, and sadly two fawns born together tend to have similar fates. When one of them suffers from malnutrition, it gets weaker and sometimes succumbs to the cold in the early morning, when the temperature is at its lowest. A short time later, the death of its sibling will often be observed.

When my two protégés are satisfied, Magalie comes to see me, and I have the idea of tasting a doe's milk. So I stroke her for a long time and then try to move under my friend like a car mechanic. I gently stroke one teat, pressing lightly, and then the milk flows gently. It's like concentrated milk infused with dried flowers and artichokes. The taste is surprising, but not bad! What's more, roe deer milk is richer in nutrition than cow's or goat's milk. In any case, it was just curiosity, and I'd rather leave it to the little fawns, who need it to get big and strong.

Sloe is incredibly intelligent, like a female Chevy. I think Courage's genes must have something to do with it. I've distinguished several families, which I've called the Six-Points (from the family of Six-Points, Chevy, Courage, and Pollen); the Bordes (the family of Sus, Magalie, and Pond); the Cobourgs; the Vaulloines; and so on. Each family is unique.

My favorite. Sloe was like a female Chevy. Intelligent, curious, and mischievous, with a real desire to learn about the world around her.

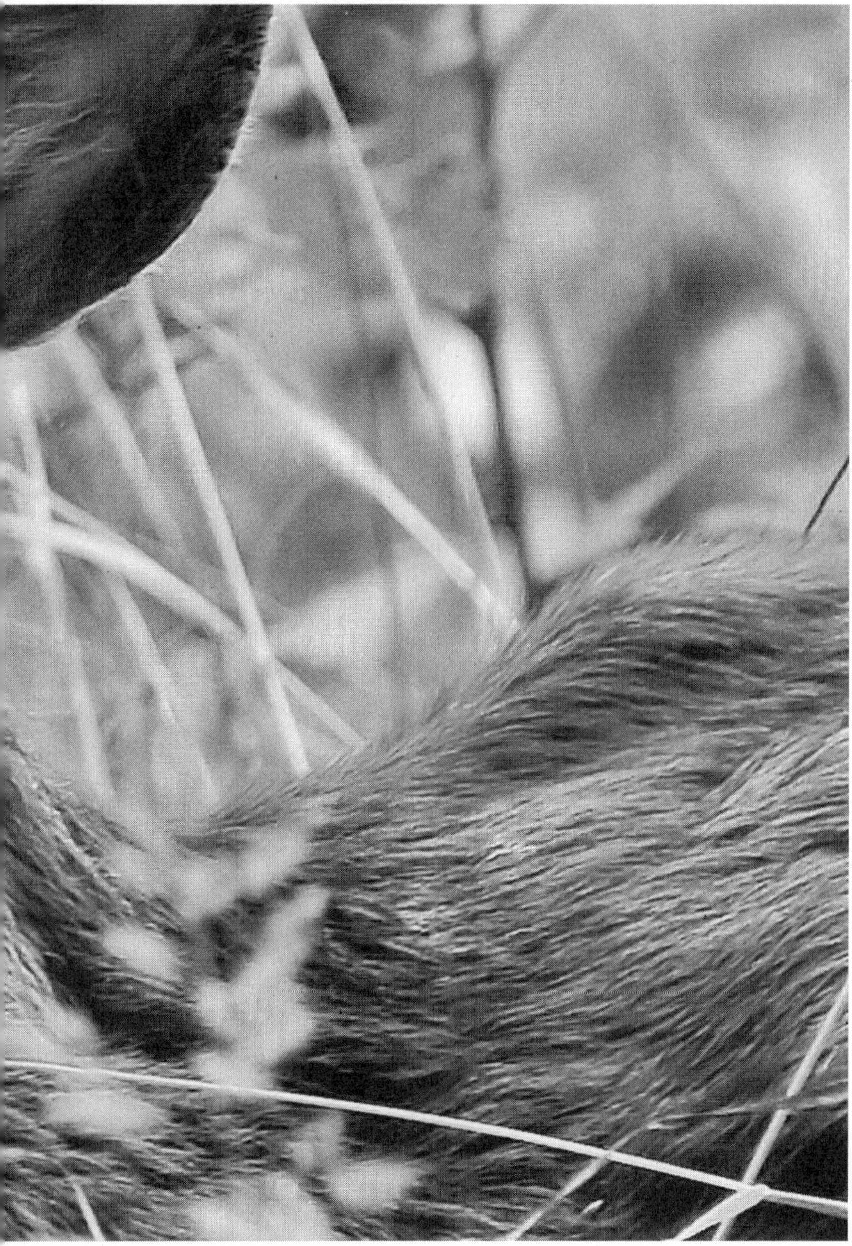

A kind of lineage with particular characteristics, such as the way the antlers grow, elongated muzzles or not, a more or less orange color of the fur, and a face with recognizable family features. Crossbreeding between families sometimes produces roe deer of surprising beauty and intelligence. I notice that the Six-Points family has a very powerful gene; each time, the result is a character like that of Chevy or his father, and now the character of Sloe. The same is true of the Bordes, who are rather reserved, and whose antlers, in the males, grow in a V shape, while in the Six-Points family they tend to grow straight and close together.

I have a lot of fun with Sloe. She sees me as being a bit like her big human brother, I think. I don't replace her twin brother, but she does hold me in very high esteem. Magalie goes off to rest in the sunlight with her son and I stay with Sloe, who doesn't want to move. We let the pair move away and go on resting at the foot of a tree. The light is beautiful and the sun's rays penetrate the canopy. Sloe is lying about four inches away from me, coiled up as usual, her muzzle under her knee. All of a sudden, with a terrible crash, a shadow takes us by surprise: a buzzard plunging down at us! Its claws literally slice open my arm and my leg—I can't believe my eyes. The bird of prey looks surprised and confused, as if it wasn't expecting to see me there. Seeing Sloe sleeping, it was tempted by the idea of hunting a fawn. Bad luck that I'm there, and the bird certainly hadn't seen me. My presence might have saved Sloe from a tragic end. The predator flies off with a shriek. Sloe, still quivering, runs off to find her mother, who isn't far away. There is blood all over my arm, and my calf is deeply gouged. Magalie sees us arriving terrified. She runs immediately to Sloe and licks her, whispers to her a little, then Sloe calms down and so do I. I take advantage of the moment to pour water from my water bottle over my wounds to clean them. Magalie comes over to me, sniffs at me, and licks me. We return to the cover of the trees to finish this emotional day.

Summer and fall pass uneventfully and, in spite of my exhaustion, I remain optimistic about the approaching winter. In fact there are still some surprises in store for me. We're approaching winter solstice. The nights are painfully long. Chevy, Fern, and Pollen change their territory. They leave the beech wood to go deep into a pine forest where logging is underway. It will bring them tender leaves and buds next spring. Sloe and her brother are still very young, while Pollen is already a beautiful yearling. I go back and forth between the two territories, which are quite a distance from each other. It is now bitingly cold and the weather is getting worse. However, one evening, a certain mildness provides balm to my heart. It's raining slightly, but not as bad as what I've known in the past. Courage joins Magalie, Sloe, Hope, and me. I snooze a little. Sloe lies down just in front of me. When I open my eyes it's snowing. The snow is falling heavily, and Sloe is covered by a thin layer of white powder. There isn't a sound in the vast forest, only the faintest crystal tinkling as the flakes touch the ground. I get up to shake off the flakes that are starting to drench my sweater. Still lying down, Sloe licks herself and sometimes tries to sniff a snowflake that falls in front of her. It doesn't stop snowing all night.

In the early morning the cold returns. The cloak of snow is not very thick for now, and it isn't yet too hard to find food. One fine sunny day passes, and I use it to rest on some fir tree branches, in the bright sunlight. Night falls, and the sky is overcast again. Some snowflakes whirl in the air, the cold gets a little stronger again, and then, after nightfall, the snow falls in abundance. An icy wind from the east freezes me immediately. The snow turns into ice. At daybreak the forest is like a skating rink. The successive layers of snow and ice make the terrain very difficult to negotiate. Magalie and Sloe nearly fall several times, and so do I. The bramble leaves are completely frozen. The does scrape the ground to get rid of the snow and the leaves, then lie down in the hole that they have just dug and rest for a long time.

When the climatic conditions become extremely harsh, roe deer are able to slow down their metabolism. So Sloe considerably reduces her activity, staying in front of me, almost motionless all day. This phenomenon is explained by roe deer's ability to reduce the absorbent surface of their bellies, allowing them to survive major and prolonged climatic events without feeling the need to eat or move, and without losing lots of weight. A kind of superpower to which, sadly, I don't have access. I look more like a pink flamingo. I lift one leg to get rid of the numbness, then the other, and so on. And the only thing I can do is to move from one territory to the other to see if everyone is all right. But it leaves me exhausted. So I reduce my activity as well; I make a fire to heat up some water and warm myself up. The only thing to do is wait patiently for it to pass. I'm starving, but I mustn't think about it. I admire the extraordinary resilience of the little fawns. They look frail and fragile, but they never complain. It's a good example to follow.

The crisis passes; the wind and rain return with more clement temperatures and life goes on. This climatic hazard has made me think again about an end to my adventure, and now I'm torn between this wild world with the roe deer that I love so much, but in which I'm gradually withering away, and the need to return to humans to survive and tell the story of my friends.

25

I'M TIRED. I'm losing my strength; I feel that in the very depths of my being. The cold, the snow, and the ice of last winter were particularly exhausting. I struggle to find food that would give me the strength that once ran through my body. My territory is stretched too thin. No leaves, no grass. Everything has been cut down: the wild cherries, the archangel, the nettles. The clearing has been turned into a field of corn. I have to travel for several miles to find anything to eat. To make matters worse, everything has been felled on either side of the main trail. Before, there were birch trees, wild cherries, ashes, hornbeams; it was a visual shield behind which we could go walking, seeing the path without being seen. Today, that shield has disappeared, and you can see two hundred yards into the forest.

I'm thinking more and more about bringing this adventure to an end. Not that I want to abandon my friends; I'd rather die side by side with them in the forest than elsewhere among humans. I know some places where no one would ever find my body. In particular I think of the suffering that my friends endure every day in the face of the disappearance of their territory, and I think it would be good, for both them and me, to relate the things you can experience when you're a wild animal. Without wishing to be pretentious, in a way I could become their spokesman.

Daguet is old, and we spend this early summer morning sleeping to regain our strength. A few hours pass, the sun rises, and Daguet wants to cross a very busy forest path. His territory is divided this year, because the young bucks of former years have become more powerful and Daguet's old bones can no longer compete with them. The anarchic growth of his antlers makes me think of the fingers of arthritic old men. His past grandeur is fading and the new generation now sees him as a sad old geezer. He gets up, grooms himself, nibbles a few nearby leaves, and then steps cautiously into the path. He wastes a little time on some brambles along the side of the clearing. A few moments later some morning walkers arrive. Daguet lifts his head, observes them for a moment, and then comes back, neck stretched, into the undergrowth where we were before. The walkers pass. We stay there for a long time, and then Daguet lies down to chew the cud.

Beech leaves. This is where Chevy was born, but this part of the forest no longer exists. It was subjected to a first cut that got rid of beeches, hornbeams, hazels, and blackthorns, then a second that cleared the oaks and the other valuable trees, before being subjected to a final clear-cut that left nothing but a desolate landscape.

After this moment's rest he gets up and browses, then sets off again toward the forest path. As he crosses, a cyclist comes down the pebbled path at full speed. Once again, Daguet resigns himself to eating a few flowers that grow inside the forest. Time passes; he steps cautiously forward, but as he's finally preparing to cross, three motorcyclists pass at full speed. This time Daguet jumps into the undergrowth, climbs a little slope, and watches the bikes disappear into the distance. One step forward, three steps back, and the merry-go-round begins all over again. Every time we try to cross to the other side of that damned road, a walker, a car, groups of tourists, or runners take us by surprise and stop poor Daguet from continuing with the marking of his territory.

The day passes, and human activity slowly becomes rarer. We go back to the road, and peace seems to have returned. The sun is about to set, and Daguet calms down, taking advantage of the quiet to nibble a few leaves, when I see someone walking their dog in the distance. Daguet sees them too and comes back again. All right, I've had enough! For the first time since I chose to live in total immersion in the forest, I decide to approach the walker.

26

"GOOD EVENING..."

"Good evening, *monsieur*."

The walker is a woman. She wears jeans, a white fleece jacket, and square metal-rimmed glasses. I look at her little dog. I'm worried that it will catch Daguet's scent on me. If it turns aggressive, I risk losing control of the situation and I'm not sure I would know how to react. I adopt an affable air, or at least do my best to.

"I should warn you, there's a big boar out for a stroll a bit farther up. For your own safety and that of your dog, you should really turn back."

"Oh, thank you! You're right. Do you know the forest well?"

"Yes, I'm a nature photographer."

We talk about animals and the beauty of the forest world as we walk back toward her car, parked in the lot outside the forest, on the edge of the village. She tells me that a road-building project is underway, that the work will start soon, and that the forest will suffer. She seems close to nature and I don't know why, but I start to talk to her about my friends the roe deer.

"How exciting! You know, you should really exhibit your photos to tell people about the life of the roe deer."

A strange feeling fills me. A feeling that I've never felt before. I'm touched by this woman who loves animals and nature. She seems to have a certain interest in defending my friends. We part at nightfall. I return to Daguet, who has finally managed to cross the path. I can't forget the face of that woman, who returns regularly to my thoughts. And the memory of her scent doesn't leave me either.

A few months later, I've resumed contact with civilization, and I'm organizing my first exhibition at Les Damps, a little village near Louviers. A crowd of people turn up to study my photographs, but also to catch a glimpse of the strange person who spent seven years, not far from their own homes, surrounded by wild animals, scaring the walkers. When I talk to these people, all my senses are on alert. I can smell their fear, their horror, dread, or suspicion. It's very hard for me, a source of anxieties the like of which I haven't felt for years.

And then, mid-conversation, a little distance away, in front of one of the most beautiful portraits of Chevy, I recognize the form that a few months ago moved me so. She smiles at me and comes over.

"Are you the one I met in the forest?"

"Yes, that's me. How are you?"

I immediately understand that my adventure will never be lonely again. And that she alone will meet my friends. On December 31, the feast day of the forest, I introduce her to Magalie, Sloe, Hope, and Sus. From now on, at least two of us know the extraordinary world of roe deer.

EPILOGUE

THE FOREST IS an integral part of the universe of roe deer and human beings. It feeds and it protects, and if each one of us watches carefully over it, that's how it will remain for a long time to come. The forest protects us against the cold of the frozen winter, it softens the heat of blazing summer, eases the violence of the wind, and prevents the advance of the desert. The forest is fertile; it brings us food and medicine. Without it, our landscapes would be nothing but desolation, and life would be reduced to the most total silence. It is the forest that purifies the atmosphere and allows us to breathe the oxygen indispensable to all living creatures. Without the forest there is no animal life, so let's respect it; let's respect the animals who live there and not, out of selfishness, forget the debt that we owe it. To live with roe deer is to live with the forest. Humans appeared on Earth less than a million years ago. Over the course of my adventure, I thought about my little story within the larger context of natural history. Who has never met eyes with a deer at a bend in the road? Most of these encounters are fleeting but, with the growth of our cities, peri-urban zones now allow many of us to come across this marvelous animal quite often. However, to come across something is not necessarily to become acquainted with it. Our human activities, by industrializing forestry, interfere in the life of deer even on the social level. Anyone who takes an interest in animal life needs to understand what a forest is. Then, in the face of the economic and industrial challenges of our age, I hope that a new approach to deer, based on a recognition of our shared lives, will let us open the door to a better integration of humans with their environment.

As Ernst Wiechert wrote so brilliantly:

The forest can only give the sense of a calm and safe place for as long as the law of cause and effect reigns manifestly there. It only starts to become a threatening place from the moment when that law loses its power and arbitrary forces seem to govern the world of trees.

NOTES

Translations of quoted material are the translator's own. The Wyandotte legend on page 85 is adapted from Georges E. Sioui, *Les Hurons-Wendats: Une civilisation méconnue* (Presses de l'Université Laval, 1994), and William E. Connelley, "Religious Conceptions of the Modern Hurons," *The Mississippi Valley Historical Review* (Oxford University Press, on behalf of the Organization of American Historians, 1922). The publisher gratefully acknowledges the Wyandotte Nation for permission to retell the story.

Elmer A. Mattot,
Senior Staff Assistant,
Physical Distribution Evaluation,
Continental Oil Company,
P.O. 2197, Houston, Texas, 77001

Dear Elmer,
  Autographed to and for you my good friend. I only hope and trust that this book means something to you, something worthwhile, something meaningful.
  Cordially and sincerely,
  William H. (Bill) Jorbert

Athens
Resident

Profit Potentials
of Physical Distribution

Profit Potentials
of Physical Distribution

William H. Joubert

AMERICAN MANAGEMENT ASSOCIATION

© American Management Association, Inc., 1972.
All rights reserved. Printed in the United States of America.

This publication may not be reproduced, stored in a retrieval system, or transmitted in whole or in part, in any form or by any means, electronic, mechanical, photocopying, recording, or otherwise, without the prior written permission of the Association.

International standard book number: 0-8144-5287-6
Library of Congress catalog card number: 70-173318

FIRST PRINTING

In memory of the late Thaddeus Street, Jr., good citizen nonpareil of Charleston, South Carolina, whose sterling character, brilliant intellect, and warm heart lifted and inspired his fellowmen. He, and his seafaring fathers for four generations before him, made Charleston the jewel seaport of the south Atlantic Coast.

Acknowledgments

ASSOCIATION with former colleagues on the faculties of the University of Florida, Florida State University, the University of North Carolina, and the University of Tennessee sowed the seeds that begot this book.

I am especially grateful to the late Truman C. Bigham, professor of economics at the University of Florida. On his advice I chose to major in the field of physical distribution. In counseling me 40 years ago, he correctly predicted that transportation as an intellectual discipline would become broader and deeper. I tried to heed his advice that I equip myself to analyze these deepening and broadening functions.

Following are other farsighted and warmhearted people whose teaching, encouragement, and philosophy helped me in studying this subject. Professor John G. Eldridge, an authority on economic thought, detected falsity and insincerity with an eagle eye. He embedded into the minds of his students, including myself, the need for accuracy, truthfulness, and an understanding of economic problems.

Montgomery Drummond Anderson, professor of statistics, business forecasting, and advanced economic theory, was a man of driving energy and incisive intellect. We endearingly termed him "Moby Dick," not for his physical but for his intellectual size. Dr. Anderson was a mathematical genius who made application of statistical methods to economic problems his life's goal. Like Professor Eldridge, Dr. Anderson fiercely challenged intellectual fakers who veered from the truth, and he instilled in his students a passion for precision.

Between 1936 and 1943 at the University of North Carolina I studied toward my doctorate under such world-renowned scholars as Herbert von Beckerath, Dudley J. Cowden, Edwin N. Bernstein, Theodore Drucker (father of Peter Drucker), Franz Guttman, and E. W. Zimmerman. These were men of broad vision and an international conception of the economy of the day.

While economic teachers and researchers at the University of Florida and the University of North Carolina did not formulate a full physical distribution theory or well-rounded concepts of intermodality, to their credit they did emphasize that man had not solved the major problems of the economy he created and that most of those unsolved problems were in the field of distribution.

When employed with the Tennessee Valley Authority between 1945 and 1953, I had the good fortune of associating with A. J. Wagner, currently TVA's chairman, J. Porter Taylor, Stefan F. Robock, and R. B. McGehee, all of whom had a genius for grasping facts and stating principles correctly in large and meaningful perspective. These men, economists, engineers, political scientists, and others of TVA's staff with whom I had the privilege of working, were guiding forces toward constructive thought.

Acknowledgments

Upon joining the Bowater Organization in 1953, I worked with Karl O. Elderkin, who encouraged me as his chief traffic officer to take an intermodal approach to all transportation problems and who listened intently when I urged that Bowater should weigh service and savings against each other in making decisions in the field of transportation and distribution.

While in the U.S. government service, I joined with N. R. Danielian in preparation of the basic studies which justified construction of the St. Lawrence Seaway project. That project, finally completed in a joint undertaking by Canada and the United States, has opened the Great Lakes to deep draft vessels and thereby given the lake ports commercial access to the oceans of the world. My association with Dr. Danielian gave me concepts concerning the value of water transportation, which I otherwise would not have acquired.

Coming closer to home in Calhoun, Tennessee, I wish to mention the contribution of my research analyst, Mrs. Gladys Baker, who assembled and codified research materials from hundreds of government reports, professional journals, and magazines and books, and made numerous constructive editorial suggestions.

And deserving of gratitude beyond measure is my wife, Anna Margaret, who created an atmosphere at home in which I could think, write, complain, and rewrite this manuscript, suffer discouragement, and perform a heavy burden of assignments for the Bowater Organization, knowing that she was managing well the household and our children, Lorraine and Rebecca.

William H. Joubert

Contents

1 Physical Distribution: The Neglected Function / 1
2 Components of Physical Distribution / 21
3 Current Problems and Opportunities / 66
4 Distribution Principles in Practice / 114
5 Future Prospects for PDM / 140
  Index / 171

1 Physical Distribution: The Neglected Function

PHYSICAL distribution accounts for approximately one-fourth of the retail dollar and for more than one-sixth of the U.S. gross national product. In many firms physical distribution costs are more than 50 percent of all operating expenses. Transportation costs alone account for approximately 20 percent of the operating expenses of the pulp and paper industry. In food manufacturing, PDM (physical distribution management) costs are more than 30 percent of sales. For all U.S. corporations, costs of physical distribution are double net profits, and two writers estimate that almost 50 cents of each dollar the American spends for material items falls within the scope of distribution.[1]

In most firms, however, procurement of raw materials, manufacture, legal, accounting, and other activities greatly overshadow physical distribution as a responsibility of management. Some company executives either disregard the fact that physical distribution is an essential

2   Profit Potentials of Physical Distribution

step between production and consumption or regard distribution as a twilight zone between raw material and ultimate consumer.[2] Physical distribution gains effectiveness only when the physical distribution manager has top-level staff responsibility for physical distribution policies and only when other staff and line officials, including local plant managers and their distribution departments, follow his policies. The main difficulty in promoting the systems approach to distribution, which cuts across departmental lines, arises from corporate organizational structures. From 1940 to the present, a kind of business organization has emerged that emphasizes specialization, segmented staff, and decentralized line responsibility. This type of organization creates virtually insurmountable roadblocks to a systems approach.

Recently McKinsey & Company, a business consultant firm, conducted a study of distribution management in 26 companies representing food processing, chemicals, petroleum, building materials, and metal fabricating. McKinsey selected four measures of efficiency in physical distribution: control information, personnel competence, distribution economics, and scope of distribution function.

Control Information

McKinsey's study found that, in order to function with optimum efficiency, companies should compile accurate accounting figures on principal segments of their distribution operation. It is equally important that the firms then utilize these data to control costs, measure results, and improve policies in such areas as inventory control,

Physical Distribution: The Neglected Function 3

plant location, transportation, and production planning. However, when queried on the subject, key executives of one sizable firm could estimate only roughly that their company's annual distribution costs ranged from $65 million to $120 million. By contrast, a building materials company with annual sales of over $500 million prepared detailed physical distribution cost reports, which enabled top management to pinpoint inefficiencies and within a reasonable period reduce its distribution costs by $50 million annually.

Personnel Competence

It requires a high degree of skill to negotiate freight rates and storage and stevedoring costs, to institute customer-satisfying delivery programs, and to pressure carriers to provide maximum service. Moreover, wide-awake transportation personnel can educate fellow executives to the need for a total look at the transportation function. Employment of high-caliber people in the distribution department is of paramount importance, and failure of management to recognize this will stultify any program to improve distribution.

Distribution Economics

Profits will suffer if management locates plants, promises faster deliveries to customers, or selects new markets without consultation with distribution officials. For example, a manufacturing company with $400 million annual sales maintained five separate plants but paid little attention to the high cost of shipping its product to distant markets. Through research the corporation found that, by expanding the number of factories from five to ten and placing them nearer destinations, it could and did save $5 million in annual distribution costs.

Scope of Distribution Function

The 26 McKinsey-surveyed companies varied enormously in their grasp of the total distribution problem. Their physical distribution procedures fell into three distinct concepts.

Traffic department. The narrowest distribution approach, adopted by eight of the studied companies, aimed only at securing the most advantageous freight rates and routes, usually with a strong bias toward railroad delivery.

Transportation. Thirteen of the companies had competence in more than one mode of transport and typically compared and evaluated transportation alternatives. Their personnel took an aggressive interest in and were successful in gaining rate concessions from carriers.

Total logistics. The most startling finding was that only five of the twenty-six companies qualified as "good" distributors. Their approach manifested itself in three ways: top executives dealt with distribution activities from a corporate rather than a functional viewpoint; transportation, traffic, and distribution personnel were unfettered by functional parochialism; and pertinent officials compiled accurate, adequate, and timely cost information. Relying on comprehensive cost data, the five "good" distributors could price out alternatives and effectuate trade-offs. For example, these superior companies readily accepted an increase in transportation costs in exchange for an improvement in competitive service or a reduction in warehouse expense. Thus by balancing economies in one physical distribution function against performance in others, such as customer service, manufacturing, and warehousing, these five companies saved markedly more in distribution than other companies in the sample.

Problem of Image

This is the age of the image, and an occupational group should, through heeding constructive criticism or self-evaluation, strive to create a favorable psychological impression. In the business arena a poor image is a handicapping liability to be expunged, a good image a valuable asset to be preserved.[3]

The physical distribution fraternity is endeavoring to modify and improve the image of distributors. But these executives are moving haltingly toward that goal in the face of numerous obstacles. Many hindrances, however, are caused by the managers themselves, and it is necessary to diagnose shortcomings and to seek guidelines to improve the image and status of those in physical distribution.

Shortcomings of Physical Distribution Managers

Physical distribution management exhibits four major shortcomings: lack of creativity, overspecialization, prejudice for particular carriers, and insufficient training.

Lack of creativity. The manager who lacks creativity is headed for a low rung on the organization ladder. New discoveries are being made so rapidly that Westinghouse Electric Corporation has found that the knowledge of graduate electrical engineers has a half-life of about ten years; that is, half of what the engineers know upon graduation will become obsolete within a decade. A reasonable estimate is that between 1930 and 1970 advances in research techniques have been responsible for 60 percent of the growth of the national income. There are too many traffic and distribution officials who buck the tide of technological advancement. A surprisingly large number of these executives lack enthusiasm for promising innovations and are indifferent to the bright promise of integrated transport, containerization, unitization of loads, and other progressive shipping ideas.[4]

Every year inventive individuals devise hundreds of new methods of freight handling via truck, rail, air, barge, express, freight forwarder, and mail at terminals, docks, warehouses, and other areas. However, many in physical distribution are insensitive to these revolutionary innovations, and some are even hostile to profit-creating advances.

Overspecialization. Most commercial traffic officers are specialists in their field and give inadequate attention to other significant functions of their firm or the whole economy. Clear-cut proof of rigid orthodoxy among these officials emerged from a recent survey by the American Society of Traffic and Transportation, the only professional society in the field of distribution. In its tests for certified membership AST&T includes one on general business, which encompasses economics, accounting, investment, price making, and other general aspects of the business world. Fifty-five percent of the candidates regarded general business as "very difficult," but only 7 percent placed the subject of traffic management in that category. Thus the run-of-the-mill traffic manager finds questions on his specialty relatively easy to answer, but he flounders when tested in a broad, unspecialized area of study.[5]

Prejudice for particular carriers. A large number of physical distribution managers are transferees from traffic departments of transportation carriers. Naturally there is a conscious or subconscious carry-over of interest in their former employers. Traffic officials who are familiar with a particular mode often fail to appreciate fully the traffic and distribution aspects and the advantages of other modes, and frequently are blind to the significance of physical distribution functions other than transportation. Though not always deliberate, these prejudgments nevertheless color the thinking and attitudes of many distribution executives. The damaging result of such prejudice is often rejection of sound physical distribution policies.

Another upshot of the industrial distribution manager's immersion in his own subject matter is his alienation from other sectors of corporate operations, even to the extent of devising his special vocabulary. Many top executives view the traffic world as a jungle of complex rates, ponderous tariffs, and peculiar ICC regulations with little or no relationship to manufacturing, sales, or finance. But that relation does exist, it is an intimate one, and failure to comprehend it can lead to serious economic errors.

Carrier and industrial traffic officials often maintain a camaraderie, which is not always conducive to "arm's length" bargaining between buyer and seller. Perhaps no other company group is as closely associated with outside interests as traffic and distribution men are with the carriers with whom they negotiate. And in few markets do suppliers dominate buyers as completely as suppliers of transportation services dominate buyers of that service.

8   Profit Potentials of Physical Distribution

Influence of carrier over shipper thinking is exemplified by the temper and editorial slant of major publications on subjects related to transportation and distribution. Since carrier, warehouse, port, and other related organizations insert 99 percent of the advertising in these periodicals, their pages naturally carry articles that promote carrier viewpoints and usually do not present adequately the problems of the shippers. In fact, shippers are without a single strong journalistic voice in the transportation and distribution world. Unfortunately there is a widespread but not altogether correct impression that various national and regional leagues, conferences, associations, advisory boards, trade groups, chambers of commerce, and other allegedly shipper-oriented groups powerfully champion the shippers' welfare before regulatory agencies, congressional committees, transportation rate bureaus, and related groups. In most instances, however, these organizations do little to uphold the shippers' cause.

Insufficient training. Another jolting reality with which most traffic, transportation, and distribution managers must reckon is that as a group they stopped their schooling too soon. They are hardworking and dependable, to be sure, but they are severely handicapped by lack of academic training. Only 24 percent of candidates for membership in the AST&T have completed four years of college, a much lower level of college training than is found in legal, medical, architectural, engineering, accounting, teaching, and other professional groups.

Following is a list of professional associations, their founding dates, and approximate present membership.[6] Each group is at least 80 years old and has a membership of not fewer than 36,000. AST&T, with 1,800 members,

Physical Distribution: The Neglected Function

Associations	Founding Date	Present Membership
American Medical Association	1847	155,000
American Association for the Advancement of Science	1848	54,000
American Bankers Association	1875	147,000
American Chemical Society	1876	79,000
American Bar Association	1878	96,000
American Institute of Certified Public Accountants	1887	36,000

has existed only 25 years. Its establishment was long overdue, and through AST&T traffic and distribution will probably achieve a greater degree of professionalism.

AST&T faces, however, the question of professionalism versus popularity. In an effort to take the pulse of the membership, the society conducted a survey in the fall of 1964.[7] The typical founder member of AST&T is a leader in the academic, industrial, or transportation world. Although this category of members is the best equipped academically of any in the society, 58 percent of them opposed a two-year college education requirement for eligibility to take AST&T examinations. Fifty-five percent of AST&T's certified members, who must make passing grades on four examinations and submit an acceptable research paper to gain membership in the society, were not in favor of the two-year college requirement. The examination program has been the backbone of AST&T. The society was organized in part to test the knowledge, technical ability, and experience level of candidates. However, as long as industry employs as traffic managers individuals with no education or training in the field, AST&T will face serious obstacles in attaining professional status for its members.

In this, the twenty-fifth year of its existence, AST&T is an established and respected member of the commercial world. However, AST&T still attracts too few people active in shipper, carrier, and education fields. Estimates of the number of people directly involved in handling freight exceed 5 million, but fewer than 2,000 belong to AST&T.

Government agencies such as the Department of Transportation, the Interstate Commerce Commission, the Civil Aeronautics Board, and the Department of Defense, all of which employ highly trained traffic personnel, produce a mere fraction of AST&T members. And there is only limited representation from persons in packaging, engineering, and warehousing, although AST&T encompasses all phases of physical distribution.

Impact of Shortcomings

Deficiencies of industrial traffic and distribution managers impose serious handicaps on their occupational growth. Following are brief descriptions of four of these drawbacks.

Low rank in management. Physical distribution departments will continue to be low on the managerial totem pole until they broaden their perspective and contribute constructively to solutions of larger problems (for example, ferreting out new and cheaper sources of raw materials and contributing information essential to location of plants, development of new markets for finished products, and adjustment to automation).

Ineffectiveness before regulatory agencies. Industrial traffic and distribution men are too frequently unpersuasive advocates before the Interstate Commerce Commission and other regulatory agencies. These quasi-judicial agencies often convince the customer-shipper appearing before them that he is dealing with conclaves that ignore the public interest and abuse the shipper instead of granting him the fair treatment to which the law entitles him.

For example, the favoritism that the ICC exhibits toward carriers that it regulates is blatant. Throughout the 91st session congressional committees harassed the ICC almost daily. At the so-called oversight hearings in March 1970 before Senator Vance Hartke's subcommittee on surface transportation, numerous witnesses castigated the commission's prorailroad, antipublic decisions with particular focus on its actions in rate increase cases; its failure to evaluate fairly evidence and testimony that shippers present; its dereliction in attacking freight car shortage; its approval of mergers without full consideration of their harmful results; its blindness to the extent to which conglomerates, giant corporate combinations of unrelated businesses, have siphoned off rail earnings to nonrail speculations, especially the case of the Penn Central Company; and its continued toleration of outmoded rate-making practices.

A review of the biographies of the present members of the Interstate Commerce Commission reveals that only two of the eleven are even remotely qualified to serve on that body. Commissioners on this supreme transportation tribunal should stand rigorous screening, as do judges of the Supreme Court. Ten of the eleven commissioners who have withdrawn from the Interstate Commerce Commission since 1960 immediately accepted positions with corporations or trade associations that they formerly regulated. One ICC commissioner resigned to become vice-president of a large railroad, another became assistant to the president of the Southern Railway Co., another resigned to represent bus operations, and another became vice-president of the Railway Express Agency, Inc. In contrast, however, during the same period no ICC commissioner resigned to join a manufacturing industry.

It is evident that carrier influence with the ICC, FMC (Federal Maritime Commission), and CAB (Civil Aeronautics Board) is much greater than that of any shipper or group of shippers. Carrier witnesses and lawyers maintain intimate friendships with the examiners and know well the inner workings of these agencies. Most shippers, however, are excluded from the informal chitchat between the regulator and the regulated. Powerful carrier trade associations, like the AAR (Association of American Railroads) and the ATA (American Trucking Association), and individual railroads and truck lines have Washington offices and maintain close personal contact with all pertinent agencies by telephone or over the coffee cup. Lobbying is, of course, not unethical, and it can be highly useful and beneficial. For example, carrier representatives can provide the commissions with facts and concepts that are needed to regulate the modes effectively. But the shippers as well as the carriers should influence decision making.

Inadequate influence on transportation legislation. Congress plays a major role in formulating transportation policy. Because it has created the federal regulatory agencies, it is the only branch of government capable of cutting across lines of authority. The decisions of the regulatory bodies are also restricted by the statutes that created them. Congress supersedes even the president in the transportation area, because the chief executive is faced with so many complex problems that he pays only passing attention to interstate transportation.[8] To be sure, shipper groups are well represented in Washington; their lobbyists and other representatives work diligently in the interests of their principals, but their efforts are concentrated in areas other than transportation and distribution (for example, in securing government contracts, tax advantages, and other favors and services). However, carrier-lobbying juggernauts such as the AAR, ATA, FFA (Freight Forwarders Association), AWO (American Waterways Operators), and CASL (Committee of American Steamship Lines) drown out the shippers' voices before congressional committees.

During its 90th and 91st sessions the Congress considered more than 1,500 bills dealing with transportation. Judged by potential contribution to the national welfare, some of these measures deserved adoption, others did not. By taking a more active, intelligent, and forceful position before congressional committees, traffic and distribution executives could influence Congress to act more effectively in the public interest. These executives could also remind Congress that the regulatory agencies are extended arms of the legislative body and should not be overly influenced by the president, by any executive agency of the national government, or by any carrier, shipper, or sectional interest.

Since 1961 Congress has experienced one fiasco after another in its attempt to enact beneficial transportation legislation. Following the failure of President John Kennedy's omnibus transportation proposals in the 87th Congress, the 88th Congress considered a modified version, termed the Harris Bill (H.R. 9903), the main purpose of which was to eliminate virtually all significant regulation of interstate transport. The House Interstate and Foreign Commerce Committee, with Representative Oren Harris of Arkansas as chairman, overwhelmingly approved this bill, which had strong railroad support. However, mainly because of opposition of truck lines, water carriers, and certain regional interests, the House Ways and Means Committee did not permit this legislation to come before the House for a vote. The significant fact is that shipper traffic managers played virtually no part in framing this legislation, in pushing it before Congress, or in killing it.

The very same was true of H.R. 5401; this bill was also sponsored by Harris but was a greatly modified and weakened version of the original proposal. The first session of the 89th Congress approved this legislation, and President Johnson signed it into law. The bill did eliminate many unlawful or "gray area" truck operators, but its approval was due mainly to rail and regulated truck line support, not to the support of shipper traffic managers.

In the 89th Congress both the House and the Senate approved penalty per diem legislation, a measure that would penalize a railroad holding and utilizing beyond a reasonable time freight cars of other rail carriers. But again shipper support was so weak, desultory, and badly organized that the House Interstate and Foreign Commerce Committee refused for months to hold hearings on the bill. When the committee finally held hearings, only three shipper witnesses appeared in support of the measure, while the other thirty-three witnesses were either railroad officials or congressmen. Thus the shippers did little to insure the eventual enactment of this bill.

Additional developments reflect the absurdity of the present situation. In 1966 Congress, having neglected for years the enactment of a comprehensive transport bill, decided to establish the Department of Transportation, (DOT), a new bureaucratic giant with an annual budget larger than that of any other cabinet office except the Defense Department. DOT is a truncated organization without clear-cut responsibility or authority. The new cabinet post has jurisdiction over safety, promotion, and research, areas for which existing government agencies in other departments were already responsible. However, the department lacks jurisdiction over four major phases of transportation—evaluation of waterway projects, maritime affairs, freight car service, and regulation. One cannot fairly charge DOT's personnel with indifference or incompetence; to date, however, the department's record is one of nonaccomplishment, mainly because Congress has failed to grant it adequate powers or to clearly define its relationship to other agencies.[9]

The Interstate Commerce Act itself is an example of the inadequacy of Congress's approach to transportation. Congress should recognize that the Interstate Commerce Act is not one but four separate acts with conflicting and inconsistent provisions. Congress should therefore recodify the act into a coherent, consistent law regulating railroads, truck lines, barge lines, pipelines, freight forwarders, and other modes of transport.

Lack of bargaining ability. Of all the desirable attributes of a distribution manager, the most critical ones are the ability to outwit and outmaneuver his counterparts in industry and the talent to persuade traffic organizations to further his company's welfare by overcoming negative, if not impossible, conditions that carrier officials often demand of shippers in exchange for publication of fair rates and provision of adequate service and equipment. Distribution managers should give most of their energy to bargaining for rates, charges, equipment, and service with individual modes of transport and with carrier rate and classification conferences, and to representing their companies before regulatory agencies, courts, national and state legislative committees, and other pertinent groups. Unfortunately the vast majority of distribution managers lack training in these key phases of their responsibility. Many companies recklessly sacrifice profits by sending untrained and uninformed representatives to bargaining tables in the tough-minded transportation world. These representatives cannot possibly hold their own against carrier professionals concerning freight rate levels, best equipment for particular freight items, and needed improvements in distribution services.

Physical Distribution Worldwide

Physical distribution encompasses both foreign and domestic commerce, and students of the subject must distinguish the similar and dissimilar characteristics of trading abroad and at home. Continued expansion of international trade is a virtual certainty. That growth will relegate to limbo those physical distribution executives who fail to keep abreast of worldwide economic trends.

U.S. government agencies, particularly the Commerce Department, have long actively encouraged American private businesses to expand their markets abroad. Commerce implements the aid program through three

Physical Distribution: The Neglected Function

subdivisions—the Bureau of International Commerce (BIC), the Business and Defense Services Administration (BDSA), and the Capital Projects Division.

BIC is a clearinghouse for foreign marketing data. For example, it issues trade lists of individual companies handling certain commodities in specific countries. Another helpful unit within BIC is the Business Assistance Division (BAD), which helps exporters to plow through the red tape of Washington. BDSA, with 100 industry specialists at work, strives to transcend obstacles at national boundaries and compiles data for industries seeking foreign markets. The Capital Projects Division assembles "packages" concerned with major foreign construction, mining, and heavy industry programs. For example, a foreign industry may not possess the financial capability to perform a sizable construction job. Once the Capital Projects Division learns of such a foreign undertaking and financial deficiency, it forms a consortium of U.S. firms to coordinate proposals of several individual U.S. companies.

Issue of Liability

Each type of carrier has its own peculiar liability standards, which may differ widely from those of other carriers. Reconciliation of these standards is a thorny and troublesome problem. For example, a railroad may accept a through international shipment at an inland U.S. point of origin for delivery via ocean carrier to the port of Cherbourg without knowing whether railroad or steamship liability standards apply. Railroads typically bear stricter and heavier liability than ocean lines. For instance, even if the steamship company damages the cargo and the railroad reimburses the shipper or receiver fully for the money loss, the steamship company is under no liability to share in that repayment.

Container Marine Lines (CML), a large containership operator, has made an attempt to overcome the liability issue by filing a tariff providing transportation from inland points in the U.S. to inland points in Europe. The Federal Maritime Commission accepted the tariff only after CML announced a separate charge for port-to-port service. In what was perhaps the first meaningful statement by a government agency on liability in international commerce, the FMC permitted CML to assume responsibility for the entire origin-to-destination movement.

For understandable reasons the Civil Aeronautics Board has not joined the FMC in the latter's attempt to solve responsibility for liability in foreign trade. Unlike seaports, airports are scattered throughout the country, and truck lines enjoy statutory exemption from regulation of the Interstate Commerce Commission for pickup and delivery of airline traffic. Thus a truck carrier that has damaged an air shipment in foreign trade has no responsibility to honor claims for loss and damage.

There is yet another touchy liability issue— responsibility for damage to export shipments upon arrival at and movement inland from foreign ports. U.S. regulatory agencies lack jurisdiction over foreign legs of joint international moves and consequently are in the dark concerning placement of damage claims against foreign port operators or transportation agencies. In the case of foreign exports via air the shipment must land in the country of destination and under existing international regulations cannot cross national boundaries without special arrangements.

The Paper-Work Problem

Today red tape cramps and at times blocks the avenues of international commerce and handicaps in one way or another all but a fraction of that traffic. It is a paradox of the age that in foreign trade, paper work is an even greater nemesis than most political and technological problems. Today a U.S. exporter cannot consummate at one time and place arrangements for through transportation from an inland origin to an inland destination overseas or secure a single-factor rate for the movement. For each international shipment the American exporter must also bear the burden of executing a dozen or more documents at an average cost per consignment of $163.

One comprehensive assault upon the red tape barrier is the Trade Simplification Bill, which the Department of Transportation introduced into Congress in 1968. The national legislature has to date rejected the measure, but it is still before Congress. The legislation would legalize publication of joint rates and institution of through service between inland U.S. and inland foreign points, permit use of through export bills of lading, and remove other shackles to world commercial progress. It would apply to interstate and foreign trade by sea, rail, air, and highway through countries and continents.

Although no organized group has explicitly opposed the bill, there is a surprising absence of supporters. The Interstate Commerce Commission, which should have a profound interest in clearing paths for commerce and trade, has made no statement concerning the measure. The Department of Justice has also remained mute for fear that the bill would vitiate its power to prosecute carriers that violate the antitrust laws.

Freight forwarders take a jaundiced view of the legislation, fearing that it would permit other carriers to bypass them in making land-ocean and air-land transportation arrangements. And motor carriers have withheld their support, arguing that freight forwarders are not carriers and have no right to the authority the bill would grant forwarders to participate in international trade.

References

1. Donald E. Horton and Mark Egan, "Should You Go Public in Distribution?" *Handling and Shipping*, December 1969, p. 57.

2. Robert P. Neuschel, "Physical Distribution—Forgotten Frontier," *Harvard Business Review*, March–April 1967, p. 125.

3. James M. Dixon, "NCDM Theme: Planning," *Distribution Worldwide*, November 1970, p. 48.

4. "Ex Cathedra," *Handling and Shipping*, February 1971, pp. 41–44.

5. "A Study of Transportation Education Needs," *Transportation Journal*, Spring 1966, pp. 5–24.

6. The data were compiled from official publications of the trade associations indicated.

7. James T. Harris, "A.S.T.T. . . . Survey of Membership: Professionalism or Popularity?" *Transportation Journal*, Winter 1965, pp. 15–20.

8. Hugh S. Norton, *National Transportation Policy: Formation and Implementation* (Berkeley, Calif.: McCutchan Publishing Corp., 1966), Chapters 8–12.

9. John McCullough, "The Shipper & the DOT," *Distribution Worldwide*, November 1970, p. 7.

2 Components of Physical Distribution

OUR next step is the exploration of the seven major component functions of physical distribution management (PDM). We will start as close as possible to the point where manufacturing ends and distribution begins, although such a break-off point is difficult to define sharply since it varies from industry to industry. We will evaluate the relative importance of each PD function and demonstrate that top management should execute these activities under coordinated centralized control. The components of physical distribution are: order planning, packaging, transportation, storage and warehousing, inventory control, stevedoring, and delivery services.

Order Planning

The customer's order sets in motion the physical distribution machinery. It is the ramrod from buyer to supplier that initiates the processes transforming raw material into delivered product. Order planning is the initial, and next to transportation perhaps the most significant, step in the logistics of business. The best-conceived business logistics system accomplishes little unless it gives priority to prompt and accurate processing of customer orders.

Order planning in a manufacturing, wholesale, or retail company begins with receipt of the itemized order. Immediately on arrival of the order at the supplier's office, the staff should analyze it carefully and adjust manufacturing, scheduling, routing, order picking, and dispatching in order to produce and deliver the desired articles promptly. The individual in charge of preparation and dispatch of the order should ascertain the optimum assortment and quantity of each item on the list. Determination of the optimum-size order requires a balancing of two expense items—ordering and inventory holding. Ordering costs are the product of the expense of a single order multiplied by the frequency of orders. The smaller the quantity ordered, the greater the ordering costs and the higher per unit inventory-holding cost.

The purchaser must bear two major categories of inventory-holding costs: (1) interest on capital invested in inventory and (2) storage charges plus losses resulting from damage in storage. For example, if interest on the value of inventory is 10 percent and risk of loss and physical costs of storage of inventory are 15 percent of the money value of the inventory, the total cost of holding the goods is 25 percent. As interest rates fall, the size of the optimum order increases. For example, a 20 percent decrease in holding costs would result in about a 10 percent rise in the optimum order quantity.

Fixed Order Quantity Versus Fixed Order Time

Order departments may place their orders for (1) a fixed quantity to be delivered at variable times or (2) variable quantities to be delivered at a fixed time. Each procedure affects inventory systems differently. For example, under the fixed quantity method, a grocery chain may order a fixed quantity of canned goods and permit a variable time between placing of the order and delivery date. Under the fixed time procedure, the receiver may schedule inbound trucks at fixed times with varying quantities in order to minimize transportation costs. Generally, the fixed quantity basis works best when no severe fleet-scheduling problems exist, and the fixed time basis is preferable when such difficulties do exist.

One irritating characteristic of double-entry accounting systems of the majority of manufacturers, wholesalers, and retailers is that they fail to identify costs associated with the time period of order cycles. A profit-and-loss statement shows old inventory plus purchases minus new inventory to determine cost of goods sold, and the accompanying balance sheet shows only the new inventory at the end of the fiscal period. The result is that neither statement throws light on the effect of varying time dimensions upon earnings.

For example, a firm with annual sales of $365 million may require an average daily inventory of $1 million. Therefore, if the elapsed time to complete the manufacture of an article from raw material to finished product is 30 days, the average daily inventory is $30 million (30 days multiplied by $1 million). If this period is shortened from 30 to 10 days, the required inventory drops to $10 million, a saving of $20 million in inventory investment.

Thus accounting systems, order cycles, and inventory planning should intermesh much more closely than they now do. At present, although order cycles may vary widely, very few order planners adjust their inventories to these variations.

Modern Systems

Processing of orders by AJF Industries, a national public warehousing chain with headquarters in St. Louis, Missouri, for The J. B. Williams Company, a manufacturer of pharmaceuticals and toiletries of Cranford, New Jersey, constitutes a modernized order-planning system. AJF handles 100 percent of the clerical work required to process Williams's orders. The public warehouse (1) screens buyers' orders by class of trade, discount, or credit; (2) prepares invoices on computers; (3) executes within 24 hours all shipping documents, selecting and packing the ordered items and enclosing packing slips and shipping orders; (4) prepays and audits freight bills, consolidating them into a single itemized document; and (5) prestamps bulk mail for forwarding to post offices in metropolitan centers.

The Williams Company first encouraged AJF to establish an automated billing system in order to improve distribution of Williams's pharmaceuticals into the Southwest.[1] Previously Williams's consignments destined for the 12-state southwestern region had been shipped via motor carrier to St. Louis. There the Williams Company separated consignments for distribution to points beyond. Increased sales and multiplying product lines, however, compelled Williams to evaluate utilization of public warehousing. Williams's complicated order-handling and invoicing system was a major block to adoption of its own nationwide warehouse system. Under the original setup customers sent their orders to Cranford, New Jersey, for processing, invoicing, and preparation of bills of lading. Surveys indicated that private warehouses in Texas and St. Louis would only increase distribution costs without improving service.

Williams then turned to the idea of permitting AJF to handle all southwestern orders. Prior to tackling the job, AJF acquainted itself with Williams's invoicing procedures, and the two companies adopted a mutually beneficial distribution system. Under the new plan a buyer in the southwestern area mails his order for a Williams product directly to AJF's St. Louis warehouse. A messenger collects the incoming order from the St. Louis post office and drops it off at the AJF warehouse, which stamps the order with date and time of arrival. A clerk at the distribution center checks each order for special instructions, credit limitations, and class of trade, and marks the customer's code number on the order. A second AJF clerk pulls the computer card bearing the buyer's name, address, and other data needed for preparation of the invoice and the bill of lading. The order is then ready for a screener, who determines the type of case to pack and eligibility for discounts and checks other invoicing information. AJF queries Williams's home office by TWX for approval of unusual terms or out-of-area deliveries. The AJF computer then prepares the invoice and bill of lading. A clerk transmits the bill of lading to the warehouse shipping staff, and the goods are picked, packed, and forwarded to the southwestern buyer. The warehouse accounting department attaches a receipted copy of the bill of lading to the invoice and mails both to the customer.

The entire process is accomplished within two days of receipt of the original order.

Major benefits which the Williams Company and other AJF clients derive from this scientific procedure are: continuous 24-hour-a-day operation; decreased lead time on inbound orders; improved statistics on distribution services and costs; and inclusion of all charges for storage, order processing, and transportation on one bill of lading.

When the Carrier Corporation reorganized its distribution structure into a total logistics system, the firm established a customer services department. That department's ability to process customer orders promptly and completely, as well as to develop production schedules related to order processing, contributed significantly to improvement of Carrier's service image. Carrier's customer services activities fall into two distinct categories: day-to-day processing of new orders and forecasting sales and production in order to meet anticipated demands.[2]

Orders arrive at a central point daily. A team of order planners, called the availability committee, works with the original copy of the order and determines the appropriate shipping origin and availability of requested articles. A taped copy is also received, which a card converter uses to imprint the order on cards. After the availability committee completes order notations on the original copy, the identification of articles available is punched into the cards. The cards are then fed into a computer, which creates a formal record of the order. The computer records the sales value of the ordered items for the accounts department and prints a copy of the order for the customer, showing origins of and other pertinent data for each item to be shipped. If the company revises its production schedules while the order is in process, the availability group records these changes on the computer and sends another notice to the customer advising him of altered delivery dates and other departures from the originally planned handling of the order. A weekly listing of the status of customer orders, showing all orders in process, provides an important control.

In addition to this computerized order program, Carrier conducts a parallel linear-programming operation, which determines the relative costs of production, inventory, and distribution and thereby optimizes profits. On examining the information generated about each of these functions, the production department is able to determine problems it must anticipate, and the distribution department can fix proper inventory levels from month to month. With computerized linear forecasts Carrier now finds it a simple matter to examine the lowest, highest, and most likely patterns of cost. Instead of living with one yearly forecast, as it had previously done, the company now has available from its individual plants estimated monthly, seasonal, and cyclical fluctuations of production, sales, costs, and profits.

Packaging

The dictionary defines the verb "to package" as to enclose in a protective covering; the noun "package" is defined as a covering wrapper or container. Easy to define and to conceive visually, a package is actually a complex psychological, physical distribution, and engineering concept that can and frequently does determine whether the enclosed product is a money-maker or a money-loser.

Consumer Packaging

Consumer packaging aims to increase sales through impact on the customer. Packaging experts, along with commercial artists and their advertising-syndicate employers, are currently achieving greater sales, but paradoxically there is vociferous consumer revolt against current packaging practices and policies. In 1966 Congress enacted the "truth in packaging" law to give the consumer the opportunity to make intelligent choices among products in supermarkets and drugstores. Proponents of the measure intended to ban terms such as "cents off," "super," and "jumbo." However, these terms still abound on packages, and the Federal Trade Commission (FTC), despite new powers given to it by the 1966 law, has hesitated to issue requirements that each food package list the amounts as well as names of its key ingredients. The FTC has also exempted from the law dozens of consumer items.

The critical shortcoming of the 1966 Fair Packaging and Labeling Act is that it empowered the government to regulate labels only as necessary to prevent deception of consumers. To add to the confusion, in May of 1969 the FTC, which possesses authority to regulate packaged household products, and the Food and Drug Administration (FDA), with jurisdiction over foods, drugs, and cosmetics, published conflicting rules on "cents off" procedures. While the FDA covers cents-off coupons as well as labels, the FTC does not restrict labels. The FDA attempts to define the "customary price" from which the cents are deducted as the average selling price in an area for the previous 20 days, but the FTC calls for the most recent regular price. The FDA demands only that the cents-off price show the reduction under the immediately preceding price; the FTC, however, declares that a cents-off reduction must set a price at least 8 percent below the customary price.

Both agencies continue to demonstrate indecisiveness. For example, in November 1970 the FTC announced that the agency would give consumers the opportunity to present in writing their views on the package descriptions, but it did not mention the need for hearings or issue a clear-cut FTC ruling on the use of misleading packaging terms.

The business community in general is deeply concerned that the surge in consumer complaints, growth in consumer power, and louder protestations of consumer groups against higher prices and shoddy goods may ultimately damage both consumers and producers. Some entrepreneurs, however, contend that political ambitions, and not concern for public welfare, motivate attacks by federal, state, and municipal officeholders on food processors and distributors. They are skeptical of the need for the 1966 act, and many wholesalers and retailers regard the unit pricing of food and related products as an unworkable concept.

The substantial expenses of posting individual prices on thousands of products and of refiguring prices every time the cost of an item changes is an added burden to food wholesalers and retailers. Profit margins of food distributors, they argue, are already razor thin. The cost of unit-pricing expenses would, they maintain, inevitably raise prices for grocery shoppers.

The issue of unit pricing is far from solution. On October 30, 1970, Safeway Stores, Inc., the nation's second-largest retail grocery chain (next to A&P Food Stores), announced that it was beginning to price its products in Washington, D.C., by pounds or pints and that it would extend this practice to its supermarkets throughout the nation. Other smaller chain stores such as National Tea Company, Jewel Tea Companies, Inc., Stop & Shop Companies, Inc., and King Soopers, Inc. are also pricing items by units. Representative Benjamin Rosenthal of New York, who worked with Safeway in organizing the new pricing system, predicts that within 10 years every supermarket in the United States will have adopted unit pricing. A study of Safeway's experiment showed 25 percent of city shoppers and 38 percent of suburban shoppers reported they prefer and purchase unit-priced items.

There is now legislation before Congress that would require packaged food items to carry the date on which the item was processed. For packaged meat or other perishables, such regulation would be logical, but it would be illogical to impose such a regulation on canned, frozen, or other processed foods which have a nearly indefinite shelf life. Food distributors maintain that the Food, Drug and Cosmetic Act has proved its worth and that to superimpose added regulations on packaging procedures would dilute the effectiveness of this basic legislation.

Industrial Packaging

The objective of industrial packaging is not to influence the consumer, but to protect articles during loading, unloading, storing, and especially for transportation. From the industrial approach a package should have strength, efficiency of handling, compatibility with unitization and palletization, adaptability to cargo boxes of transport conveyances and to delivery demands of customers. Progressive packagers view the subject of industrial packaging from three standpoints.

Consumer versus industrial packaging. Psychological appeal of packaging frequently conflicts with the equally important need to protect the contents. For example, cornflakes boxes are thin, high, and wide in order to maximize the face size of the package. But while achieving the psychological goal of display appeal to housewives and children, these dimensions inflate handling expenses by utilizing excessive space in transportation conveyances and warehouses and on shelves.

Protection. To achieve protection of contents, the packager must tailor the box to withstand heat, cold, water, pressure, vibration, impact, and compression. Alert management will underscore the significance of protective packaging but at the same time will recognize that overpackaging is wasteful, underpackaging hazardous, and repackaging highly expensive. Although it is difficult to measure a package's ability to withstand damage, several procedures are helpful: controlled laboratory analyses, test shipments, and on-the-spot observation. Use of all three may be necessary because a package may rate high in laboratory tests but still be unable to withstand the rigors of transportation. Although the price of a strong protective package may be high, this expense must be balanced against the cost of a weak package requiring use of expensive racks, redesign of mechanized handling systems to avoid dropping or gouging the package, and other handling costs.

Accessibility. Typical manufacturing executives, order

planners, and consumers desire an easily accessible, convenient package. In contrast, transportation executives, warehousemen, wholesalers, and retailers rate resistance to pilferage as more important than accessibility in packaging. Resolving this conflict among those performing the variegated tasks of handling, designing, and constructing packages is a continuous problem.

Design of Packages

Design includes such features as shape, size, configuration, weight and other tangible characteristics of the box, case, can, or other container. Appropriate design is a prime determinant of the package's effectiveness throughout the distribution cycle. As part of their professional training, packaging engineers and designers should work briefly as dockmen or local truck drivers, so that they can understand the relationship of packages to trucks, trailers, and handling equipment and thus reorient package design toward elimination of damage.

By modifying size, shape, and methods of opening and closing, many companies have standardized their boxes through fewer and improved variations. These modifications have achieved meaningful economies in procurement, production, materials handling, warehousing, and packaging. For example, Shuford Mills, Inc. of Hickory, North Carolina, redesigned its package to achieve a 40 percent reduction in cube, a 2-pound decrease in weight, and elimination of 14 separate interior sections.

Transportation costs. Other things being equal, a low-density package means poor stacking strength, occupation of extra cubic feet in freight cars, trucks, barges, ships, or planes, and thereby inflation of transportation costs. Achievement of high-density loading economizes on the transportation outlay. For example, extracting water from juices, stowing tires in compressed form, and using square instead of round bottles and flexible instead of rigid packaging materials produce economies for the carriers involved and therefore cheaper freight costs for the shippers.

Jewel Companies, Inc., of Chicago, one of the largest food distributors in the United States, has adopted an ingenious innovation in packaging its paper sacks.[4] Previously Jewel received paper bags from Richmond, Virginia, in railroad boxcars. As an experiment, the Richmond shipper loaded an open flatcar with a 97,500-pound shipment of paper sacks on 60 pallets, protecting each pallet with heat-shrunk plastic film. The flatcar moved 940 miles from Richmond to Jewel's Chicago warehouse without loss. Jewel has now substituted flatcar for boxcar delivery, because the former improves payloads by 44 percent, permits more economical use of pallets, and allows loading from ground level.

Pricing. Experienced distributors closely scrutinize the correlation between prices and price per package. Wise pricing policies encourage customers to purchase package sizes with the highest price-cost ratio. Distributors who ignore that fact frequently adopt price-packaging policies that deliver the product at a loss. For example, a sportswear manufacturer packed his entire output in units of 12, despite the fact that 60 percent of his orders were for single items. Therefore, to assemble many consignments, the manufacturer had to change the package quantity from twelve to six so that he could ship 86 percent of his orders in standard packs. The company thus gained an increase in standard-order quantities that permitted construction of a mechanized distribution center—an impossibility if the company had continued to package in units of 12.

Role in Total Physical Distribution System

Marketing management tends to evaluate the package by its effect on sales, and packaging management views it mainly as a protective device. Physical distribution managers, however, should see packaging in a broad perspective, giving full weight to factors of sales and protection, but at the same time concentrating on the design, size, and other aspects of the package that increase the effectiveness of the total distribution pattern.

Paddle and Saddle Sportswear of St. Louis, Missouri (a division of Puritan Fashions, Inc.), is an apt example of a firm that increased its profits by adopting scientific packaging. The company distributes women's sportswear (including blouses, skirts, sweaters, shirts, pants, and shorts) from Farmington, Missouri, to points throughout the country. These sports items are sent to Farmington from a number of manufacturing plants, and the Farmington operators unpack them and box outbound shipments to customers. Deciding to double the volume of Farmington's outbound shipments, the top management of Paddle and Saddle found that it first had to make fundamental modifications in packaging. The firm had to weigh possibilities such as revision of order planning, redesign of the package, use of palletization and mechanized handling, and adoption of new identification marks for inventory.

The company finally determined that the new packaging system would consist of three parts: (1) an attractive unit package, which would hold six dozen garments in a number of varieties and sizes and which would stack five to eight boxes high and move via conventional transportation modes; (2) a tote container, which would be manually packed from the top, would stack eight or nine high in trucks and three high in storage, and would be capable of storage for up to six months; and (3) a shipping packet, which would be loaded manually from the top and closed by semiautomatic strapping equipment, would provide protection in transit and would carry identification and corporate markings on the top surface.

These components reduced the company's packaging costs alone by 25 percent and overall distribution costs, including packaging, stock handling, storage, ordering, and shipping, by 32 percent.

The banana industry has produced another striking example of productive innovation in packaging. Mother Nature encases bananas in attractive yellow peels which in themselves appeal to the consumer. But the peel is soft and gives the fruit little protection from handling damage. However, the tough stalks on which the bananas grow defy the most cunning destructive devices. One cannot economically burn, smash, or grind them. Thus product damage and banana stalk disposal were formidable industry problems. Previously bananas on the stalk were moved from Central America by freighters to warehouses in the United States. There they ripened and were then cut from the stalk, packed in returnable boxes, and delivered to wholesalers and retailers. The expense of handling materially reduced profits all along the distribution line.

To halt that profit drain, banana companies instituted a few simple, but profit-producing, changes. They developed a strong, well-ventilated paperboard box into which were packed the "hands," clusters of five to seven bananas. Banana pickers took these strong boxes into bananas groves, pulled the "hands" from the stalks, and cut, weighed, and packed the fruit in the field. The beneficial effect on the banana industry was dramatic. Stalks remained on the tree where they naturally decayed; the uniform rectangular package reduced damage and lowered transportation costs through more efficient utilization of space and use of pallets. As a clinching advantage, the new packaging permitted a gas-ripening process, which left the banana peel unblemished and much more appealing to the housewife. This packaging innovation was largely responsible for the increase in the annual import of bananas into the United States from $165 million in 1965 to around $200 million in 1970.

The Technical Impex Corporation of Waltham, Massachusetts, a book distributor for a number of publishers, utilizes a computer to determine all packing arrangements before an item is even picked from the shelf. That is, the computer produces the pattern of packages and packing arrangements that guides the human packers. The computer prints instructions on where to place commodities on hand-operated trucks. Prior to printing these picking sheets, the computer has already predetermined box sizes and assigned boxes to individual bins on these trucks. The picking sheet directs the picker to place a given quantity of items into each bin. The computer has already determined the quantity of books that will fit horizontally in this specified container. To make these calculations possible, the computer has been fed the inside dimensions of the bin and the dimensions of each book. The book dimensions are recorded to a hundredth of an inch to prevent cumulative error and the skewed stacking that can result if large quantities of books with different dimensions are stacked together. The computer performs in a few thousandths of a second procedures that would take packers minutes to determine through trial and error; and it avoids selection of oversized boxes, thus simplifying the packing job.

Upon completion of order picking, a checker inspects each order for correctness, places the books loosely in the proper size box as indicated on the computer-printed shipping label, and pastes the shipping label on the box. The packer then determines that the box contains the proper number of books, packs the books properly, and seals the case. After packing, the boxes are weighed, and the actual weights are compared with computer-projected weights. This is the last of several checks by shipping personnel to eliminate short shipment.

The Technical Impex Corporation's computer picking and packing system creates several cost-saving advantages, including elimination of a vast amount of time-wasting paper work, quick turnaround of orders, and maintenance of a continuously accurate record of inventory. Other advantages of the computer system are simplification and improvement of reporting, automatic billing, improved control of received goods, more accurate inventory checks, and special services such as generation of mailing lists. A final and outstanding advantage is that by predetermination of the final packing pattern the computer is able to prepare the exact number of shipping labels the boxes require.[5]

We are now witnessing a period of ingenious innovations in packing and packaging that has no precedent. H. H. Scott, Inc., which manufactures compact stereo cassette players, needed an improved method of containing these delicate instruments to prevent damage in transit.[6] Scott's objective was to create a package that would hold the contents snugly and resist breakage. The firm posed its problem to the supplier of its plastic player housing, the Worcester Moulded Plastics Company.

Following analysis, designers and engineers of WMPC recommended, and Scott adopted, a plastic foam insert. These inserts are made of expandable polystyrene, which is manufactured by the Sinclair-Koppers Company, Inc. The inserts are first used to ship the housing of the cassette players from the molder to Scott's plant. The top half is then used as an assembly tray for installation of the sound system of each cassette. (The player is assembled upside down in order to expose its parts conveniently to operators on the assembly line.) The housing is securely nested in the foam insert and moves through the assembly line in that position. At the end of the line testing personnel remove the player from the insert, examine and test dials and other parts, and replace the instrument in the foam insert. When the cassette player is fully manufactured, it is covered with the bottom half of the foam insert, placed into a corrugated case, and shipped to final destination.

The polystyrene inserts have eliminated the need for conventional protective packaging, decreased the number of steps in assembly of the players, reduced direct labor costs by 15 to 25 percent, lessened required storage space from 2,500 to 1,000 square feet, sharply lowered damage and transportation costs, and cost 35 percent less than previous packaging.

Transportation

When Alfred Marshall, a leading economist of the early 1900s, wrote that transportation, not manufacturing, was the dominant economic fact of his age, steam railroads carried the lion's share of the world's overland freight. Motor transport was in its infancy. In the United States railroads had annihilated waterway transport. Ocean steamships carried freight from country to country in exploding volumes, and Great Britain was the world's leading commercial country, with the United States, Germany, Japan, France, and the Scandinavian countries swiftly rising competitors.

Since Marshall's time world economic institutions have survived two world wars. There have been continuing and repeated conflicts among nations. In this turbulent era transportation occupies and will increasingly occupy a central part of the world economic stage.

American businessmen have been continuously affected by striking changes in speed, efficiency, and size of the nation's transport system. These advances influence all phases of physical distribution, from costs of inbound and outbound freight to packaging, order planning, inventory control, warehousing, and volume and cost of paper work. Businesses that fail to keep pace with the zooming progress in transportation face danger of extinction. Let us take an overall look at recent changes in the American transportation industry. The percentage of the nation's ton-miles of freight that the major modes of transportation carried in 1940 and in 1969 are:

	1940 [7]	*1969* [8]
Railroads	61	41
Motor vehicles	8	21
Waterways (including Great Lakes)	19	16
Pipelines	12	22
Total	100	100

These official ICC statistics show that the railroads have lost ground, that motor vehicles and pipelines (private and public) have expanded their share of the total, and that water carriers have held a fairly constant share of the nation's freight. Airlines (although not listed because as yet they haul less than 1 percent of the nation's ton-miles) have surged into the transportation picture and now account for the majority of the nation's common carrier passenger miles. Airplanes are hauling expanding volumes of mail, express, and freight, and nothing stands in the way of this expansion.

Railway Transport

U.S. railroads are striving desperately, but with little success, to halt the decline in their share of the nation's ton-miles. Technological innovations, mergers and consolidations, revised approaches to rate making, managerial reorganizations, and other attempted solutions have failed to regain for the railroads the preeminence in the nation's distribution system which they once held.

Within the last 20 years one exception to this decline has been the Southern Railway Company, which serves almost every commercial center in the Southeast. In 1964 Southern Railway sparked a progressive upsurge in railroading with the acquisition of 100-ton grain hopper cars and establishment of carload freight rates 60 percent below those applicable to grain in boxcars. That step, aimed to meet competition of barge-truck delivery of grain from the Northwest into the Southeast, was only the first in a long series of innovations. The Southern Railway was the first railroad to use a wood-chip car with a carload minimum of 24 units (cords) and to give lower rates to shippers who loaded larger quantities in each car. The Southern was also the first rail line to introduce wood-rack cars with a capacity of 32 to 36 cords of pulpwood and to extend lower rates to shippers who loaded more than 28 cords per car.[9]

Paper transported via rail tended to suffer severe damage in transit, largely because of poor loading patterns. Rolls of paper 72 inches high, 36 inches in diameter, and weighing 1,800 to 2,800 pounds do not load easily, and the slightest impact will cause serious damage. The Southern Railway was the first carrier to construct 60-foot hydracushioned underframe cars. These vehicles have totally replaced 40-foot and 50-foot cars and have reduced customer damage complaints to near zero.

Freight-carrying rail vehicles of 150- to 200-ton capacity are now common, and larger equipment is anticipated. This trend extends to flatcars handling truck trailers and containers, gondolas hauling steel, tank cars moving oil, and flatcars and boxcars hauling lumber. Three-deck steel auto-rack cars, each with capacities of 12 to 18 new automobiles, have enabled the railroads to regain the preponderance of lucrative automobile tonnage previously lost to highway and water carriers.

Automation in railroad classification and freight yards, computerized freight car control, television observation of organization of trains in freight yards, and more powerful locomotives are increasing car utilization, which means additional freight-carrying capacity. However, despite their claims to the contrary the nation's railroads are not keeping pace with American transportation progress. Instead of striving to increase their own natural competitive advantage over other modes, they often use their tremendous political power to damage other types of carriers as well as themselves. The consequence is that they continue to suffer a downtrend in their share of freight ton-miles.

Motor Transport

The sharp uptrend of motor carrier freight continues, and new technology in this field will probably increase the truckers' share of freight traffic. In 1956 Congress authorized the 42,500-mile Interstate Highway System at a cost then of approximately $25 billion and has since authorized expansion of that system. In 1968 the total distance of roads and streets under the jurisdiction of all levels of government in the United States reached 3.68 million miles, including 532,000 miles of municipal roads and streets and 3.152 million miles of roads in rural areas. About 814,000 miles of all roads and streets in the United States are unsurfaced; 1.3 million miles have surfaces of granular material, gravel, crushed stone, or slag; 1.57 million miles have surfaces ranging from bituminous materials to portland cement. While the United States continues to improve and expand its road system, important links are also being formed with other countries. The final section of the Pan American Highway, which will span North America and South America and be the longest continuous highway in the world, is nearing completion. When this great road is finally open to travel, motor carriers will be able to drive on paved roads from Alaska to the tip of the Southern Hemisphere, a distance of 21,000 miles.

In many respects technology is moving ahead faster in the motor carrier industry than in any other phase of the nation's distribution system. While the index of rail employment declined from 100 in 1959 to 70 in 1969, the comparable index for motor freight transportation increased from 100 to 129. It is most significant that motor carrier freight revenues now exceed total rail revenues. Motor carriers are now the single most important transportation agency in this country. The reason for the tremendous advance in motor carrier transportation is the technological innovations that have been made in nearly all phases of trucking.

Pipeline Transport

The pipeline, a shadowy, seldom seen mode of transportation, moves crude oil, gasoline, gas, water, and other products and long has been a substantial but unheralded segment of the national transportation network. Pipelines are a cheap, efficient, and reliable form of transportation. At present 220,000 miles of pipe move half of all U.S. petroleum products and according to reliable estimates are 1,400 times safer than railroads. The nation's $5 billion pipeline network was built entirely by private capital, in sharp contrast to past and present government grants to railroads, airports, harbors, highways, and ocean shipping.

Water Transport

The nation's domestic and foreign water carriers are not lagging in the competitive race. Thirty years ago a typical barge tow on the inland waterway system was comprised of a towboat of 300 to 1,500 horsepower with 8 to 12 barges and a cargo of 5,000 to 10,000 tons. Today's tows dwarf those. Towboats of 6,000 to 10,000 horsepower propel 40 or more 200-foot-long barges, 5 abreast and 8 in line. Some tows now plying the lower Mississippi extend 1,400 feet in length, and their barges are carrying to market more than 40,000 tons of cargo.

Lightninglike progress is occurring in all phases of ocean commerce. Both bulk and general cargo deep-sea carriers are placing larger merchantmen into service. Repeated political and military crises near the Suez Canal have stimulated construction of giant tankers, which navigate around the Cape of Good Hope and thus bypass the Suez Canal in journeying between oil fields of the Mideast and petroleum markets in the Western World.

Freighters capable of 20 to 25 knots are rapidly replacing those with speeds of only 15 knots. Self-loading and unloading bulk freighters on the Great Lakes and open seas are increasing in number, speed capability, and size. The rapidly growing fleet of container and roll-on/roll-off ships is replacing the conventional lift-on/lift-off break-bulk freighter. Ocean transportation companies are building new containerships, some of which will handle up to 1,000 standard 40-foot containers.

Storage and Warehousing

During the last half century storage and warehousing have cast off the old and taken up the new with a speed and vengeance unmatched ever before in this allegedly staid and inert area of physical distribution. A few decades ago distributors conceived warehouse buildings in two-dimensional terms of square feet of floor space, not in three-dimensional terms of cubic feet of storage space. Not long ago warehouse workers hoisted and shifted articles by hand or with hand trucks and other primitive tools and operated elevators with pulleys and ropes. Typical warehouse buildings were multistory with severe restrictions and limitations on weight and size of upper-floor loads. Warehousemen placed little emphasis upon utilization of space, width and location of aisles, and scientific shipping and receiving techniques.[10]

Time has drastically changed that picture. During the 1950s and 1960s industry and commerce developed fundamental principles of warehousing, such as direct assembly-line flows of warehoused items, utilization of pallets, unitization of loads, and scientific layout of warehouse space. Managers of storage and warehouse buildings now recognize that location is of prime importance.

For example, market-slanted warehouses should be near points of consumption and thus afford distant manufacturers close-to-market services and customers a reliable manufacturer-representative in close proximity. Production-oriented warehouses, on the other hand, should be situated near points of manufacture and be collection centers for goods manufactured nearby. Their fundamental purpose is to take goods from factories and plants and place those articles into channels of trade.

Public Warehouses

The relatively new systems approach to physical distribution has revived interest in public rather than private warehousing, and each year shippers now distribute merchandise worth over $50 billion through public facilities. There are now approximately 10,000 public warehousing establishments in the United States with annual revenues exceeding $1.75 billion. Public warehouses offer realistic advantages to the manufacturer. They spot-stock a truckload of a commodity and upon receipt of customer's orders immediately deliver to destination. They permit manufacturers to place inventories at a wide variety of locations in anticipation of customer demand.[11]

They also offer immediate distribution. The public distributor may receive from the manufacturer one shipment of a combined order of several customers; the distributor then separates the individual orders and delivers the items at the convenience of each customer. These services produce two major advantages—reduced carload or truckload freight rates on consolidated inbound shipments and elimination of troublesome small outbound shipments from manufacturers.

Railroads have long granted the "storage in transit" privilege, which enhances the profitability of shipper use of public warehouses. For example, under that privilege manufacturers may route goods to an intermediate distribution warehouse and thence to the ultimate customer on the same through all-rail rate that would have applied if the shipments had moved from first origin to ultimate destination without an intermediate stopoff. This arrangement enables the manufacturer to dispatch his finished products immediately to intermediate stopoff points and the customer to receive shipments much earlier than if the merchandise had to move from the distant factory. The only added charges for the manufacturer are for loading in, loading out, and storage at the intermediate stopoff point. But these charges would also apply if the shipper had to pay the full local rail rate to the distribution center and the full local rate from that center to the customer. The balance of the through rail rate is much below the local rate, and that fact makes storage-in-transit arrangements of tremendous advantage to shippers and receivers.

Another benefit of public warehousing is freedom to plan physical distribution policies. For example, Balanced Foods, Inc., a large distributor of food products in North Bergen, New Jersey, and other origin points, assigns its administrative and operating functions to a public warehouseman. The latter performs receiving, inventory control, accounting, credit, billing, and shipping functions for Balanced Foods. The company estimates that adoption of the public warehouse program reduced its distribution costs at least 15 percent and even more importantly improved service and accelerated growth of sales.

For its products whose sales volume is large and relatively constant, Diamond Crystal Salt Company utilizes public warehouses. This large manufacturer of sodium chloride for food and industrial purposes leases space in 15 public warehouses, which store the company's packaged salt and in some places screen and package the product for grocery stores. DC also uses public warehouses for bulk highway salt, most sales of which are in winter and therefore highly seasonal. DC selects for winter storage points that handle construction materials in spring, summer, and autumn. In many warehouses DC's bulk salt provides year-round employment of warehouse labor, equipment, and space, and thus DC receives low storage rates from this ingenious off-season program.

E. I. Du Pont de Nemours & Company produces a multiplicity of chemical-based products at Wilmington, Delaware. The world-renowned manufacturer requires space in about 50 public warehouses to meet approximately half of its storage needs. Following extensive experimentation and research, Du Pont's distribution executives found many aspects of company-owned warehouses costly. These officers found that land acquisition and building expenses for warehouses were exorbitantly high; conveyor systems, forklift trucks, hand trucks, pallets, racks and bins, and dock levelers added an additional cost burden, and warehouse labor costs were difficult to manage. Hidden costs crept into every area of private warehouse operations.

Requirements of Small Business

In contrast to huge business complexes with highly sophisticated distribution facilities, small businesses cannot afford computer systems, elaborate materials-handling equipment, staff experts, or highly paid consultants. Small companies, however, can profit from public warehouses similar to that of Acme Fast Freight, Inc., a freight forwarder in St. Louis, Missouri. The distribution center is situated in the terminal yards of the St. Louis Southwestern Railway. The structure is 1,000 feet long and 300 feet wide, and covers seven acres with 325,000 square feet of floor space.[12] Acme's mammoth facility boasts three 750-foot freight platforms, 194 back-in, truck-loading spots with automatic dock levelers for inbound and outbound piggyback and highway trailers, and six rail tracks which accommodate 96 railroad cars. A steel fence and numerous strong floodlights surround the area to provide maximum security.

The ultramodern structure is a marvel of sound planning. It has a two-mile in-floor dragline, which transfers daily about 5 million pounds of freight. Coding devices direct switch carts along the dragline to various bays, spurs, and track and spot locations. Clerks insert dual magnetic selector probes in each cart; these probes activate electronic underground switches, which route each cart to its destination. Excellent communication speeds the transfer of a vast variety of freight. A public address system from the central office and shortwave walkie-talkie radio between office and platform supervisors provide close teamwork between management and workers. Acme employed a competent consulting firm to train the terminal's personnel thoroughly, and in three months the consultants raised Acme's efficiency level from 1,200 to 1,500 pounds per man-hour.

Vest-Pocket Distribution Centers

Whereas Acme has a huge warehouse to serve numerous small concerns, a number of large enterprises, including Western Electric, Owens-Corning Fiberglas Corporation, and H. J. Heinz Company have adopted a "vest-pocket" distribution concept to serve major cities at reduced cost. This innovation uses idle property in urban and suburban environments for warehouses. Such small properties, including parcels of land as well as buildings, may be adjacent to railroad tracks or interstate highway interchanges, or they may be farm facilities near airports, which airplane noise has made uninhabitable by man or animal.

The vest-pocket approach turns "problem properties" into productive distribution parks. Harrison, New Jersey, established the first one by subdividing a six-acre tract that had not been used in two decades into fourteen separate parcels. Owens-Corning Fiberglas and H. J. Heinz have erected highly effective distribution centers on these locations.

Inventory Control

Inventory control is that phase of physical distribution concerned with management of the number, weight, and money value of goods on hand. They may be raw materials, goods in process, or finished articles; they may be in bulk or packaged form and may be at the factory, wholesaler, retailer, or other business establishment. To the wholesaler or retailer inventories usually consist of finished items, whereas the typical manufacturer often maintains and manages inventories of materials in every stage from origin in ocean, lake, field, or forest to finished product.

Management of inventories is a key phase of the distributive chain. For example, business forecasting now recognizes that under a free enterprise system a rise in the ratio of inventories to sales is a storm warning for action to rectify the imbalance between production and consumption. In other words, overaccumulation of inventories is a forerunner, some would argue a major cause, of business slowdowns.

A simple example will show the nature of inventory control and the necessity for individual business to avoid overstocking or understocking. A clothing firm purchases 1,000 lots of men's shirts, f.o.b. origin. Lead time from placement of the order to receipt of shipment is 10 days, and the firm sells 500 lots in 10 days. Therefore, to avoid exhaustion of stock, the retailer should order 1,000 lots when his stock reaches 500. In other words, the order point would be 500 and the order quantity 1,000. The average inventory would be 1,000 lots (500 minimum plus 1,500 maximum, divided by 2.) [13]

The annual cost of maintaining a comfortable lead

time is the product of number of units times value per unit times the annual cost of carrying those items. For example, if the value per unit is $10 and the annual carrying cost 25 percent, inventory costs of the f.o.b. origin policy would be $2,500 ($10 × 1000 × .25).

Purchasers f.o.b. origin can debit their inventory account in three ways: on shipment from origin, on receipt of the bill of lading, or on actual receipt of the goods. In crediting inventory accounts, sellers f.o.b. destination can also choose among three alternatives: they can credit inventory when the articles leave the shipping room, when they are sold (whether shipped or not), or when they are received by the customer.

Another decision the manager of a company's inventory must make is how to record the number of physical units and the money value of those units. A firm purchasing f.o.b. origin usually records the number of units as it receives them in order to calculate order points correctly. It also records the monetary value of the goods when received. But if the accounting department recognizes inventory only when goods reach the warehouse, the accountants will question whether the high cost of air freight reduces inventory costs, even if air shipment reduces lead time from ten days to one day. Accountants tend to consider inventory for costing purposes as one-half the quantity regardless of the terms of purchase and refuse to permit speed of delivery to decrease monetary cost of the inventory.

A sale made f.o.b. destination multiplies this accounting error. At time of sale many firms debit cost of goods sold and accounts receivable and credit inventory and sales income. That is, sellers remove inventories from their books, even though they still hold title to the goods in transit. If sellers debit the money value of their inventories at time of sale and buyers credit their inventory accounts upon receipt, a vast amount of phantom inventory, unrecorded on the books of either buyer or seller, exists. Under such conditions physical distribution managers of both the buyer and the seller, trying to balance inventory against other distribution expenses, have no facts to convince top management that reduction in lead time lowers inventory costs.

One solution to this problem is to have accounting departments divide inventory into cycle stock (that portion associated with the choice of an order quantity), transit stock, and safety stock (to protect against variability of sales). Financial records will then reflect more accurately actual money value of goods on hand, adequacy of current inventory, and cost of goods sold.

Stevedoring

The natural harbors of the Atlantic, Gulf, Pacific, and Great Lakes shores are U.S. national assets of the first magnitude. Nature has endowed this country with sea and lake ports without peer on earth. They account for 75 percent of the nation's $60 billion annual foreign trade and generate high levels of income, domestically and worldwide. At waterfront interfaces stevedores have transferred literally billions of tons of cargo between land and water carriers, but strangely authorities on physical distribution management have not regarded stevedoring as a distinct distribution function. However, transfer from dock to ship and ship to dock of foreign and domestic exports and imports and the relationship of that transfer to other steps in the distributive process make stevedoring a vital phase of physical distribution.

Depending upon the rules and customs of individual ports, stevedoring companies take jurisdiction of general cargo at some point between the waterfront transit shed and ship, move the cargo to shipside by forklift truck or other conveyance, and transfer it into ship's hold. Aboard longshoremen shift and arrange the freight to secure efficient stowage. The lag of technological progress in this key field is in all probability wider than in any other phase of distribution and is a critical deterrent to achievement of full employment in the United States.

From 1950 to 1960 the number of longshoremen in the United States decreased from 71,763 to 60,302, and the decline is accelerating. Mechanical devices such as forklift trucks, huge cranes, large capacity freighters, self-loading containerships, and other improvements are rapidly shrinking the stevedoring population. In addition the longshoremen's strikes have driven many dock workers to other occupations, and most of these laborers will not return to the waterfront.

Dock management and labor, the federal government, and the general public have gradually recognized that hand stevedoring is an outmoded, demeaning, backbreaking occupation. It is an anachronism from the 1700s for toiling, sweating human beings to handle with sheer muscle and brawn break-bulk cargo piece by piece between docks and ship holds, using only bare hands and the baling hook, itself a primitive tool. Under the present shape-up hiring system, each stevedore is hired from day to day. The typical stevedore employer does not register, or even identify, his longshoremen.

Unfortunately labor-management strife on the nation's

waterfronts has long constituted a hobble to ocean-borne commerce and has reverberated harmfully throughout the nation's economic system. For example, between 1958 and 1967 work stoppages on the docks of the Atlantic and Gulf coasts totaled 159, involved 293,211 workers, and were responsible for a loss of 3,396,288 man-days. The 1968–1969 walkout on these waterfronts was perhaps the most disastrous longshoremen's strike in American history. A rundown of major developments in this conflict will throw into focus the destructive nature of these recurring labor-management confrontations.

In July 1968 the International Longshoremen's Association (ILA) which controls the actions and policies of dock workers from Maine to Texas, announced the following demands to stevedoring companies: an increase in hourly wages from $3.62 to $6.00, a cut in the work week from 40 hours to 30 hours; double-time pay for all work outside regular working hours; a 2-year contract; a guaranteed annual income of 52 weeks a year (the existing guarantee was 40 weeks); payment weekly instead of monthly; 16 paid holidays a year and 6 weeks paid vacation; pensions of $400 a month following 20 years service (the existing benefit was $175 a month); the privileges of stripping, loading, checking, and maintaining containers at the piers; minimum work gangs per hatch of 17 men for both conventional freighters and containerships; separate periods for loading and discharging containerships; and establishment of a royalty fund of $4 per ton for all bulk cargoes.

The New York Shipping Association (NYSA) represented management in Boston, New York, Philadelphia, Baltimore, and Hampton Roads on the issues of wages, hours, and contributions to pensions and welfare funds but indicated that guaranteed annual income and other items were "more appropriate for local bargaining." The shipping association sought: complete freedom in managing ship and terminal operations; assurance of available manpower; freedom to use new equipment without limitation; no restriction on container transport; and compulsory retirement of older workers.

By late September 1968 the demands of labor and the offer of management remained miles apart. On September 30, in order to avoid a threatened strike, President Lyndon B. Johnson invoked the Taft-Hartley Act and appointed a three-man arbitration board to report to him by October 2. Many workers had already abandoned the docks, but a federal court order returned them to work on October 1, and the 80-day Taft-Hartley cooling-off period began. That expired on December 20, following which the longshoremen again left the piers.

Finally, in mid-January 1969 the NYSA and the ILA reached agreement. They signed a three-year contract which provided a $1.60 an hour package for wages, pensions, welfare, vacations, and holidays. The toughest issue at the bargaining table was the ILA's fear that the container would destroy longshoring as a livelihood. To resolve that point of controversy, the new agreement guaranteed dock workers against loss of jobs resulting from increased use of containers, extended ILA's jurisdiction over stuffing and stripping of less-than-trailerload containers and containers with consolidated shipments within a 50-mile radius from any port. However, the New York stevedores refused to return to work until all ports had settled, and it was not until mid-April 1969, when Beaumont and Port Arthur, Texas, ratified their contracts, that the strike at long last ended.

The walkout was the most crippling waterfront strike in the nation's history. The number of ships immobilized by mid-January 1969 was 342. The strike closed the National Sugar Refining Company plant in Philadelphia, which laid off 700 employees; New York City, Yonkers, and Baltimore sugar refineries laid off about 2,000 workers; and ocean shipment of grain completely halted. New York freight forwarders and other maritime industry employers suspended between 20 to 50 percent of their employees. In New York City alone the strike deprived more than 5,000 Teamsters (mainly truck drivers) of employment. It is conservatively estimated that the aggregate monetary loss attributable to the strike exceeded $5 billion.

Dock Labor and Containers

There remains a chasm of misunderstanding between waterfront management and labor concerning the container. Stevedoring companies stress that containerships are more than ten times as productive as conventional freighters in terms of cargo loading and discharging, number of longshoremen required, and length of time in port. Utilizing high-speed shoreside gantry cranes, fewer than 40 longshoremen, handling freight at an average of 600 to 800 tons an hour, can discharge a containership in 24 hours. In contrast, the discharging rate for a conventional freighter with 5 hatches worked by 100 stevedores averages 60 tons an hour, thus requiring 5 to 7 days for unloading.

The ILA argues that containers reduce the number of cargo handlers, permit faster turnaround of vessels, and

Components of Physical Distribution 57

require fewer ships, thus reducing total employment on the waterfront. The union insists that its members should not sacrifice their jobs and income to the containers. The truth, however, appears to be that containers create more and better jobs at the docks than they destroy. For example, on the East Coast of the United States in 1968–1969 there were more than 75,000 longshoremen at work on dock and dock-related jobs, as against 71,000 in 1964. The roll-on/roll-off containerships, like the newly built *Ponce de Leon*, offer significant examples of the creation of employment on the waterfront.[14]

Dockworkers serving the *Ponce de Leon* have switched from using baling hooks to trucking chassis and containers through the huge side portals of the great vessel. One longshoreman with 20 years experience who has been trained to work the *Ponce de Leon* asserts that he likes the new job because it pays more than hand stevedoring did and gives him a sense of dignity. In his view highly skilled "trailer jockeys" are now the most important men on the docks. Other former longshoremen have become traffic directors and shepherd cargo to 5 loading decks inside the *Ponce de Leon*. They operate red and green traffic lights similar to those on city streets. A crew is also employed to tie down trailers, heavy equipment, and automobiles, work that is much less back-breaking and demeaning than manual handling of cargo.

The president of Transamerican Trailer Transport, which owns the *Ponce de Leon*, contends that automation does not necessarily stifle worker enthusiasm and dignity. He recalls that in the old days brawn was the sole requirement of longshoremen. Now, however, loading the *Ponce de Leon* requires that dock workers have talent and judgment, and this executive states with enthusiasm that his company is getting an outpouring of these qualities from former stevedores.

Delivery Services

Delivery functions are mainly concerned with placement of goods at customers' warehouses or at the sites of consumers of the product. Delivery encompasses activities such as unloading into warehouse or store, establishing drayage arrangements at destination (including monetary allowances to receivers who perform their own drayage), and other related services. It is a key function because in a society of free choice the manufacturer or distributor must place goods at the customer's door satisfactorily or face loss of accounts to competitors.

Spiegel, Inc., one of the largest mail order houses in the United States, has improved customer delivery service by installing a new ordering system for handling "will call" business in its 273 catalog order stores.[15] Catalog orders are an expanding segment of the company's $300 million annual nationwide sales, and a large proportion of these sales is "will call" business, wherein the customer telephones, mails, or brings in an order and returns 48 to 72 hours later to claim it. Formerly Spiegel stores mailed will-call orders to the company's Chicago headquarters. The Pittsburgh store, for example, would mail orders to Chicago each evening. But when the mail failed to arrive in time for the following day's shipments, as frequently happened, a whole day was lost in serving the customer.

To remedy this difficulty, Spiegel in 1966 installed a

Digitronics Corporation's Data-Verter® order-entry system in 20 Chicago area stores and tested it for a year and a half. The system uses an adding-machine input device, a highly reliable magnetic tape recorder, and an economical acoustic transmitter (which permits transmission of orders from stores to home office by telephone).

Following success in the 20-store test, in 1968 Spiegel adopted the Data-Verter order-entry system in all its 273 catalog-order stores throughout the United States. Spiegel stores had previously written individual sales slips for each item which exactly duplicated the customer's order. Separate stores forwarded unchecked sales slips to the Chicago office, and two days would often elapse before an error was discovered. With the Data-Verter system Spiegel assigns each ordered item a seven-digit "Random Access Generated Mail Order Processing" (RAGMOP) number, which is the disc address of a stocked unit. The system insures increased order-entry accuracy and immediate correction of errors at the store level.

Each store keeps RAGMOP numbers for 300,000 commodities on microfiche and executes order forms showing the following data: cash or credit, customer initial, RAGMOP number, quantity, size, and price. Each store also enters store number, data, and order information on an adding-machine device that records these facts on magnetic sound tape. The tape is mounted on an acoustical transmitter, and the store is then ready for a telephone call from the home office. Between 2:30 and 5:10 P.M. each day five telephone operators in Chicago telephone each store to secure order data. Prepunched dialing cards permit telephone calls about every two and one-half minutes. Local Spiegel stores place the acoustical transmitters on an amplifier and transmit the information to Chicago at the rate of 1,000 lines per 3-minute call. Five Data-Verter recorders receive the sales data and note them on paper tape. That evening the tape is read onto an IBM 2671 paper-tape reader, which records sales data on magnetic tape. The magnetic tape is then passed through an IBM 360 Model 30 computer, which checks the data against four disc packs containing information on Spiegel's 300,000 catalog items.

Following this, an IBM 1403 printer produces sales tickets, which become an order-picking and shipping ticket. The following morning items are shipped to Spiegel's individual stores, which reassemble them for will-call, pickup customers. With these innovations Spiegel now meets promised delivery times of 48 to 72 hours 100 percent of the time, as against only 30 to 35 percent prior to installation of the new program, and has reduced to near zero sales-slip errors.

Montgomery Ward & Company, Inc., another large seller by mail order and local stores, has in recent years effectively overhauled its delivery of replacement parts. The company annually supplies 3.5 million replacement items for merchandise such as television sets, large and small appliances, bicycles, motorcycles, lawnmowers, and tractors.

In the past, if the firm's regional distribution center, one of ten in the country, did not have a part in stock, the disgruntled customer waited four weeks or more for arrival of the order. In such an instance, the Montgomery Ward distributor had to order the part from its supplier and receive, repack, and reship it to the buyer. Under the new plan described below, Montgomery Ward now gets most parts to the customer two days after the order is received.

As an initial step toward solving this problem, Montgomery Ward redesigned storage facilities at the replacement-part distribution centers to eliminate wasted motion in order picking and delivery. Prior to June 1967 Montgomery Ward's 10 distribution centers operated independently of each other. Orders for parts from more than 500 retail outlets and 1,200 catalog stores flowed into each distribution point. There clerks processed orders manually, referring to a file to determine whether ordered items were in stock. The process was slow, awkward, and required a mass of paper work.

Under the new system, MW distribution centers in the East, West, and South deliver only fast-moving parts such as radio and TV tubes and bicycle chains. In addition to supplying fast-movers to economically adjacent stores, the central warehouse in Chicago stocks slow-moving parts for the whole country. This main parts center is situated only seven miles from Chicago's O'Hare Airport, at the crossroads of major freeways and near a main post office. The large central parts center of Montgomery Ward is strategically placed for creating economies in distribution. Up to 75,000 pounds of parts fly monthly from Chicago to distribution points which coincide with parcel post zones.

When the new system achieves full efficiency, Montgomery Ward proposes to computerize the Chicago operation. When a parts center itself stocks an ordered item, the computer will send back an order-picking number and a mailing label. The computer will print out an order-picking number and label at the Chicago central point. If the part is out of stock at the ten centers as well as Chicago, the computer will print a purchase order to the proper supplier.

Montgomery Ward's modernized customer service program has shaved distribution costs across the board. Introduction of computer processing of orders has lowered labor costs. Maintenance on hand of a larger variety of parts has decreased the nuisance and expense of special ordering. (Prior to revamping parts distribution, Montgomery Ward failed to stock 40 percent of ordered items, now such failures are only 18 percent of orders.) The company now purchases articles in larger volumes, gaining the advantage of bulk prices and discounts. The firm has also reduced the number of distribution centers from ten to four, and thereby further slashed operating costs while improving service to customers. And the combination of air freight, air express, and airmail, the latter permitting final delivery to customers within parcel post zones, has sharply cut Montgomery Ward's mailing costs.

Most subscribers to and buyers of newspapers become irate if their favorite dailies are not delivered on time, in proper condition, and at the appointed place each day. Newspaper readers insist upon, and receive, the ultimate in delivery service. But the pressure of demanding readers is small compared to the strict and exacting delivery demands with which newspaper publishers bombard the manufacturers of newsprint paper. To remain in this highly competitive market, newsprint producers must meet the delivery schedules that publishers-customers demand or sacrifice sales to other paper companies.

Newsprint is a great and growing business in North America and the world. The demand for newsprint on this continent increased from 9.8 million to 10.3 million tons between 1966 and 1970. During those 5 years consumption in the United States climbed from 9.1 to 9.5 million tons. At the same time world production capacity

Components of Physical Distribution 63

rose from 21.2 to 24.9 million tons, Canadian production from 8.4 to 8.5 million tons, and U.S. production from 2.4 to 3.3. million tons. Great corporate complexes battle for newsprint markets both here and around the world. Some of these manufacturers are the Bowater Organization, the Abitibi Paper Company, Limited, International Paper Company, Consolidated-Bathurst, Limited, Crown Zellerbach Corporation, MacMillan Bloedel Limited, Price Company Limited, Great Northern Paper Company, Southland Paper Mills, Inc., Kimberly-Clark Corporation, and several others. There are 44 newsprint mills in Canada and 23 in the United States.

The Bowater Organization strives to outdo the delivery services of its rivals in all markets. Within the bounds of ethics, legality, and fair play Bowater leaves no stone unturned in the hour-to-hour struggle to improve delivery and maintain and expand its market outlets. Further, Bowater traffic officials place publishers in touch with dependable local drayage companies who will efficiently transfer newsprint from railroad team tracks or warehouses to customer pressrooms. If the newsprint customer provides his own drayage from team track or warehouse to pressrooms, Bowater makes fair delivery and unloading allowances for such drayage. Bowater also provides helpful hints to destination handlers of the product, instructs newspaper officials concerning types of forklift trucks most adaptive to handling bulky paper rolls, and in some instances makes forklift trucks available to customers on a lease or purchase basis.

A strong motivation for providing excellent delivery service is that the price each manufacturer charges for newsprint is nearly the same as his rivals'. Newsprint prices have also remained relatively constant; the price per short ton in 1957 was $135 and in 1971 around $158. Newsprint sales are on a delivered basis with freight allowed, a fact which gives origin mill traffic officials control over the freight from origin to destination. Another factor which upgrades the significance of newsprint delivery service is that differentials in quality are not wide and therefore are not a major determinant of customer choice. So the newsprint manufacturer finds that the only competitive edge available to him is in the arena of physical distribution, particularly delivery services.

References

1. "Public Warehousing with a Personal Touch," *Transportation and Distribution Management*, October 1968, p. 37.
2. "Automation Speeds Order Scheduling and Processing," *Traffic Management*, June 1970, p. 66.
3. Walter F. Friedman, "The Role of Packaging in Physical Distribution," *Transportation and Distribution Management*, February 1968, p. 34.
4. "Jewel Pioneers Bulk-Ship Method," *Distribution Manager*, March 1969, p. 43.
5. "Computer Pre-arranges Picking and Packing," *Modern Materials Handling*, September 1970, pp. 56, 57.
6. "Foam Packaging Insert Really Goes All the Way," *Modern Materials Handling*, May 1970, p. 98.
7. *National Resources and Foreign Aid* (Washington, D.C.: U.S. Department of the Interior, 1947), p. 28.
8. *Eighty-fourth Annual Report of the Interstate Commerce Commission*, 1970, p. 77.
9. *Annual Reports of the Southern Railway Company*, 1968, 1969, and 1970. Each of these reports records the technologi-

cal achievements of this rail line, which surpass those of any other railroad company in the United States.

10. *Warehouse Operations: 1969* (Washington, D.C.: General Services Administration Federal Supply Service), p. 5.
11. Donald E. Horton and Mark Egan, "Should You Go Public in Distribution?" *Handling and Shipping*, December 1969, p. 59.
12. Phil Schreiner, "Designed for Today's Total Distribution," *Handling and Shipping*, November 1969, p. 62.
13. Lewis M. Schneider, "Inventory in Transit—Fact or Phantom," *Transportation and Distribution Management*, January 1969, p. 30.
14. James M. Dixon, "Longshoremen Take the Wheel," *Distribution Worldwide*, October 1969, p. 77.
15. "R.A.G.M.O.P. Spells Improved Customer Service," *Distribution Manager*, February 1969, pp. 31–33.

3 Current Problems and Opportunities

THERE are problems as well as opportunities in physical distribution management (PDM). Perhaps the most promising opportunity is to upgrade PDM to its deserved status in corporation organization, and the toughest problem may be the lack of information that is needed to measure the true worth of PDM. Serious students of distribution advocate intensification of research throughout all phases of this field. They realize the need for assembling many more organized facts concerning the economics of the subject, improved engineering techniques, the proper role of government as regulator, promoter, and operator of pertinent sections of the field, and numerous other phases of this complicated area of economic life.[1]

Problems in Transportation

This is the era of scientific breakthroughs and the knowledge explosion. Thomas J. Watson, Jr., chairman of the board of IBM, has said that the dexterity, knowledge, imagination, and ingenuity of people have been the wellspring of our progress, both technological and cultural. *Fortune* indicates that from 1929 to 1957 improved education of labor, plus the general advance of knowledge, was responsible for 50 percent of the rise in national income. During the same period expansion in plant and equipment added only 14 percent to the U.S. income figure.

However, in management of all modes of transportation, there is puzzling resistance to change and reluctance to adopt innovations and new cost-saving ideas. This laggardness is probably the most glaring and crippling shortcoming of the American transportation system. True, carriers now operate unit trains, cushioned underframe boxcars, double-bottom tractor trailers, superpowered towboats, mammoth barges, and electronic computers, and have adopted other progressive advances.

However, these highly publicized steps do not present a true picture. The United States lags far behind many nations in instituting super-high-velocity rail travel. Most railroads have not yet purchased the newest type freight cars or adopted yard improvements, computer systems, scientific personnel policies, and other up-to-date programs. Many portions of our vaunted highway network are outmoded, poorly built, worn out, or unsafe. At numerous sea and river ports longshoremen handle cargo the same way they handled it a hundred years ago. Throughout the distribution field the majority of trade unions drag their feet against virtually all labor-saving automation. Poor location, inadequate lengths of runways, illogically designed terminal buildings, and inefficient operation of many airports are a blight to air freight and passenger movement.

Original, courageous, solution-seeking research by able thinkers should precede innovation. But one finds a paucity of such minds in transportation and distribution. No public or private organization is performing transportation research comparable to the great studies of the Federal Coordinator of Transportation in the mid-1930s or those of the Board of Investigation and Research in the early 1940s. For example, the 1963 transportation census, which cost the American taxpayers about $5 million, included a report on the transportation of paper articles. Although the Census Bureau used Bowater's Tennessee mill as a sample firm, Bowater's traffic department found nothing in the census report of practical value to the company or the public. No new findings appeared in the widely publicized Mueller Report, Bricker Report, or Weeks Report, all of several years ago. The Doyle Report of 1961 did have some excellent sections, but the government has not implemented the recommendations of General John P. Doyle's study.[2]

There is an urgent need for sound scholarly and practical research in transportation by universities, colleges, and research institutes, and by the federal government. The president, Congress, regulatory agencies, and the transportation industry and its clients need facts to formulate a sound and practical transportation policy. But research findings are not currently filling this need. Transfer to the Department of Transportation (DOT) of 38 government agencies means that with DOT we now have 39 rather than 38 government bureaucracies which are performing research of doubtful value in transportation. Reading the first three annual reports of DOT is a disappointing experience, since there is little evidence of sound useful research which could guide the United States in improving transportation and physical distribution. Originally DOT's research program included such subjects as: the national corridor project (the Boston-Washington Metroliner); impact of abandonment of the Rutland Railroad; a simulation model; and intermodal coordination. The department's research team has also studied ship subsidies and methods of rehabilitating the merchant marine. Lately DOT has undertaken studies of freight rate structures, railroad mergers, causes of financial difficulties of the railroad industry, the effect of transportation costs on consumers, and other related subjects.

Much of DOT's research, however, has been and still is vacuous and apologetic. For example, its officials in a monotonous repetition defend vigorously the Interstate Highway System, the department itself, mobilization of technical capabilities to maximize the advantages of all modes, removal of institutional and political barricades to progress, and centralization of leadership to support broader social, economic, and national security objectives in transportation. DOT has issued many recommendations without adequate prior study of complicated problems. For example, it has publicly announced support of user charges on the inland waterways, heavy financial subsidization of unprofitable railroads, and stringent restrictions upon the trucking industry in the name of safety.

The Interstate Commerce Commission became 84 years old in 1971 (created in 1887) and has begun to show the rigidity of age, a deplorable aspect of which is creeping cynicism toward research. The commission long held the reputation for employment of high-caliber economists to conduct inquiries into unstudied areas of transportation and distribution. For many years ICC researchers were in step with or ahead of developments in industries that the agency regulated.[3] However, the quantity and usefulness of ICC research data has sharply declined. Also, the ICC and DOT have not yet drawn jurisdictional lines between the types of research that each organization should properly perform. For years other departments, commissions, bureaus, and special study groups within the federal government have ground out research studies on distribution matters. But as one scans these mountainous compilations of statistics, charts, narrative analyses, and other documents, he finds wastelands barren of incisive thought, impartial analysis, and practical, useful findings.

If the operations of the transportation industry remain substantially unchanged, another national economic depression similar to that of 1929–1939 would almost certainly create a clamor for nationalization of transportation. Those who would abhor such an occurrence should isolate and identify the most crucial problems in transportation. Only scholarly, penetrating research, however, can accomplish this goal; unfortunately the present flood of transportation literature does not possess either quality.

Distribution Courses

In the 1940s, 1950s, and 1960s universities with colleges of business and economics discontinued their course offerings in transportation and distribution. They took these misguided steps on grounds that such courses are too specialized, impractical, and unpopular with the students. However, the recent growing importance of the subject of distribution, the improved teaching of and better literature on the subject, tied in with dramatic technological progress in the field, have restored student interest and reversed trends of intellectual hostility toward distribution courses. Seven or eight years ago, one could have counted on the fingers of one hand the number of institutions of higher learning that offered courses in PDM. Many colleges once ranked courses in transportation among the most essential of their business curricula but later abandoned them. However, the reversal of that phenomenon has been dramatic. Today one can, for example, study courses in distribution and transportation, in contrast to purely marketing courses, in such prestigious universities as Harvard, Yale, Chicago, Northwestern, and Stanford and in nearly all state-supported universities and colleges.

There remain serious obstacles to persuading college students to major in the field of physical distribution. It has been held that there is no recognized body of theory to teach. And it is difficult to persuade college students to select such a narrow major as physical distribution. There is also a lack of career opportunities in the field. No student entering college expects or should expect to make driving a truck or switching a railroad engine his life's work. This last difficulty will be overcome, however, when corporate management recognizes the importance of PDM.

Volume Versus Capacity

Since the end of World War II American transportation corporations have failed to achieve the freight-carrying capacity necessary to meet expanding transportation and distribution demands. From 1954 to 1970 the aggregate number of operational freight cars owned or leased by Class I railroads declined from 1,726,000 to 1,473,000. During this period average capacity per car rose from 53.7 to 67 tons, but total capacity of all cars rose from 93 million to only 99 million tons. The worsening freight car shortage is symbolic of the inadequacy of rail management to fulfill their responsibility to operate efficiently. Secretary of the Interior J. A. Krug's Marshall Plan Report of 1947 explained that the railroad industry, government officials, and car manufacturers were attempting to ease the freight car shortage by attaining a car construction level of 10,000 vehicles per month.[4] But the railroad industry has yet to reach that goal. Shortages of suitable boxcars is a threat to national well-being. The eastern lines are not building cars, and they are holding and using new cars of the southern and western lines at a ridiculously low per diem charge.

The Interstate Highway System and U.S. highways in general present death traps for passenger travel and bottlenecks for freight trucks. Road congestion is literally choking many cities to economic death. At the same time the motor carrier industry is not providing an adequate number of trailers to haul the nation's highway freight load. Like the railroads, the motor carriers have been unable to meet the demand for their services.

The United States has a shamefully underdeveloped inland waterway system. The Florida Cross-State Canal, which the federal government recently abandoned, and the Warrior-Tombigbee cutoff in northwestern Alabama are at least 20 years overdue. Informed observers refer to U.S. ships serving military forces abroad as "rustbuckets." Observers bemoan the fact that the American merchant marine is rapidly declining into junk. And one visiting many of the nation's major seaports is surprised to witness their ramshackle condition, filth, and slovenly operational techniques.

Small Shipments

From many angles shipments below 5,000 pounds, particularly those below 500 pounds, offer the most vexatious transport problems. But the so-called small shipper is most often a giant corporation, and small consignments are usually valuable articles requiring speedy delivery and careful freighting. The table on the next page shows the trend from 1950 to 1968 in the amounts of freight revenues that small shipments have produced for the various modes of regulated transport. (Total revenues nearly tripled during this period.)

Several years ago railroads decided that financial losses on less-carload freight were so heavy that they should work toward abandoning this type of freight, and they have nearly accomplished that goal. (The number of freight cars handling such loads declined from 1,809,000 in 1960 to 31,573 in 1970.) Shippers of small items have been placed in a precarious position by the elimination of railroad less-carload freight, truckers' rejection of small items or exorbitant rates on this type of shipment, congestion of terminal facilities handling small loads, decline of the Railway Express Agency, and bureaucratic limitations on parcel post.

In early 1968 the ICC established an ad hoc committee to report specifically on the problem of small shipments. That committee, composed of commissioners Laurence K. Walrath, Rupert L. Murphy, and Virginia Mae Brown, made the trucking industry the scapegoat for the tribulations of small shipments. The group found

Total revenue of regulated carriers of

	Direct Carriers					
Year	Motor LTL Classes I & II	Rail LCL Classes I & II	Bus-Express	Water Carriers°	Air Freight	United Parcel Service†
1950	$1,026,817	$355,780	$ 7,791	$ 8,866	$ 43,559	N/A
1951	1,045,309	354,215	8,951	9,149	47,498	N/A
1952	1,197,863	354,256	10,651	7,413	55,107	N/A
1953	1,322,555	323,676	12,509	8,733	59,444	N/A
1954	1,332,577	275,550	13,441	7,798	59,268	N/A
1955	1,465,240	282,922	15,521	7,451	74,800	N/A
1956	1,629,207	274,677	17,757	6,666	78,779	N/A
1957	1,776,502	254,247	21,350	6,297	88,637	N/A
1958	1,803,456	214,249	24,302	7,685	91,664	$ 995
1959	2,088,784	185,595	29,335	7,763	107,946	2,122
1960	2,122,914	154,373	33,102	5,751	116,154	4,907
1961	2,274,628	126,339	37,526	4,200	124,929	11,603
1962	2,501,476	100,779	42,914	6,182	144,617	24,569
1963	2,647,958	76,160	47,426	9,404	165,048	37,069
1964	2,827,075	62,044	54,005	944	198,257	58,999
1965	3,100,257	52,533	r61,024	14,386	239,312	92,785
1966	3,400,238	41,249	r64,652	11,420	276,073	116,898
1967	3,487,910	39,075	r71,769	15,778	309,626	163,645
1968	3,871,258	35,756	83,841	16,192	367,302	205,254

N/A Not available.
r Revised.
° Includes Classes A and B water carriers and maritime carriers.
† United Parcel Service was considered a local carrier from 1950 to 1957, and did not report intercity service. Revenue figures are only for intercity shipments.

that there is no single solution to the problem and urged the ICC to undertake a multiple-level campaign against small shipment ills, including the following steps: enactment of legislation to empower the ICC to revoke certificates of motor carriers that refuse to agree to route and small shipments, 1950–1968 (in thousands).

		Indirect Carriers				
REA Surface	REA Air Express	Freight Forwarders Class A	Parcel Post	Air Parcel Post	Totals	Index 1950 100
$284,308	$22,901	$ 70,502	$381,000	$ 13,000	$2,214,524	100.0
282,814	30,675	81,205	402,000	19,000	2,280,816	103.0
355,949	32,365	93,234	447,000	28,000	2,581,838	116.6
349,699	34,239	93,205	451,000	26,000	2,681,060	121.1
327,531	33,249	92,365	543,000	29,000	2,713,779	122.5
334,865	40,316	101,332	551,000	30,000	2,903,447	131.1
348,717	42,106	108,152	552,000	33,000	3,091,061	139.6
316,841	36,857	111,804	543,000	36,000	3,191,535	144.1
323,529	40,990	112,254	539,000	35,000	3,193,124	144.2
339,196	46,300	129,689	531,000	40,000	3,507,730	158.4
N/A	50,000	131,719	561,000	43,000	3,222,920	145.5
N/A	N/A	143,052	579,000	47,000	3,348,277	151.2
313,300	54,100	150,384	576,000	52,000	3,966,321	179.1
313,100	58,600	152,229	575,000	57,000	4,138,994	186.9
327,800	67,400	156,206	587,000	65,000	4,404,730	198.9
350,000	80,000	155,450	621,000	75,000	r4,841,747	218.6
343,531	86,293	184,026	628,000	91,000	r5,243,380	236.8
334,807	86,954	185,745	645,341	118,631	5,459,281	246.5
287,097	93,600	196,937	646,209	199,689 ‡	6,003,135	271.1

‡ Includes heavy-weighted pieces of first-class mail beginning Jan. 7, 1968 (Public Law 90-20, Dec. 16, 1967).
Source: Interstate Commerce Commission, *The Role of Regulated Carriers in the Handling of Small Shipments*, Statement No. 67-2.

rate arrangements on low weight consignments; assembly of more complete data on service failures with strong emphasis upon service fitness and the requirement that motor carrier certificates of public convenience and necessity describe in detail the service they will perform; and institution by the commission of appropriate court action to compel common carrier truck lines to provide service for small shipments.

The ad hoc group severely criticized carrier "selectivity." It noted that some carriers with statutory mandates in the Interstate Commerce Act to handle all traffic lawfully tendered them were rejecting shipments at will. In one typical situation a carrier regularly accepted interline shipments of 200 pounds or more but refused lighter packages with the notation, "no service available." Reports of the committee charged that performance standards of regulated truck lines were below those which the public deserved. The committee also advocated that the ICC strike from common carrier certificates of motor carriers issued prior to 1943 clauses that limited transportation to truckload lots.

In appearances before this committee, motor carrier executives contended that in general on truckload shipments of 38,000 to 42,000 pounds they just break even, on shipments between 1,000 and 6,000 pounds their costs are sky-high, and on shipments under 1,000 pounds they suffer unbearable financial losses. Accountants of these haulers produced figures that revealed that shipments of 1,000 pounds or less comprise about 84 percent of their total number of movements and 20 percent of the weight moved, but that these small shipments contribute only 30 percent of motor carrier revenues and produce an operating ratio (expenses over revenues) of about 106.

To mitigate criticism of motor carriers, the American Trucking Association has organized carrier committees, which work through regional rate bureaus in tackling small shipment problems. These committees deal directly with complaints of lack of service and, so the truckers contend, have resolved many problems between small-lot shippers and carriers.

The ICC's ad hoc committee indicated that shippers of small items can make several contributions to solution of the problem. One is to remodel their shipping docks to dovetail more readily with carrier equipment; a second is to improve packaging techniques; and a third is to pool pickup and delivery at isolated points by more extensive utilization of shipper associations and freight forwarders.[5]

Documentation and Paper Work

Bills of lading, delivery instruction, licenses, dock receipts, waybills, insurance forms, certificates of origin, inspection reports, vessel manifests, freight bills, consular invoices, export declarations, and bonds of various kinds are essential for trade to move smoothly within and beyond the borders of a nation. Documents are also necessary to alert accounting, shipping, receiving, and other departments concerning the nature and weight of the shipment and correct procedures for handling. The paper work mountain in transportation and distribution has reached a nearly unendurable size. Preparation of foreign trade documents alone costs U.S. shippers about $7 billion annually.

Anyone with experience in domestic and foreign trade is aware of the mountain of paper work he must prepare daily and send and receive in order to consummate delivery of freight of almost any kind.[6] Any intercity shipment requires some kind of stamp or signature. Shippers and receivers are legally required to have written data on the type and contents of consignments, insurance, evidence of delivery and receipt, and evidence of ownership of title or change of title of transported items. For example, a consignor in the United States must prepare at least 18 separate documents to export a shipment from Chicago to Paris, and en route the same consignment will generate at least double that number of documents before it finally reaches destination.

To solve the problem of excessive documentation, the Department of Transportation, the Interstate Commerce Commission, and private organizations such as the Transportation Data Coordinating Committee (TDCC) are attempting to slash through the paper work jungle. Computers have entered the picture and are already mitigating the document burden. Also, the growing volume of container shipments requires fewer documents per ton of cargo than break-bulk cargo.

One of the most advanced innovations is the Transport Internationale Routier, or "carnet" system, in use by other countries but not yet by the United States. Under this system a shipment can originate in one country, travel through several other nations, and finally terminate at a foreign destination without interruption or delay en route.[7] Carnets are prepared at origin and accompany the shipment. Inspectors at border points recognize valid carnets and tear off proper pages at key stopoffs. It is a mystery why the United States has refused to adopt all phases of this highly efficient documentation system; other countries, particularly those in Europe, have utilized it with great success for the past seven or eight years.

The Transportation Data Coordinating Committee adapts computer techniques to physical distribution management and aims to produce the up-to-date statistical data that physical distribution managers now lack and badly need. TDCC coordinates electronic data processing of transportation data in order to make such information useful in instituting shipments and in compiling statistics.

TDCC began its work by establishing five "task forces" of shippers, carriers, and other transportation users. These groups devised standard codes for the transportation industry and reviewed these codes following tests and recommendations by interested shippers and transportation agencies. The carrier symbols of TDCC identify individual corporations and their transportation equipment. The geographical area is also codified in order to speedily pinpoint locations of consignors and consignees and best routes of transport between them. TDCC's tariff code group concerns itself with instructions by shippers to carriers concerning publication of rate and routing guides.

TDCC's chief executive emphasizes that unfortunately transportation agencies now issue separate code symbols, rates, tariff formats, bills of lading, freight bills, waybills, receipts, and commodity descriptions. He stresses that in the 1970s a basic need is uniformity of documents, so that the nation's transportation network will provide intermodal distribution service with easily identifiable administrative procedures guided by data that computers will produce accurately and quickly.[8]

Many question why the Department of Transportation, the Interstate Commerce Commission, the Federal Maritime Commission, and the Civil Aeronautics Board do not make freely available to carriers and the public data that the TDCC proposes to issue at an exorbitant price. For example, composition of a common waybill format, regardless of mode or commodities, would make it relatively simple for major shippers to provide regulatory bodies with essential data in readable form. These data would replace the existing haphazard compilation of governmental transportation statistics, virtually all of which are long out of date and nearly useless when they finally appear.

With intelligent computer programming, for the first time it is now possible to develop transportation data with accuracy and precision. Whether a private agency, namely TDCC, should exploit that advancement at a monetary profit or whether the federal government should provide that information free to the public is an unsettled question.

Improved Transportation Technology

Improved transportation and materials-handling technology is gradually convincing some corporate executives of the high productive potential of PDM. Perhaps PDM has been subordinate to other phases of the economy because the cycles of progress could find no niche for it or evaluate its true worth. There is a multiplicity of explanations for the surging economic changes under way in physical distribution, and only now are we beginning to delineate and define them. We will now discuss some recent steps forward in transportation and other areas of PDM.

Improvements in Railroading

Viewing the broad spectrum of railroading in both its positive and negative hues, one detects several trends which could lead to a brighter day for this most troubled, yet most essential, of all means of surface transport.

Rail unit trains. Several railroads have instituted a type of service in which entire trains, each with up to 200 fully loaded freight cars, start from origin, bypass congested terminal centers, and speedily deliver several million pounds of freight at a destination many hundreds of miles away.

One version of this system is the Rent-A-Train plan of the Illinois Central Railroad Company, the most important and progressive north-south rail carrier in the Mississippi Valley. One purpose of the new concept is to open foreign export markets to the large part of mid-America's farm area that does not have access to low-cost barge transportation. The Illinois Central charges the shipper $1 million annually if the train consists only of IC-owned cars and $700,000 if the train is composed of shipper's or receiver's cars. If a unit trainload is composed of both carrier and shipper equipment, the yearly charge is $700,000 plus $3,489 for each IC car used. The Illinois Central imposes an additional ton-mile rate, subject to a minimum of $5 per train-mile, loaded or empty. The railroad publishes unit-train charges on bulk corn, oats, and wheat in covered hopper cars from stations in Illinois to five seaports on the Gulf of Mexico. The carrier guarantees a minimum average running speed of 25 miles per hour with provision for self-penalizing reductions of charges for delayed arrivals.

The Interstate Commerce Commission approved the Rent-A-Train system as a form of annual discount rates but found that in certain respects the proposal is unlawful. For example, the ICC ruled that omission of provisions for alternating Rent-A-Train rates with carload rates did not comport with the Interstate Commerce Act.

Recently the Interstate Commerce Commission rendered another significant decision on unit-train rates. Manufacturers of steel at Sault Ste. Marie, Ontario, and of cement at Alpena, Michigan, annually use approximately 240,000 and 500,000 tons respectively of steam coal. This commodity moves from mines in eastern and southern regions of the United States to Toledo, Ohio, for transshipment via lake vessels. The railroads maintained depressed carload rates from these mines to Toledo for such transshipment, but to destinations other than Sault Ste. Marie and Alpena the rates were based on minimum annual tonnages less than tonnages the complainants shipped. The principal contention was that the lower rail rates to points other than Sault Ste. Marie and Alpena were unjustly discriminatory. The ICC found, however, that the railroads were justified in establishing the depressed rate level to prevent loss of traffic to pipeline transportation.

Centralized traffic control. Another practical and already working innovation is the electronically controlled freight terminal yard. For example, one man sitting in a tower at the Southern Railway Company's Citico Yard (Chattanooga), John Sevier Yard (Knoxville), Inman Yard (Atlanta), or Norris Yard (Birmingham) can control the coupling of hundreds of freight cars into six or seven trains, each with more than a hundred cars. He accomplishes this by observing flashing lights and radar-recording devices, and by manipulating a few simply operated switches within his reach. This method of making up trains is far superior to archaic procedures of the past when even in the largest classification yards lantern-swinging switchmen guided locomotive engineers, who leaned out of their cab windows and shifted freight cars back and forth. In line haul, as apart from terminal operations, centralized traffic control has allowed abandonment of double tracks on many railroads, and has created other economies for rail transportation.[9]

Large damage-free freight cars. As noted above, the railroads are now placing into service freight cars with nearly double the capacity of corresponding vehicles of 10 years ago. For example, giant 60-foot hydracushioned underframe boxcars have expanded loads per car, increased revenues per carload, and justified reduced freight charges on many items.

Logical consolidation of railroad corporations. Another movement aimed to improve railroading is the merger and consolidation of numerous separate railroads into fewer and fewer large regionwide systems. For example, absorption of the Nashville, Chattanooga, and St. Louis into the Louisville & Nashville Railroad was beneficial from the standpoint of the railroads' stockholders, the shipping public, and the southern region. The merger of the Southern Railway and the Central of Georgia Railway has also resulted in worthwhile economies.[10] Combination of the Norfolk & Western Railway and Baltimore & Ohio into one system has also been a profit-creating venture for the carriers. The same can be said for consolidation of the Burlington, Great Northern, and Northern Pacific railroads. Logical consolidations of railroad corporations do aid and further the public interest. The existing 66 Class I railroads resulted from tens of thousands of consolidations and mergers beginning in the 1830s and extending into the 1970s.

However, it does not follow that *all* recent consolidations have had or will have positive results. Witness, for example, the Penn Central fiasco, which has been nothing less than a national economic disaster.[11] In fact, the thesis that a few large railroad systems, say four or five, can better serve the whole public than the present sixty-six Class I railroad corporations is highly debatable.

The specter of government ownership lurks in the shadows, and the railroad industry's stampede toward consolidation, which will reduce to near zero constructive competition in the industry, has created deep concern among many shippers. It is unlikely that the public will tolerate a privately owned railroad system from which competition has evaporated and in which a few giant privately owned rail corporations dominate rail transport throughout the entire United States.

Abandonment of unproductive rail lines. The average miles of Class I railroads operated in the United States declined from 219,000 miles in 1960 to 210,000 miles in 1970, a significant shrinkage in view of the concomitant rapid growth of the nation's production. However, most of the abandonments were well thought out and fully justified. It makes no sense to compel privately owned corporations, many already in dire financial straits, to operate unneeded trackage that drains millions of dollars from their coffers.

Increasingly scientific freight rate structures. The railroad industry is in general organizing freight rate structures that are relevant to modern needs and times. For example, many rail lines now quote heavy-volume rates, already described above. Another new type of charge is the incentive rate. Under this pricing system carriers give shippers incentives to increase loads per car by setting one rate for a conventional carload minimum weight, say 100,000 pounds, and a much lower rate on all tonnage above that minimum. These lower incentive rates reduce the overall average freight bill submitted to the shipper and enhance railroad revenues. There has also been developed a system of multiple car rates. Under this system the carload rate for a number of cars used by a shipper is less than the single carload rate.

In a category by itself is piggybacking, which has allowed an intermodal tie-in between rail and highway transportation to the benefit of shippers, railroads, and motor carriers. Rates per ton on commodities loaded in trailers on flatcars (TOFC) are typically lower than single truckload rates. Piggybacking is a long overdue intermodal arrangement between rail and highway transportation. When piggybacking began, in a far-reaching action the ICC and railroads and truck lines established five plans of TOFC rates based on ownership of freight cars and trailers and methods of loading, unloading, and delivery of trailers.[12]

Highway Transportation

Between 1950 and 1970 the percentage of the nation's intercity ton-miles, public and private, which the motor carriers carried, increased from 16 to 21. The aggregate intercity ton-miles hauled by all carriers rose from nearly 1.2 billion to more than 1 trillion. Recently Pacific Intermountain Express, as well as Consolidated Freightways, both huge trucking organizations, established transcontinental highway service. Previously these lines had operated principally west of the Mississippi River and joined with lines east of that boundary for transcontinental hauls. Now PIE and CF offer through single-line service from the Pacific to the Atlantic coasts. In other words, the United States now has full transcontinental common-carrier trucking service, something the railroads do not not yet offer.

The trucking industry has made advances far beyond those the railroads have achieved. The explanation of this faster acceptance of improved technology is that the trucking industry is much more competitive than railroading. Improved transportation technology in the trucking industry may be briefly summarized. There are now much larger, more efficient trailers and semitrailers than existed 10 or 15 years ago. Recently a 30,000-pound trailerload was about the maximum that a truck rig could accommodate. Now an individual trailer can haul as much as 50,000 pounds. Design of novel single-purpose highway equipment to meet unique industrial needs is another achievement of the motor carrier industry. Specialized equipment is used because: it serves several points, which conventional trucks and other modes cannot; it often provides pneumatic self-loading and other economies in loading; and it permits delivery of the product on tighter schedules.

An example of specialized truck equipment is the cryogenic tank truck, which hauls oxygen, hydrogen, or other chemical elements in liquid form at far below zero temperature. Highway tank trailers also handle products like asphalt at temperatures double the boiling point. Pneumatic pressure highway trailers now haul 76 different dry bulk commodities, which are able to flow, including cement and grain, and hundreds of other solid, liquid, and gaseous products. The major drawback of specialized truck trailers is that they are costly to construct and maintain and must return empty on 95 to 100 percent of their trips.

Interstate Highway System. The Interstate Highway System of more than 42,000 miles is about 65 percent complete. All routes are at least one way on four lanes and six to eight lanes in and near large cities. With controlled access, wide curves, and absence of stoplights and rail crossings, the IHS permits high-speed, safe, nonstop driving for many miles.

Originally the U.S. government authorized a $25 billion trust fund to construct the Interstate Highway System. Taxes specifically marked for deposit into this fund include: 4 cents a gallon on motor fuel; 10 percent on manufacturers' wholesale price of trucks, buses, and trailers; 10 cents per pound on highway vehicle tires and tubes; $3.00 per 1,000 pounds on total gross weights of vehicles of more than 26,000 pounds; 8 percent of the manufacturers' wholesale price of truck and bus parts and their accessories; and 5 cents per gallon on lubricating oil if used for highway purposes. But a major problem of the Interstate Highway System is the rapid rise in costs of construction. The federal government and the states have already expended $37 billion on this undertaking, as compared to the original $25 billion estimate. The final cost may well exceed $50 billion.

The Interstate Highway System permits a sizable saving for commercial carriers. They can maintain sustained high speeds with a minimum of braking and stopping. Such advantages open the door to use of more powerful engines. These carefully constructed highway routes also permit operation of bigger, better, and safer vehicles.

In June 1970, John A. Volpe, secretary of transportation, proposed before the road subcommittee of the House Public Works Committee a program which would assure permanence of the interstate system but at the same time provide for scaling down of IHS priorities in order to finance noninterstate highway construction. The DOT chief recommended an increase of over $9 billion through fiscal 1976 for further extension of the system; a continuation through 1972–1973 of present levels of expenditures for primary and secondary road systems other than the IHS; and continuation through 1973 of existing levels of expenditure on highways on public lands. The secretary declared that the central issue was not the amount spent on highways but the overall adequacy of expenditure on transportation in general. He maintained that for the future the United States needs a better balance between federal investment in highways and that in subways, bus systems, and rail passenger lines, which he feels have been neglected.

In testimony before the same committee, the managing director of the American Trucking Association opposed diversion of highway tax revenues to areas other than the federal highways. The trucking executive argued that the existence of nonhighway needs were a poor excuse for inflicting injustice upon the owners of motor carriers.

The IHS trust fund has worked so successfully in financing and constructing the four-lane superhighway network that governmental leaders now favor diverting those monies to other transport purposes and also creating a single trust fund for other modes of transport. Under a bill which Senator Gaylord Nelson of Wisconsin has introduced, monies in the interstate fund would be diverted to development of alternative transport modes, such as mass transit and pollution-free urban vehicles. The Wisconsin senator would create a $4 billion a year "Transportation for People Fund" to finance alternatives to the automobile on city streets and thwart a second round of interstate highway building. The secretary of transportation has also expressed support for the idea of a single fund for transportation.

Between 1956 and 1969 truck owners paid in taxes about 42 percent of construction costs of the Interstate Highway System. The trucking industry maintains that the IHS is financed by the truckers and thus does not place a burden upon the federal government's general budget and does not hurt other government programs. Motor carriers argue that it would be a gross inequity to divert highway funds to subsidize other modes of transport.

Another obstacle to increased efficiency of motor carriage has been failure of the government to update size and weight standards for the Interstate Highway System. The House and Senate public works committees are considering measures which would authorize the states to increase these limits. DOT supports these bills but would delay application of them for three years while it develops new safety standards.

Some congressmen oppose any increase in vehicle size and weight limits and have blocked legislation to increase these standards. They have introduced a bill into Congress to establish a 15-member presidential commission to compile data needed for a hard look at the justification for larger trucks. These reluctant legislators recognize that organizations such as the American Association of State Highway Officials have compiled some pertinent data but fear that the average citizen does not understand these facts. The congressmen recommend further research, particularly on safety, because experts of the National Highway Safety Bureau have testified before

Congress that governmental highway officials have insufficient knowledge of the relationship between the design of a highway and the size of tractor-trailer rigs that the highway can accommodate. The pertinent legislation is still in committee and other transport legislation will probably supersede and nullify it.

About 15,000 trucking firms hold interstate operating authority. It has been contended that 500 common carriers and 1,500 special commodity carriers would be sufficient to fill the demand for motor carrier service.[13] The nation's regulatory system may be supporting inefficient motor carriers by setting rate levels for average rather than most efficient motor lines. The trend has been to consider as representative the needs of carriers that produce 75 percent or more of total revenues and to ignore the needs of carriers whose revenues comprise the balance.

The specious reasoning supporting this policy is that, since those carriers doing 75 to 80 percent of the business are faring poorly, higher rates are justified for all carriers. Major truckers agree that if competing giant-sized companies did not lose volume to the small ones, the large truck lines could operate more efficiently. The physical distribution managers of shippers face the following destructive cycle. Small carriers drop rates to attract business; big ones then suffer losses and appeal to the ICC for rate increases, and the ICC advances all motor carrier rates. Following that, small operators cancel marginally low rates to increase net profits. Soon thereafter the "bigs" further reduce their rates, attract more traffic, and compel the small carriers to drop their rates to survive. The vicious circle then begins all over again.

Multiple trailer operations. To fulfill expanding shipper needs and requirements, motor carriers have turned to new equipment, one of which is the multiple trailer. Initially the twin trailer, one tractor pulling two trailers, operated only over primary roads classified as interstate limited-access highways. As early as 1956, 18 states allowed twin trailer operations. Other states have since eliminated their restrictions, and now 33 states permit twin trailers on public highways. At present 28 states permit 65-foot twin trailers.

A number of states in the East and Southeast totally forbid operation of multiple trailers. These limitations seriously hamper nationwide hauls of large loads per truck unit, a restriction that strongly influences truck movements, particularly in the high-density eastern states. It is probable, however, that in the near future all 48 continental states will allow twin trailer operations, provided advocates of this equipment can convince the public that such units are not a safety hazard.

Opponents of big trucks declare that these vehicles are damaging the nation's paved highways at a cost to taxpayers of hundreds of millions of dollars. A recent report of the government accounting office (GAO) charged that about $200 million is already needed to repair cracked pavement. GAO, the watchdog of federal spending, contends that virtually all superhighways need an added layer of concrete to patch cracking. Crucial cause of this damage, so GAO maintains, is heavy trucks. GAO recommends placement of an extra inch or more of asphalt concrete atop damaged interstate highways to enable them to withstand traffic 20 years in the future. GAO alleges that mistakes in design due to misjudgments of road engineers about weather, underlying soil, and truck weights have caused cracking and buckling of the roadways.

Motive power systems. Diesel engines have dominated the motor carrier industry. Technology has developed lightweight, high-speed diesel motors operating at more than 300 horsepower. However, dominance of the diesel is not assured. General Motors Corporation recently announced that its engineers have devised and the corporation is building gas turbine engines for trucks and buses aimed primarily for multiple trailer operations. GM estimates the original cost will exceed that of the standard diesel engine by 10 percent, but because of its sturdiness and low fuel consumption the turbine will be more economical to operate in the long run.

Motor carrier terminals. Trucking companies are placing most new terminals on fringes of industrial parks close to the Interstate Highway System and at stopoff points on inner-city land cleared for urban renewal. They usually equip these terminals with conveyors (either towline or roller systems with electric controls) and allow room for expansion. They also strive to perfect transfer techniques. For example, in some companies the truck driver, having positioned his trailer at a dock, connects the floor-mounted conveyor in his trailer to the terminal conveyor. At the press of a button two interlocked conveyors unload the freight automatically; electric sensors read coded markings on the freight, and it is moved by conveyor from the truck's tailgate into the receiver's warehouse.

Inland Waterways

In its lumbering and hotly controversial fashion, inland waterway transport has implemented improvements in routes, equipment, and navigation techniques. The

United States now has nine-foot navigation throughout the inland waterway system and along the Atlantic, Gulf, and Pacific intracoastal waterways. In addition, the Great Lakes water routes have long served many metropolitan areas in the Northeast and Northwest.

Within a few years this country will have even deeper channels and more extended waterway routes throughout the central heartland. For example, the Missouri, Arkansas, and Trinity rivers will offer transport service to points now closed to barging. The U.S. government will improve channels on the Mississippi and Illinois waterways and dredge other rivers to practical navigation depths.

Automation of waterfront dock facilities at Port Elizabeth, Philadelphia, Baltimore, and other ports on the North Atlantic, South Atlantic, Gulf, and Pacific coasts has reduced delays in handling water-borne tonnage. This mechanization has benefited all concerned, even the affected trade unions. As noted previously, the longshoreman who felt he had a vested interest in an outmoded job changed his mind when he developed additional skills and made the docks more productive.

The U.S. Corps of Engineers is designing a deeper, wider, and improved Panama Canal and another canal across the Isthmus of Panama. One possible route is through a narrow section of Nicaragua. Construction of additional canals with modern methods (use of atomic instead of dynamite explosives, for example) and deepening, widening, and improving the existing Panama and Suez canals would facilitate waterway commerce between highly populated areas of the earth.

Oceans cover about three-fourths of the earth's surface, and spectacular advancements have been made in oceanic transport. Competitive forces have motivated shipbuilders to construct larger, speedier ocean freighters and tankers. Containers are now capable of hauling up to 1,200 containers at speeds of 22 knots and discharging 15,000 tons of cargo in 24 hours.

Container Transport

Containerization, a relatively new approach to distribution, is among the most important PDM developments of the twentieth century. The current container explosion compares with the commercial revolution of the 1600s, the Industrial Revolution of the 1800s, and electric, electronic, nuclear, and other earth-shaking innovations of the twentieth century. Containers are drastically modifying banking, insurance, and investment procedures. They are changing governmental practices, redesigning waterfronts, and reshaping patterns of foreign trade. Just as the automobile obliterated the village blacksmith, the container should eventually destroy the occupation of hand stevedoring. Package designers have entered the container act. For example, packages for various articles are being keyed to fill the inside space of containers.

The container of this decade is a highly engineered, usually rectangular-shaped box or chest, 8 feet high, 8 feet wide, and in lengths of 20, 27, 35, or 40 feet. Container dimensions vary widely, and standardized modules remain in the future. A U.S. organization, the American Standards Institute (ASI), has tried to establish standard dimensions for containers. However, both the ASI and the International Standards Organization (which attempts to do internationally what ASI tries to do domestically) have powers only to recommend and not to enforce container rules and regulations. Relentless laws of economic costs will eventually dictate worldwide adoption of harmony and uniformity in dimensions of container equipment.

Materials for constructing containers are mainly aluminum, steel, and plywood. However, container manufacturers are still researching in many fields, among them plastics, for the ideal container construction material. Giant-size forklift trucks, cranes, conveyor belts, and other handling gear transfer containers into and out of warehouses or open container parks, from rail flatcars to truck chassis, or from land carriers onto decks or into hatches of conventional freighters or into cells or onto decks of containerships.

Although containerization frees shipper, carrier, receiver, and governmental agencies from many shackles, the container shipper still faces a number of roadblocks. At some places containers are in short supply, at others there is an oversupply. This imbalance is due in large part to failure of shippers and carriers to utilize container boxes continuously and efficiently. Container companies face stone walls of separatism between the different modes of transportation. A glance into ancient history should shame us. In the first century Roman merchant ships sailed from Rome to Ceylon, loaded precious cargo, then sailed to the African East Coast, and unloaded their exotic freight onto the backs of camels. Camel caravans then carried the imports to ports on the Nile, where slaves loaded the freight on barges for delivery to inland points or to ports on tributaries of the Nile. Nineteen centuries ago intermodal transport was the rule, not the exception.

The Federal Maritime Commission found that in 1969

only 13 of 27 ocean rate conferences of the United States permitted containership operators to allow discounts in rates on containerized cargo, despite the tremendous economies each ship gains from carrying container instead of break-bulk cargo. Controversy over equalization of rates between European and Atlantic Coast ports, fear that low freight-of-all-kinds rates on container freight will divert high-value cargo from break-bulk to container ocean carriers, and opposition to establishment of two-way ocean container rates have impeded development of container transport.

Let us note some of the *must* breakthroughs that the containers will achieve. Foremost is solution of the critical shortage of transportation equipment. Railroads themselves have for years refused to view realistically their own shortage of freight cars. Utilization of rail equipment must also improve. It is doubtful that the United States can continue to tolerate the appalling facts that a railroad boxcar moves loaded an average of only 23 days a year and stands idle or moves empty the other 342 days and that 80 percent of railroad freight and classification yards are in unsound condition.

Domestic shippers must utilize the best routes of rail and motor transit from origin to destination. It is ridiculous for shippers to rely on motor carriers that travel routes that are 100 to 200 percent circuitous. And certainly shippers should not subject high-priced containers with high-value cargo to such roundabout routing. The container is the most logical of all intermodal transport equipment, and pooling of containers on a regional, national, and world basis is an absolutely essential next step in the nation's distribution pattern.

During 1969 containers carried more than 11 percent of ocean-borne general cargo on the all-important North

Atlantic route. It is the opinion of many that with improvements in design and structure the container will eventually haul 50 to 80 percent of merchandise freight over that route. Our society must entirely restructure its freight rate-making process. The container should expedite that breakthrough. As noted, some railroads, for example the Santa Fe, are already running full container trains and quoting rates per container.

Air Transportation

By 1975 the volume of commercial air travel will be triple that of 1970. Lockheed's C-5A, which was tested recently, can carry cargo exceeding 500 tons. Unfortunately, the C-5A has weaknesses in its wing structure which the manufacturer has not yet corrected, but there is little doubt that the C-5A will eventually achieve its potential.

Airplane manufacturers have also developed the Boeing 747, which is nearly as large and efficient as the C-5A. In addition the Boeing 747 has airspeeds of 625 miles per hour over a 5,000-mile range, and can shift freight from origin to destination around the world. Airways have also devised ingenious and practical air express, freight, and container rates different from those published by the railroads, truck lines, and waterways and adapted to the airlines' particular needs and problems.

The United States as a Land-Bridge

When the container revolution emerged as the transport sensation of the twentieth century, many thought that one of the wonders it would accomplish would be creation of land-bridges across North America and Euro-Asia. The theory was that full containerships would sail, for example, from Tokyo to Seattle, where mechanized equipment would swiftly lift the boxes directly onto rail cars, which would speed the cargo to New York for transfer into containerships bound for England. While carriers must sustain high costs of loading and discharging container boxes at seaports on the Atlantic and Pacific coasts, land-bridge enthusiasts argue that land-bridge routes will eventually compete with and replace all-water intercontinental routes through the Panama and Suez canals.

At the request of the Department of Transportation, Litton Systems, Inc., analyzed various land-bridge proposals. Litton found that international land-bridge services could open a $200 billion market for U.S. railroads at the expense of steamship lines serving six trade routes. For example, the Gulf Coast could lose traffic, which now travels through the Panama Canal, to the Pacific Coast, but in turn the Gulf Coast would attract traffic headed south which now moves outbound via the Great Lakes. A further finding was that containerized traffic would possibly divert from existing routes to unit trains approximately 3.1 million tons by 1973 and 8.5 million tons by 1983.

McKinsey & Company, in an earlier study, concluded that if rail and sea distances are equal, rail cost per container would fall below that of a ship with a capacity of fewer than 600 container boxes. But if the containership had a capacity greater than 600 containers, the mileage involved would determine which mode was lower in cost. The McKinsey researchers found that an Atlantic to Pacific transcontinental trip of 3,000 miles would be cheaper

per containerload than a 6,000-mile all-water voyage through the Panama Canal.

United Cargo Corporation pioneered the first land-bridge attempt in July 1968. UCC tried to secure special low rates via the steamship routes, Asia–U.S. Pacific Coast and Europe–U.S. Atlantic Coast, as well as depressed transcontinental rail rates across North America. UCC's objective was to secure rates low enough to compete with the all-sea movement via the Panama Canal. The nonvessel operator—UCC—proposed to put into land-bridge service 1,000 containers, 100 of which would move in full loads in each direction every 10 days.

Canada may have advantages over the United States in land-bridge arrangements. For example, Canada has two major transcontinental coast-to-coast railroads, whereas the United States does not have a single transcontinental rail carrier. Another Canadian edge over the United States is that Canada's major east coast ports are nearer Europe than is New York; and Vancouver, Canada's leading west coast port, is closer to Yokohama than is San Francisco or Seattle.

Railroad Encouragement

The Norfolk & Western and Union Pacific Railroad have announced joint low-level transcontinental rates, which start at $660 per container for single 40-foot containers and decline to $510 per container when the volume tendered reaches or exceeds 31 or more carloads. The previous domestic rate was $700 per container, compared to the relatively high freight-of-all-kinds (F.A.K.) rate of $80 per ton. The F.A.K. rate may have been excessive because the direct overland route did not attract traffic even with the time saving it promised.

Atchison, Topeka & Santa Fe Railway statistics show that containerized freight moving between the western United States and Europe and between the eastern United States and Asia through the all-water Panama Canal route totals 9 million long tons, 4.8 million in imports and 4.2 million in exports. The railroad estimates that the volume susceptible to containerization moving on the Atlantic between the United States and Europe is 17 million long tons.

ATSF officials calculate that if each container holds 20,000 pounds of freight and railroads carry two containers per flatcar, this freight volume would generate the following annual containerloads and carloads: via the Panama Canal, 1 million containers and 500,000 carloads; via the Atlantic through United States ports, 1.9 million containers and 950,000 carloads. By comparison, long tons of freight susceptible to containerization between the Orient and Europe for 1967 were as follows: Orient to Europe, 1,100,000; Europe to Orient, 550,000.

The Santa Fe's enthusiastic predictions have not materialized. Exorbitant and ever-heightening port costs on the East and West coasts are one blockade to development of a land-bridge movement. Construction of containerships with capacities of 1,200 boxes and speeds of 24 to 28 knots have made the all-water route through the Panama Canal, Europe-to-Asia, and Asia-to-Europe much more attractive than any present land-bridge route.

Uncertainties of the Concept

There are other uncertainties plaguing the future of land-bridge freighting across both Canada and the

United States. One is that the Asia-to-Europe rail route across the Soviet Union is shorter, faster, and cheaper than land-bridge routes across the United States and Canada. Another cause of apprehension is the attitude of the formidable and rapidly expanding Japanese shipping industry, which likes the long ocean hauls through the Panama and Suez canals. At present the heaviest international water-borne container flow is between Europe and eastern U.S. ports; the next largest tonnage is between the Orient and eastern U.S. ports; and the third largest is between the Orient and western U.S. ports.

Containerized Japan-to-Europe commerce is far less remunerative for shipowners than shipments from Japan to the U.S. Pacific Coast. For example, the waterway distance from Yokohama to San Francisco is 4,536 nautical miles, as against 12,483 miles from Yokohama to London. Differences in ocean distances, which vitally affect ocean shipping costs, are not reflected in ocean rates. For example, on three representative commodities from Japan container rates per long ton are: electrical goods—$37.60 to European ports, $38.25 to U.S. West Coast ports; synthetic fiber—$39.42 to European ports, $35.25 to U.S. West Coast ports; canned fish or fruit—$29.36 to European ports, $31.00 to U.S. West Coast ports.

The truth is that not every student of the subject is convinced of the feasibility of the land-bridge concept. U.S. Maritime Administrator Andrew E. Gibson pours cold water on land-bridge proposals generally. He feels that greater efficiencies could be gained by reducing documentation, standardization of containers, modernization of port facilities, and centralization of planning for inland movements of ocean containers. Mr. Gibson observes that a nearly fatal handicap of the land-bridge idea is delays in interchanges between trains and ships. He also questions the potential time saving of rail transit across the United States as against all-water transit via the Panama or Suez canals.[14]

Loss and Damage

Any nation's transportation objectives should be the speedy, safe delivery of freight traffic. The modes of transport that provide the best customer satisfaction and service should attract the shipper's business. But loss and damage to freight in transit is a virulent blight afflicting the railroad, trucking, barging, and other transport industries. For years all modes have striven to deliver freight damage-free, an objective that shippers encourage carriers to achieve. However, over the last decade the loss and damage picture has worsened. For example, in 1960 damage claims paid out by the railroads were approximately $100 million. In 1968 rail damage claim payments rose to $182 million. In 1970 (year ended September 1970) rail claims exceeded $226 million, an increase of 13.2 percent above the total for the corresponding period in 1969.

The sad fact is that damage losses come directly out of the already paltry earnings of the rail carriers. In 1969 claims ate up 1.69 percent of rail revenue and wiped out one-fifth of total rail net income. Rail management insists that it desperately seeks ways to halt this tragedy of waste, but one sees very few positive results.

Truck lines suffer equally in loss and damage payouts. Their payments for damage in 1968 were $188 million. In 1969 this payout grew to $229 million. Similar reliable data on claims paid by airlines, barge lines, ocean carriers, and other modes of transportation are not available. Physical distribution managers are becoming more and more concerned over failure of transportation agencies to place solution of damage problems foremost among their immediate objectives.

At the start-up of its Tennessee paper mill Bowater utilized conventional 40-foot boxcars and adopted a unit-load method in which wide-banded steel strapping encircled 2 units of 18 or 20 rolls of paper in each end of the vehicle. However, other shippers of paper products and many railroads opposed the Bowater approach and there was widespread disagreement on the subject of transit damage. Rail-shipper-publisher investigations disclosed that all loading patterns, including Bowater's floating unit load, were far from perfect. Finding that it could not overcome the damage menace by styles of loading, in 1955 Bowater's traffic department began to place heavy emphasis upon impact registers to pinpoint locales and causes of transit damage. These registers are clocklike machines that record on a special tape the speed per hour at which boxcars couple, and date and time of each coupling with an impact.

By 1960 Bowater's Tennessee mill had purchased 10 impact registers, and the Southern Railway had 20 others in Bowater's service. The one important fact those recorders taught was that an overspeed impact or any heavy shock of a longitudinal nature would almost certainly damage newsprint in boxcars. These instruments also revealed that about 90 percent of damage occurred in switching and classification yards.

Unit loading, careful selection, cleaning and preparation of boxcars, use of impact registers, and the determination of the Southern Railway and Bowater slightly ruffled the gremlin of damage but by no means eliminated it.

Introduction of boxcars with hydraulic draft gears was a crucial step forward in the assault upon newsprint transit damage. Originally the Southern Railway assigned 285 units of this equipment to Bowater's Tennessee mill by stenciling on each car the instruction "Return to Calhoun When Empty." Upon completion of the Louisville & Nashville Railroad track into Calhoun in 1962, the L&N purchased and placed cushioned boxcars at Calhoun. For a while these super boxcars retarded transit damage and produced additional benefits. Formerly the company loaded into each conventional 40-foot car only single tiers of 36 to 40 standard newsprint rolls. At present, with double tiering and use of doorway space, Bowater loads 112 rolls of 60 inches long and 38 inches in diameter in a 60-foot boxcar.

However, despite the contribution of cushion cars to damage-free delivery, the menace of transit damage lurks and repeatedly strikes home, and Bowater is still in pursuit of a foolproof remedy. On several occasions the company has loaded and dispatched a boxcar of newsprint, followed it in an automobile, and checked its contents at each interchange yard, step by step, until it arrived at destination. In the endless struggle to achieve undamaged delivery, the company continually switches from one rail route to another, from truck to piggyback, or from rail to truck or barge delivery.

Publishers of metropolitan newspapers, hard pressed by deadlines of five or six newspaper editions daily, demand that the newsprint sheet run swiftly and continuously through their automatic rotary presses. These machines, whirling at lightning speeds, are extremely sensitive to physical defects in the paper. The steel-hard paperboard core around which the newsprint is wrapped must be almost exactly straight and true, so that the core tightly fits the revolving bars of the press. Pressroom operators reject even slightly flat cores which can cause damage to the expensive presses.

These demanding operators also frown upon scuffed, scarred, starred, or out-of-round rolls, which can and often do stop an entire printing operation. Out-of-round rolls cause 40 percent of web breaks in a typical newspaper plant. Following such a break, the highly paid operators must waste time threading the newsprint back into position before the presses can resume printing. Delay in issue of a newspaper edition, plus overtime labor which breaks frequently require, can become very costly to publishers.

To reduce damage to newsprint, several publishers have constructed ultramodern warehouses and installed highly automated handling and record-keeping equipment. These innovations have lessened the frequency of damage, improved the accuracy and speed of reporting losses, lessened confusion concerning responsibility for damage, minimized the concealed damage problem, and created a more cooperative understanding among the railroads, Bowater, and publishers.

The Oklahoman is the pioneer in this field. At the receiving dock of that newspaper's warehouse, skilled forklift drivers carefully remove newsprint rolls from boxcars and place them on a conveyor. Inside the warehouse a device called a Trak-rak, which runs on overhead tracks and is equipped with a vacuum lift, picks the circular packages off the conveyor and stacks them. A single operator of the Trak-rak can stack newsprint rolls six high at any point in the building. According to the production manager of *The Oklahoman*, the automated warehouse has reduced damage to newsprint from around 6,000 pounds a month to practically zero.

The *Dallas Morning News* has also constructed a mechanized warehouse facility and adopted advanced techniques for storing newsprint. The warehouse manager found that by stacking the rolls end on end, the bottom roll will support a weight of nearly five tons. As against that, a single roll of newsprint stored on the side (or bilge) will soon flatten on the bottom under its own weight. Other newspaper companies which have instituted efficient warehousing and handling of newsprint are the *Miami Herald*, the *Miami News*, the *Jacksonville Journal*, the *Newark Star Ledger*, the *Winston-Salem Journal Sentinel*, and the *Charlotte Observer*.

But serious newsprint damage problems persist throughout Bowater's U.S. market area. Some pressroom managers continue to carry rolls of paper from railroad team tracks in rickety drayage vans and pickup trucks and to roll the paper off the tailgates of the vehicles onto old automobile tires lying flat on the pavement. Others utilize inefficient hand trucks, vintage 1800, for shifting the rolls. Many pressrooms that possess expensive forklift trucks equipped with special rubber-lined clamps employ drivers who do not operate the trucks or clamps properly.

National Freight Damage

The nation's rail lines have announced that they are engaged in a dynamic, far-reaching, four-point damage prevention campaign to: determine causes of freight damage, improve efficiency of car equipment, pressure their operating personnel to avoid rough handling, and augment the effectiveness of damage prevention organizations.

However, the attitude of the Association of American Railroads toward loss and damage is intriguing. That organization has not published results of this four-point damage abatement program. Instead the AAR prints an endless stream of accusations against shippers and the nature of commodities as the culprits responsible for damage of freight in transit. For example, one recent article in *Traffic World* attributed the increase in rail damage claim payments to: increasing movements of high-value freight; high cost of repairing and reconditioning damaged items; failure of shippers to load damage-free rail cars properly; and failure of railroads to obey impact limits which the railroads themselves had adopted. Thus three of the AAR's four causes of damage are based on the nature of the commodities shipped and shipper neglect, and only one is attributed to railroad equipment and operations.

An exceptional rail carrier that strives aggressively for undamaged delivery of their shipments is the Atchison, Topeka & Santa Fe, one of the nation's largest and most profitable rail corporations. Seventeen special agents in the Santa Fe's freight-handling department regularly evaluate damage reports in order to identify troublesome commodities and anticipate potential claims. These division officials then assign these reports to damage specialists for thorough investigation.

The all-around, in-depth nature of the Santa Fe's attack upon damage waste may be summarized as follows: use of photographs to pinpoint particular problems for shippers; dispatch of experts to trouble points as soon as the Santa Fe discovers such damage-causing locations; attendance by pertinent employees at frequently held "Local Better Handling Meetings" (in a recent year 84 committees held 945 such meetings with 24,224 in attendance); display of the Santa Fe's damage prevention movies, *Impact* and *Pay Day*, as well as comparable movies of other railroads and the AAR; infliction of discipline upon employees responsible for overspeed impacts; organization of seminars for freight claim departments, division special agents, transportation inspectors, and transportation agents; and installation of specialized freight car equipment, including about 9,000 shock-control cars.

However, the manager of better freight handling of the line recently admitted that despite his best efforts his carrier still has serious loss and damage problems. The Santa Fe's total 1969 claim bill was $13,072,881, or $2.02 per $100 of freight revenue, compared to $2.06 in 1963.

Perhaps the most widely read and most influential publication in the field of physical distribution, *Traffic World*, also brands shippers for failure to solve the loss and damage problem. The weekly periodical charges that shippers fail to package and reinforce their shipments adequately and that they press carriers for speedy delivery without recognizing that speed causes damage and refuse to attack known causes of repetitive damages.

But a large group of conscientious shippers are bucking the waste of damage in transit. For example, Scott Paper Company, one of the best-known manufacturers and converters of paper products, is earnestly seeking to dam this leakage of profits. Scott's corporate traffic manager espouses *claim prevention,* not *claim collection,* and impresses that policy upon Scott's carloaders as well as customers and railroads.

Following are the main components of Scott's broad-scale assault on the damage problem: conducting annual damage prevention contests among Scott's mills, converting plants, and warehouses; appointment of an intracompany claim prevention committee, which continually reminds Scott's packaging and loading personnel that a good or bad image of the firm is created in the customer's mind by the condition of the contents of each boxcar of Scott's freight; and organization of a traffic and distribution operation section charged with eradicating transportation damage. Operators of Scott's distribution warehouses and the paper company's customers describe damage they find in a freight car or truck received from any Scott origin. The company screens such information and deals directly with loading crews to improve loading of future shipments.

Viewpoint of a Packaging Authority

Manufacturers of paperboard boxes, cartons, and other containers are peculiarly sensitive to mishandling of freight. The Fibre Box Association, members of which consume about 10 million tons of paperboard annually in manufacturing boxes to package rail freight, keeps a sharp eye on damage trends. In public hearings before rail classification committees shipper witnesses have testified that less than 1 percent of freight packaged in fiberboard boxes incurred damage. Yet the claims bill of the railroads bounds continually upward.

Executives of the FBA charge that the annual statement of the Association of American Railroads on damaged freight, *Freight Loss and Damage,* serves little purpose. Box makers complain that these figures provide poor guidance in delineating the fine line between too much and too little packaging.

For example, the AAR report lists thousands of products under 37 commodity groupings. A few of these, such as cotton in bales, sugar, newsprint paper, and refrigerators, are quite specific. Unfortunately other groupings overlap and are confusing. In 1969, for example, 9 percent of the total payout for claims was classified as "all other." This catchall grouping included such diverse items as drugs, paints, electrical instruments, plastic articles, chemicals, paper and paper articles, aircraft, and hardware.

Fiber box experts maintain that their boxes are so dissimilar that a single aggregate damage claim figure is virtually useless in apportioning to the fiber box such causes of damage as: failure in the strength qualities; weaknesses of outer shipping containers; inadequate strength and thickness of glass in bottles or jars; and substitution of brittle, easily breakable plastic for glass bottles.

The AAR's report divides total rail claims payments among eleven causes of damage, which the fiber box industry declares are so vague that they have little practical use. For example, the AAR pigeonholes 60 percent of total damage under a catchall category, "improper handling—all damage not otherwise provided for." Fibre Box Association officials have recommended that the AAR update its loss and damage statistics by: compilation of damage payments by a central agency with that specific duty; computer analysis of these data to show shipper, origin, commodity, consignee, and type of packaging; and more frequent issue of loss and damage claims data.[15]

The rail lines appear blind to the fact that damage costs are a major waste of their earnings. Assembly of much more accurate, complete, and up-to-date damage statistics and computer analysis of those data is a must. The feasibility of computer analysis has been proven by the Chicago, Milwaukee, St. Paul and Pacific Railroad Company, and the Southern Pacific and Union Pacific Railroads, which have adapted their entire freight claim procedures to computers. A concerted joint effort by shippers, receivers, and carriers, using relevant up-to-date statistics would in all probability halt the erosion of rail earnings by damage claims.

One area deserving intensified study is the extent and effects of vibrations in rail transit. Many experts conjecture that railroad vibrations, even on firm roadbeds, may cause more damage than head-on impacts. There is some evidence that vibration caused most of the damage to Bowater's newsprint when this company utilized the steel-strapped unit loads. Quite often Bowater's boxcars would arrive at customer docks with severely damaged lading, but the impact register tape would show no significant impacts during the entire journey. The problems of vibration and swaying, caused by uneven roadbeds, curves, and other factors, remain to be solved.

References

1. John F. Magee, "The Logistics of Distribution," *Harvard Business Review*, July–August 1960, pp. 94–99.

2. *National Transportation Policy*, The Doyle Report, 1961.

3. Hugh S. Norton, "Economics and Economists in the Interstate Commerce Commission," *ICC Practitioners' Journal*, May–June 1969, p. 1649.

4. J. A. Krug, *National Resources and Foreign Aid* (Washington, D.C.: U.S. Department of the Interior, 1947), pp. 29–30.

5. *Eighty-first Annual Report of the Interstate Commerce Commission*, 1967, pp. 86–88; 1968, pp. 15–16; 1969, pp. 8–10; and 1970, pp. 13–14.

6. Joseph S. Coyle, "Stepping Across the Data Gap," *Traffic Management*, December 1969, p. 77. Jack W. Farrell, "How Consultants View Today's Paper Work Patterns," *Traffic Management*, August 1970, pp. 41–45.

7. *Carnet* (New York: United States Council of the International Chamber of Commerce, 1969), pp. 1–8.

8. *Closing the Data Gap in Transportation* (Washington, D.C.: Transportation Data Coordinating Committee, 1969), pp. 1–19.

9. The difficulty is that despite the availability of Centralized Traffic Control, Automatic Car Identification, TRAIN, and other advances in the railroad industry, fewer than one-half of the 66 Class I railroads have adopted these new ideas. *Railroad Review and Outlook* (Washington, D.C.: Association of American Railroads, January 1970), pp. 5–7, 13–15, 24–26, and 32–35 presents rail management's view on their innovations.

10. For an up-to-date discussion of railroad mergers see *Eighty-fourth Annual Report of the Interstate Commerce Commission*, 1970, pp. 28–30.

11. Association of American Railroads, *R & E Series, No. 664*, Fourth Quarter, 1970. The Penn Central suffered a net railway operating deficit in 1970 of $315 million, as against a deficit of $68 million in 1969.

12. Although piggybacking is only 15 years old, the railroads are now carrying more than 2.3 million loaded trailers annually. See *Revenue Freight Loaded by Commodities and Total Received from Connections* (Washington, D.C.: Association of American Railroads, December 1970), p. 7; *Eighty-fourth Annual Report of the Interstate Commerce Commission*, 1970, pp. 42–44.

13. Barrie Vreeland, "One Point of View," *Distribution Manager*, March 1969, p. 19.

14. *Journal of Commerce,* July 24, 1969.
15. Thomas R. Lynch, "The Freight Loss and Damage Picture—One Year Later" (speech before the Pulp and Paper Traffic League Seminar, Murray Bay, Quebec, June 27, 1966), pp. 2–6.

4 Distribution Principles in Practice

AN encouraging number of companies in different industries have applied physical distribution management principles to their operations with effective profit-creating results. They have adapted these principles in a variety of ways, depending upon the nature and type of enterprise. Mere realization that in the broad spectrum of activities between manufacturing and sales there are critically important distribution functions has meant improved business organization for individual firms, entire industries, and widespread economic regions.[1]

Following are case studies of application of scientific PDM in five diversified categories: mining industries; raw-material-oriented firms; market-oriented firms; consumer-oriented firms; and farm-oriented firms. The examples cited demonstrate that variegated types of enterprises gain by meshing scientific distribution programs into their organizational pattern. The central point is that the distribution function has a wide and significant place in the economic society.

Mining Industries

Extraction of minerals from the bowels of the earth extends back to earliest recorded history. Egypt became a world power immediately upon its acquisition of the valuable copper deposits of the Sinai peninsula about 4000 B.C. According to the *Holy Bible*, the Philistines subjugated the Jews by depriving them of the use of metals. The Roman Empire reached its zenith following attainment of control of rich mineral resources in Spain.

One moves into the twentieth century and the area adjacent to Tampa, Florida, to discover many revolutionary innovations in physical distribution of phosphate rock, a mineral mined near that seaport. Chemical compounds composed with phosphorus are essential items for soil fertility and human life itself. For example, the basic ingredients of commercial fertilizer are potassium, nitrogen, and phosphorus. Plants take phosphorus from the soil, and by eating plants, man and animals obtain that essential element. Phosphorus is necessary for normal growth of bones, nerves, and brain cells, and insufficient ingestion of phosphorus is a major cause of human deformities. Fortunately many common foods are rich in phosphorus, including wheat, eggs, milk, fish, nuts, beans, and peas. Prior to World War II North Africa, Soviet Russia, and the United States, in that order, originated most of the world's phosphate rock supply. Following the war, U.S. production jumped far ahead of Russia and North Africa and now exceeds that of the rest of the world combined. The U.S. Department of Commerce estimates that world consumption of phosphate will double by 1975 and triple by 1980.

Phosphate rock was discovered in Florida in the

1880s. The state's Bone Valley region, located within a radius of about 20 miles from Tampa, contains the world's richest phosphate mines. They account for 73 percent of the nation's output of this life-fostering product. In 1968 aggregate production of the Bone Valley mines, which 8 chemical companies operate, was 31 million tons. On retrieval from strip mines near Florida's west coast, phosphate rock is ground and graded in various BPL (bone-phosphate-lime) grades. These categories are then processed into commercial products such as triple superphosphate, which results from treatment of ground rock with phosphoric acid and diammonium phosphate. The last is produced by treatment of the rock with anhydrous ammonia and phosphoric acid.

Railroads serving Bone Valley, including predecessors of the present dominant company, the Seaboard Coast Line Railroad Company, have provided necessary transportation for the mineral. In 1968 transport of phosphate rock produced $100 million in revenue for the SCL (30 percent of the carrier's gross freight revenues). In the past the railroad had utilized two phosphate-loading terminals at Tampa. The carrier reached these facilities over tracks that ran directly through the most congested part of Tampa's central city, adding half an hour to every train run. The municipal government adopted restrictions that prevented rail operations through the city at certain times during the day and limited train lengths to 75 cars. The railroad realized that it had to abandon this cross-city operation and did so.

In an admirable cooperative venture the railroad, phosphate rock and related companies, and federal, county, and city governments in central and west coast Florida constructed new rail tracks, deepened channels in

Tampa Bay, and erected new dock facilities. Thus physical distribution of phosphate rock and fertilizers was reorganized via rail, barge, truck, and steamship to domestic and world markets. The Seaboard Coast Line completed a new $13 million waterfront marine terminal, Rockport, in east Tampa.[2] More than 85 percent of the rock mined in the vicinity of Tampa moves through that port. Net tons of rock are about 86 percent of Tampa's total port traffic. Since 1960 transshipment of phosphate rock has expanded by about 70 percent, raising Tampa to the fourth most important port on the South Atlantic and Gulf coasts.

Included in the 268-acre phosphate terminal is a hump yard of eight tracks, plus seven holding and four receiving tracks, a total of seventeen miles of rail track. Trains traversing the 30 to 50 miles between mines and port enter receiving tracks where the hopper cars are classified at a speed of one every 84 seconds and then placed on holding tracks. The layout is designed to keep loaded cars moving smoothly to shipside and empty cars returning to the mines.

SCL has converted 1,250 open hoppers into covered hoppers equipped with flip tops. The attached covers fasten securely when the cars are upright. Following uncoupling of the cars from the locomotive, the lead car of a cut of cars to be unloaded is automatically positioned at the dumper. When the dumper rotates the car, the car's top slides a few inches laterally, disengaging the hooks on the lower side and allowing the flip top to open and the lading to fall out of the car onto a conveyor, which is geared to an unloading speed of 3,000 cars per hour. The conveyor moves the rock from the dumper to ship or storage or from storage to ship. The storage building is a clear span, 270 feet by 890 feet, and can accommodate about 148,000 tons of 6 grades of phosphate rock.

The key to fast loading of ships is speedy rotary dumping of cars, which discharges phosphate rock in half the time as bottom dumping. Phosphate material en route via the conveyor to a ship passes through a sampling station, which scientifically separates grades of rock into specific hatches of each vessel. The shore-loading boom has a shuttle conveyor with rotating deflector to control loading into any type of craft, be it small barge or large freighter.

The new terminal has created conveniences for all concerned. For example, in 1962 Tampa elevators loaded the mineral at a rate of 1,500 tons an hour. The modernized facilities load at an hourly rate of 3,000 tons. The railroad expects the capacity of its new terminal to reach 10 to 12 million tons per year. The volume compares with 3½ million tons at each of the two terminals that the new one replaced.

Advantages of the new terminal are: (1) rotary dumping, which speeds unloading of cars; (2) increased utilization of cars; (3) better service to shippers; (4) fewer car shortages; and (5) faster turnaround of steamships. The new waterfront terminal and adoption of a systems approach to distribution has kept the Florida phosphate industry competitive worldwide.

A large mining corporation that has adopted a profit-creating logistics program is the American Smelting and Refining Company (ASARCO), which in 1968 had annual sales of $630 million, a net profit of $77 million, and retained earnings of $236 million. The company's annual transportation bill exceeds $40 million. ASARCO mines, smelts, and refines copper, silver, lead, zinc, and other nonferrous metals. While copper is the concern's major product as measured by tonnage, substantial amounts of silver, lead, and zinc also flow through the corporation's refineries.

Transportation holds major attention in ASARCO's highest councils, and its executives have acquired extensive know-how in solving transport problems. For example, in 1956–1958 the board chairman of American Smelting was responsible for construction of a well-located, 120-mile railroad across the Andes, proof of the breadth of interest and depth of knowledge of the company's top management in the field.[3] Although American Smelting's corporate traffic department employs 34 people, many other traffic officials share the total PDM responsibility. District traffic managers at San Francisco, Houston, and Whiting, Indiana, plus the traffic manager of the Federated Metals Division, have full operating responsibility for specific areas. In essence, while reporting to the central unit, each district office is within itself a complete distribution entity.

Shortly after the founding of the company in 1899, the management appointed its first transportation vice-president. Since then ASARCO's management has maintained a well-informed interest in transportation. According to company policy, the vice-president of traffic is a member of the corporation's major advisory committee, which consists of all general officers. In developing facilities, traffic personnel thoroughly analyze manufacturing and warehousing location sites, and following site selection, staff technicians refine relevant logistics information. There is close interdepartmental liaison. Traffic supervisors of ASARCO cooperate with their counterparts in engineering, marketing, and mining and play an integral part in determination of the cost of pricing and selling American Smelting's products. Inbound shipments are carefully scrutinized. Traffic analysts insert routings on purchase orders and clear invoices for accuracy of freight costs prior to final processing.

As is true of most large smelting corporations, railroads haul the preponderance of ASARCO's workload. Two specialized cars regularly serve ASARCO—copper-concentrate cars, which replaced conventional gondolas; and copper-anode rack equipment, which manufacturing plants can load and discharge much more readily than conventional boxcars or gondolas and which haul much heavier loads per car than conventional cars.

After some study, Baldwin-Lima-Hamilton Corporation, the nation's largest builder of freight cars, constructed for ASARCO a special car with sides canted slightly inward. The slanting sides permit loads to fall freely. The Southern Pacific and Santa Fe have purchased a substantial fleet of these vehicles, while ASARCO itself operates eight at its large lead smelter at Glover, Missouri.

The anode cars hold anodes in fitted racks. Three of these conveyances replace five boxcars with a resultant 40 percent reduction in number of cars per train. The ASARCO plant at Perth Amboy, New Jersey, found that anode cars created $15,000 annual savings in handling costs. At El Paso this special equipment reduced loading costs by $32,500 annually. One man can load a car in twenty minutes, whereas it requires three men an hour to fill a conventional gondola. Thus the special cars permit a ninefold increase in efficiency of loading.

Barge movements play an important though irregular role for ASARCO. Drawbacks of barging are heavy loads

(1,200 tons per shipment), slow transit times, and other deficiencies, but ASARCO frequently finds that slowness in transit (actually free storage) is desirable and that low barge rates are highly beneficial.

During the mid-1950s ASARCO instituted a new copper-mining operation at Toquepala, Peru, and expanded its export staff by 14 employees to handle ore shipments there.[4] The Toquepala project confronted ASARCO's traffic department with formidable challenges. The large mine was 11,000 feet above sea level and over 120 miles from the coast. The company built a railroad from the mine to the oceanfront, where it constructed a seaport at Port Ilo, including complete town facilities.

This new South American enterprise immediately faced a myriad of distribution obstacles. A Peruvian customs office imposed stringent regulations and required execution of numerous forms before approving export of copper. Ocean freight costs from Peru to San Francisco spiraled steadily upward, handicapping ASARCO's capability to compete with rival European processors. There were increasing stevedore charges at the corporation's refinery on San Francisco Bay. ASARCO solved the last problem by installing gantry cranes to replace ship's gear to speed unloading at the waterfront and by using conveyors instead of trucks from pier to furnace storage area.

To depress hikes in ocean freight costs, American Smelting's export traffic department acquired a broader understanding of ship operations and inner workings of shipping conferences. The new policy, which included consummation of a shipper-ocean carrier agreement in August 1955, assured adequate economical ocean service.

The traffic department's early and continuous involvement in the new Peruvian undertaking has produced substantial gains. Transportation executives of ASARCO estimate that the 1955 shipper-carrier agreement alone controlled from Toquepala a freight volume of 300,000 tons and saved the corporation a net of $4 million on construction freight.

Today the harbor of Port Ilo bustles with activity. ASARCO accumulates stores in a New York warehouse for transshipment by container to Peru. Customs are cleared at Port Ilo where stevedores strip the freight for movement overland to final destination. Large tonnages of outbound copper flow over Port Ilo's pier on a "free in" basis, the company doing its own loading. The firm estimates that in a nine-year period pier handling has improved by 35 percent through advances in equipment and education and training of personnel.[5]

Raw-Material-Oriented Firms

Industries drawn toward raw materials give cost of delivery of those basic essentials major weight in selecting production sites. For example, the paper-manufacturing industry is raw-material-oriented and has in recent years located many new mills in pine forests of the South.

Weight loss from raw material to finished product in the paper industry is striking—about 5,000 pounds of wood make 2,000 pounds of newsprint. So naturally paper mills locate near wood supply. The policy of paper firms is to own substantial amounts of wood-producing land, preferably close to mills, and to purchase the rest of their needed pulpwood and wood chips in open markets. Transportation represents 40 to 60 percent of the delivered cost of pulpwood, but pulp mills minimize the distance pulpwood must move.

International Paper Company, the largest paper manufacturer in the world, recently instituted novel modifications of its physical distribution pattern. The firm has completely reorganized its traffic department into a physical distribution setup and has opened new vistas of international transportation by placing in service the LASH vessel, the *Acadia Forest*.

Since its inception, the company has continually expanded and introduced new ideas into forestry management and paper making. Today annual output of primary products by the 33 pulp and paper mills owned by IP in the United States, Canada, and throughout the world is 7 million tons. In addition International Paper operates 81 converting plants. Various divisions of the corporation in the Northwest and Southeast manufacture lumber, plywood, and millwork items. Through subsidiaries IP also operates paper mills in Germany, Italy, Colombia, Ecuador, and Puerto Rico and converting plants in France, Germany, England, Spain, and South America. IP's overseas division, which coordinates all export marketing other than newsprint, shipped 15 percent of the corporation's total North American output to foreign markets.

IP's management has considered several approaches to solving mounting distribution difficulties. One was to convert break-bulk freighters into special paper carriers, but this was found to be uneconomical. Another possible modification was to containerize IP's paper packages. However, the heavy weight of containers and pallets rendered them impractical for hauling paper products. So the company's distribution researchers turned to the LASH concept.[6] The *Acadia Forest*, the LASH vessel that IP acquired, is 860 feet long, 107 feet wide at beam, and 34 feet below waterline when loaded and cruises at an average speed of 20 knots. With a gross tonnage of 39,000 she carries in 14 hatches a total of 73 barges stacked 5 or 6 high. The barges loaded with the paper are lifted on and off the ship by a 510-ton capacity traveling crane. The *Acadia Forest* is making a particular gain for IP in transporting linerboard, which has a stowage factor on conventional vessels of 90 cubic feet. LASH barges have reduced that factor to only 70 cubic feet. On woodpulp, another important IP product, the corporation has gained 10 cubic feet per ton in stowage space.

Market-Oriented Firms

Every company that constructs a plant bases its placement upon a market. That market may be local, regional, national, or international. Regardless of product, managerial decisions and location of competitor's plants determine placement of the facility. Corporate officials orient plants to markets in order to minimize transport costs or to secure larger portions of trade. When transportation costs are a significant part of delivered costs, propinquity to markets is a major factor in location.

An example of the market as a key location factor is the Du Pont sulphuric acid plant at Richmond, Virginia. Du Pont's facility was placed there to serve the corporation's other two plants near Richmond, one of which manufactures textile fibers and the other, celluloid film. It requires only sulphur, air, and water to manufacture sulphuric acid, which weighs three times as much as the sulphur from which it is manufactured. In other words, the closer Du Pont's sulphuric acid facility is to the two plants it serves, the cheaper the total inbound and outbound distribution costs.

The site selection of the Celanese Corporation at Rock Hill, South Carolina, was influenced by needs of the textile industry in the Carolinas. Another example of the market as a factor in location is establishment in the South of firms manufacturing specialized farm machinery, including the mechanical cotton picker, and small farm tractors.

Steelcase, Incorporated, a market-oriented firm, is the nation's largest manufacturer of steel office equipment and harmonizes its traffic, marketing, manufacturing, and computer functions to meet customer demand. The corporation's management leaders emphasize three important areas of physical distribution: [7]

Computer processing. Cathode-ray tubes and optical recognition equipment speed distribution data through two IBM 360-40 computers.

Automatic materials handling. In the shipping department of the Grand Rapids warehouse (a 320,000-square-foot structure) towlines, conveyors, and automated sorting systems speed order preparation.

Strategic utilization of private trucks. Seventy-five percent of Steelcase shipments move in common motor carriage, but its private fleet has steadily expanded. These proprietary carriers reduce packaging costs, avoid rapidly mounting charges of rented trucks, and improve delivery service.

Plough, Incorporated, which handles such products as St. Joseph's Aspirin, Coppertone, Mexana Powder, and other consumer drugs, provides another instructive example of up-to-date physical distribution. The corporation's sales in 1968 totaled $122 million with a net income of about $15 million, which was 4 times the earnings of 1958. This middleman for consumer drugs has erected two new distribution centers, one in Toronto, the other in Memphis.[8] Plough has adopted private trucks to provide customer-tailored transportation service. Plough's motor fleet includes 35 trailers and 10 city trucks. In 1968 Plough's over-the-road units made 744 trips, an average of 15 a week, and hauled around 50 million pounds of freight. The cost was a relatively low $1.30 per hundredweight.

Plough's tractor trailers perform two functions: transportation of items from plants to warehouses situated at Miami, Florida, Carteret, New Jersey, and La Mirada, California, and direct delivery to consumers. The firm makes truck deliveries on a 28-day cycle along 4 routes to a 20-state area of the South, Southwest, and Midwest to wholesalers of Plough's International Distributors Division. Truckloads average about 40,000 pounds, and dispatchers strive to route the vehicles to destinations near supply locations in order to load materials for back-hauls. This back-haul freight consists of bottles, chemicals, and other products. In 1924 Plough began selling in foreign trade, and now services 140 markets abroad. Motor carriers haul Plough's products to New Orleans for export; there they load such imported articles as radios and hardware items for International Distributors.

With its outstanding financial strength Plough purchases instead of leasing its truck equipment, and employs its own drivers. However, rising costs of equipment, parts, and drivers' wages have created problems for Plough. Plough's executives feel that its private motor fleet will grow as production and sales expand; they also believe that common carriers will continue to handle substantial volumes of the firm's traffic.

An important advantage of the private truck operation

is that Plough can dispatch drivers at any time and thus schedule shipment to arrive at the receiver's convenience. This flexibility is a particularly valuable attribute in delivery of seasonal commodities. For example, drivers in sleeper cabs can replenish the stock of suntan lotion at Carteret by speedy runs from Memphis, a service that common carriers cannot match. In emergencies Plough can deploy its own trucks much more quickly than for-hire carriers.

Computer printouts of incoming orders to the International Distributors Division are the basis for determining loads and routes. As IDD receives order information, it notes destinations on a large wall map. Following the Thursday noon order deadline, IDD combines delivery sequences to fill each trailer and loads so that the trucks will effect delivery of a trailer near a source of back-haul freight. Each week a Plough driver services 75 customer orders. With pickups en route he travels 1,600 to 1,800 miles through 12 states. When shipments to a single customer do not justify a 100-mile out-of-route journey, Plough employs a local for-hire carrier to make delivery. For example, shipments destined for Greensboro, North Carolina, are given to a local carrier at Raleigh for movement to Greensboro.

Following long study, IBM's traffic department manager found that careful adaptation of freight to pallets increased density and thereby reduced the rate per pound. The company's distribution manager decided to test this system. Utilizing standard 88-inch by 125-inch air-blind pallets, the IBM center built a low-profile dolly for loading and moving these pallets and persuaded several truck lines to install roller systems in their trailers. IBM then made two successful test shipments of electronic components from the United States to IBM's London offices. The freight items originated at IBM's distribution center in East Fishkill, New York; drivers trucked them to Kennedy Airport for a night flight to London.[9]

IBM prepalletized its highly valuable and fragile products at the plant. Jet Air Freight, an experienced air shipper, was IBM's forwarding agent. A JAF official nursemaided the first flight of two pallets, weighing 6,375 and 5,394 pounds respectively. Arriving at London's Heathrow Airport, the consignment moved quickly through Pan American's freight terminal. It was then whisked to IBM's London warehouse by local trucker. Both pallets were broken down at that point and transshipped to individual consignees.

Currently the United States representative for IBM's world trade is the East Fishkill center. Controlling millions of pounds of freight, this origin sends 62 percent of IBM's assignments by air. Of that percentage 70 percent crosses the Atlantic to Europe and Africa, 20 percent moves to the Far East, and 10 percent to South America.

This new system of palletized export shipments produced a number of benefits for IBM and those with whom it deals, including: (1) reduced handling for the carrier; (2) reduced damage; (3) immediate application of lower freight rates for volume shipments; and (4) simplified paper work. When IBM utilizes the services of an air freight forwarder, the amount of paper work for both carrier and IBM shrinks even further.

Pressed Steel Tank Company, headquartered in Milwaukee, Wisconsin, was founded in 1902. Its products are compressed gas cylinders and other pressurized vessels. The outbound tonnage of Pressed Steel in 1969 was 55 million pounds; 55 percent was shipped by rail, 8 percent by piggyback, the remainder mostly by truck. Terms are f.o.b. origin at Milwaukee, so that the customer derives benefits of distribution savings. Carload movements, which include stopoffs, enable PST to reach inland markets by carrying shipments to a common point.[10]

The tank manufacturer has recommended carload shipments to team tracks where customers can make pickups in their own trucks. The difference between carload and truckload rates produce savings. Many customers can enjoy reductions by picking up the tanks themselves because dealers in industrial gases are usually located outside the city near railroad facilities and are accustomed to using tank cars.

Pressed Steel has been increasing its participation in TOFC consolidations, especially since the railroads relaxed their 60–40 mixing rule. (In a piggyback shipment, 40 percent of the freight in each trailer must be one item. The 60 percent can be a mixture of other articles.) PST has found that piggybacking is lower in cost than less-truckload lots. The TOFC trailers from Milwaukee move under Plan II½, Plan III, or Plan IV. PST arranges for drayage at both origin and destination, sacrificing savings to gain improved service. A 35,000-pound consolidated shipment can proceed by piggyback from Milwaukee to Houston at a total freight cost of $449.38, as against a carload charge of $665 on a minimum load of 32,000 pounds. However, in shipments from Milwaukee to Philadelphia the carload rate is $45.50 less than the truckload rate.

To serve the Chicago area, PST utilizes a drayage concern with interstate authority. Following delivery in Lake and Cook counties to points near Chicago, the contract carrier picks up the freight for return trips. He has grandfather rights southbound from Milwaukee, and PST assisted him in getting the back-haul authority from the ICC.

Many industrial traffic departments must handle all paper work and clerical chores associated with the inbound and outbound movement of their company's product. However, PST in adopting a physical distribution concept has shifted routing functions formerly performed by traffic to accounting, purchasing, and shipping. The traffic manager has become what Pressed Steel terms a problem solver. He informs sales and marketing executives on how to reduce transportation costs, while satisfying customer delivery demands. The result has been improved all-around distribution service.

The PST traffic executive not only supports domestic sales efforts, but also cooperates with the international division in developing special rates and methods of shipment by attending conferences in order to compete with British, Italian, and Japanese producers of steel tanks. The traffic manager has shown that he can make money for the company and has advanced to a top executive level with the title vice-president–operations.

PST has weight agreements with the railroads that give the company control over freight rates. The shipper furnishes the tare weights of its cylinders to customers and to the Department of Transportation whose safety regulations govern specifications of containers of hazardous items. These average weights were calculated by computer. The agreed weight list is one of the items that the PST traffic department has turned over to the shipping department. The shipping and traffic departments have written a manual of shipping instructions, a routing guide, a rail rate and truck rate guide, a list of commodity rates, and a series of instructions for shipments in foreign trade.

PST prefers to buy transportation service of common carriers rather than provide its own transportation, which it formerly did. However, the company found that its trucks were not as efficient as common carriers. Its business was cyclical, and the private fleet could not handle heavy loads at the top of the season and allowed equipment to stand idle in the off-season.

Independent steel distributors are one of the fastest-growing industries in Great Britain. Since 1953 these firms' share of the market has expanded from 15 to 27 percent. The trend has been toward larger plants and longer production runs. Since renationalization of the steel industry and formation of the British Steel Corporation, this trend has been accentuated.[11]

Founded in 1789, Druce became a public company in 1954 and immediately set upon a period of rapid expansion. This growth has resulted to date in acquisition of five other steel-distributing firms and takeover of companies of allied interests, including steel-cutting firms and a trucking company. This expansion has resulted in a chain of Miles Druce distribution centers. Each center has a warehouse and a sales office. The centers are in Glasgow, Scotland; Hebburn-on-Tyne, Leeds, and Manchester in northern England; Birmingham in the Midlands; Brandon and Suffolk in eastern England; Colnbrook near London; and Bristol in western England. Sales for the Druce group of companies exceeded $43 million in 1968. The stock of 20,000 different items is maintained at the various warehouses to supply 25,000 customers.

The leading steel distributor in the United Kingdom, Miles Druce & Company, Limited, has continuously explored methods of establishing better customer service and minimizing costs of distribution. One of the company's primary aims is to supply customers within 24 hours of order placement. To achieve that objective, Miles Druce has expanded its network of distribution centers, planned more efficiently designed warehouses, and streamlined its managerial organization.

The latest facet of the company's program to expedite customer service, integrate the operations of its distribution centers, and realize other benefits of centralized control of a widely dispersed organization has been installation of a real-time computer system. The system, a UNIVAC 1050, is located at company headquarters at High Wycombe, Buckinghamshire, about 30 miles northwest of London. Westrex teletypewriters, using telegraph lines for data transmission, link the center to the eight major distribution points.

The central processor has a main memory of 32,768 characters, which can be accessed in an average time of 4.5 microseconds. Peripheral equipment consists of a FASTRAND memory drum providing storage for 44 million characters, 4 magnetic tape units, a card reader and a high-speed printer. Information on the FASTRAND can be accessed in an average time of 92 milliseconds. Within the FASTRAND unit is contained a complete record of stock items at all eight distribution centers, as well as essential customer information such as name, reference number, and address, plus addresses of specific places where customers may desire delivery.

Orders received by telephone or through the mail at any of the sales offices are entered on a sales order form, which is passed to a teletypist by means of a document conveyor belt. The itemized data on this form are teletyped to High Wycombe. Each item on the order is identified by a code (such as CA 02110), in which the alphabetical characters represent the product group, the first two digits refer to the type of product, the third is a check digit, and the last two figures indicate the length of the material.

The computer processes the order by referencing the customer file and checking the stock file for availability of the items required. Orders are then sent to the warehouse nearest the customer. Simultaneously information concerning the customer and descriptions of the ordered items are recorded in the computer's memory bank.

At each warehouse the Westrex terminal prints out a six-part order form giving specifications of each of the items. Distribution of the form is as follows: one to the salesman, another in the sales office file, the third to the customer, a fourth to the warehouse supplying the items, a fifth to the customer as a receipt which he signs and returns to Miles Druce, and a sixth to headquarters as notification that the warehouse has shipped the material.

While the customer is on the telephone, the system allows a salesman at any branch office to interrogate the computer concerning the volume of stock of particular items held at all warehouses. In response to an inquiry about a particular item, within seconds the computer will transmit a list to the inquiring sales office, detailing type of steel, lengths, and number of pieces of steel on hand at each warehouse.

While business hours each day are reserved for real-time order processing, the evening hours are reserved for the batch-processing of information. Forms that list shipments completed during the day are attached to original orders and sent to the computer. Thus stock records in the FASTRAND memory bank and the stock ledger on magnetic tape are updated.

Miles Druce feels that it has realized a number of important advantages from its revised distribution program, including prompt service, information for use by the sales department, easier location of ordered items, better stock control, and a reduction in money capital tied up in inventory.

Consumer-Oriented Firms

Sperry & Hutchinson Company (S&H Green Stamps) has built a distribution center in Hillside, Illinois, with 9 million cubic feet of storage space (300,000 square feet of floor space, 30 feet high). This center serves more than 150 redemption centers throughout the Midwest and handles in a single system more than 2,000 commodities received from 700 suppliers. Long before the new distribution center originated its first shipment, a mock-up of the system was filling sample orders to discover best patterns for running orders through the center. Now in operation, the highly mechanized distribution facility employs a sophisticated computer complex to feed orders through the system.[12]

General Logistics Corporation, a consulting firm, established the general configuration of the system. Rapistan Incorporated organized the system design and cooperated with S&H engineers and other technicians in developing the operating plan and computer programming. The materials-handling machinery follows the "queue theory," which provides a buffer between supply and demand that averages out variables in the system and its throughput. Processing an order calls upon the system to perform four basic functions:

1. Order picking on four conveyor lines, each 500 feet long and reaching one-fourth of the total stored items.

The computer divides each order into quandrants to program activities on each of the four lines. Large and small orders are fed into the system in a sequence that balances order-picking time equally among the four lines.

Before an order clerk begins filling his assigned part of an S&H store order, he drops onto the conveyor a colored "locomotive" tote box in which he places a copy of the order for merchandise in his aisle. Upon placement of the last item of the order on the conveyor, the order picker drops a "caboose" tote box of the same color on the conveyor. On the side of each tote box is a piece of retro-reflective tape the size of a quarter that triggers electric eye scanners. These scanners activate equipment to bring together the items that have been picked and to dispatch the completed order to the proper truck at any one of six loading docks used for outgoing shipment. The sequence is programmed in advance to assure a smooth flow of merchandise to each trailer waiting at the loading dock.

2. Amassing quadrants into trains on Rapistan Automatic Pressure Control (APC) conveyors. This permits accumulation of long lines of cartons without buildup in pressure.

3. Interchange of trains from four order-picking lines to three truck-dock accumulation lines. Computers release trains with precise timing to avoid collisions and obstruction of other lines. Segments of individual orders are programmed to arrive at their assigned truck docks together and in correct quantities.

4. Accumulation of cartons on the truck docks. Here cartons queue on three accumulation lines for immediate loading into truck trailers.

Empty pallets are placed on the return conveyor,

which feeds them onto a vertical conveyor and delivers them to a forklift truck position when each stack of pallets reaches the desired height. The pallets are then used for incoming merchandise.

Every step from original paper work to the truck-dock conveyor is programmed scientifically. The S&H Corporation gets optimum productivity from both men and machines and fills orders faster and more accurately than ever before.

Farm-Oriented Firms

Just as some industries are mining-oriented, raw-material-oriented, and market-oriented, there are also farm-oriented industries. One of these is the grain industry, and the world's largest grain assembling and distributing company is Cargill, Incorporated, with headquarters in Minneapolis, Minnesota. This concern has a large, versatile, intermodal distribution program directed by managers with driving force, skill, and effectiveness. Cargill leases approximately 1,100 large covered hopper cars and 500 tank cars for the carriage of its solid and liquid grain products. Since Cargill's private car fleet represents less than 1 percent of its total annual rail capacity requirements, the company relies heavily on railroads to supply in excess of 300,000 cars a year.

Cargill's water operations are also extensive. For distribution on the inland waterway system, the corporation charters two towboats and owns two towboats of its own. It also owns or charters 190 dry-bulk cargo and tank barges.

Interestingly enough, Cargill's truck fleet is not growing because the company has found that for-hire carrier charges are cheaper than the company's operation of its own trucks.

Fruit and vegetable growers, shippers, exporters, and retailers are keenly mindful of what speed via air can do to broaden their markets. The airlines too are conscious of gaining revenues from this mammoth potential tonnage but are sorrowfully rejecting most of it for lack of profitable rate structures, suitable routes, and necessary equipment.[13]

During the 1960s California's strawberry producers began airlifting their product to East Coast and European destinations in increasing quantities. In 1968 a record 45,336,524 pounds were flown from San Francisco and Los Angeles International Airports. Strawberries became the No. 1 item among all fruits and vegetables shipped by air. These berries represented 75 to 80 percent of all airborne produce. For example, that year 35 other types of air-freighted fruits and vegetables, plus 2 categories identified as "miscellaneous oriental vegetables" and "miscellaneous commodities," added up to only 14,836,238 pounds.

Strawberries are picked in the morning, cooled during the day, delivered to the airport in the evening, and reach their markets the following morning. Growers usually notify the airlines in advance, but there have been an uncomfortable number of no-shows, and many flights have departed on schedule with money-losing gaps in the cargo hold. The LD (belly) containers designed for the combination 747 jumbojets may represent a turning point in overcoming these difficulties. The shippers are excited about this container because it allows them to stack the berries by hand. It eliminates pallets, which cost $4 each, steel strapping, and paperboard sleeves.

Driscoll Strawberry Associates in California is the nation's largest strawberry shipper, cultivating some 1,400 acres of that crop. Driscoll turned to air freight in the 1960s and began shipment in the Paul Bunyan Box, a large aluminum container introduced by American Airlines in the late 1950s. The company's biggest production year was 1968, when it shipped 21 percent of its production by air. In 1969 Driscoll's production dropped about 15 percent, but the airlines took 25 percent of the total tonnage. Since 1968 all the company's shipments to the New York, Boston, and Hartford markets have been airborne. However, the steep upswing in rates may drive this shipper back to highway delivery.

Driscoll's management maintains a fine balance between distribution costs and profits, a critical equilibrium in the perishables field.

References

1. Robert P. Neuschel, "Physical Distribution—Forgotten Frontier," *Harvard Business Review*, March–April 1967, pp. 125–126.
2. Robert Roberts, "SCL Builds Marine Phosphate Terminal," *Modern Railroads*, August 1970, p. 60.
3. Jack W. Farrell, "ASARCO: Traffic At the Top Level," *Traffic Management*, July 1969, p. 51.
4. Jack W. Farrell, "Worldwide Control Gains Better Market Service," *Traffic Management*, July 1969, p. 62.
5. Jack W. Farrell, "Establishing Logistics in an Undeveloped Region," *Traffic Management*, July 1969, p. 70.
6. "Shipper Spurs LASH Concept," *Container News*, December 1969, p. 18.

7. Jack W. Farrell, "Advanced Logistics: Steelcase's Total Commitment," *Traffic Management*, December 1969, p. 45.
8. "Drug Company's Trucks Supplement For-Hire Service," *Traffic Management*, June 1969, p. 53.
9. Kendric Taylor, "IBM World Trade Tries Its Hand at Do-It-Yourself Palletization," *Air Transportation*, Mid-December 1969, pp. 9–11.
10. "The Traffic Manager as a Sales Stimulator," *Traffic Management*, March 1970, pp. 79–82.
11. James M. Dixon, "Moving Steel by Computer," *Distribution Worldwide*, September 1969, pp. 60–63.
12. "Computer/Controls Police Distribution Center Material Flow," *Transportation and Distribution Management*, January 1969, p. 21.
13. Richard Malkin, "Giant Potential with a Giant Headache," *Cargo Airlift*, August 1970, pp. 6–9.

5 Future Prospects for PDM

PDM executives, professional organizations, and educators should equip themselves to advise students that physical distribution is a desirable occupation. The next 10 to 30 years should hold bright promise for those entering this field. As has been noted, physical distribution has been an overlooked link in the economic chain; however, in the future it will undoubtedly receive the attention and weight it merits.

There is already a severe shortage of well-trained managers in physical distribution, and this situation will worsen before the tide turns. Like the short supply of schoolteachers that fomented a critical problem in pre-college education from 1960 to 1968, shortage of PDMs has created a crisis in the nation's economy. By 1970 federal government aid alleviated the schoolteacher shortage, but no such aid is in prospect for offsetting the diminished supply of PDMs. It appears that managerial obsolescence in physical distributon will accelerate at an alarming pace. The superb distribution management of today will be the mediocre one of tomorrow. Forty-year-old traffic managers must continue their education just to keep pace with newly developing forces. Top executive management will soon learn that the best physical distribution policy is to separate men from boys on the basis of excellence. The distribution manager faced severe challenges in the 1960s and will buck even more serious ones in the 1970s. No distribution system of the 1970s will be competitive unless it is based on a fully integrated, computerized information system.

At present an individual with talent, drive, and dedication has little incentive to become a physical distribution manager. Sales-minded, finance-minded, or production-minded corporate management hardly recognizes that efficient physical distribution is a basic requirement for profitability. Because of that blind spot, business firms discourage talented young men from choosing physical distribution as a career. But experience often changes management's attitude.

For example, one firm with annual sales of $300 million established a distribution department and appointed a director of distribution. Manufacturing and marketing executives recognized the need to trade off costs against each other to attain optimum results, and they checked with the new distribution director before making key decisions affecting distribution costs. The distribution manager proposed many ideas to reduce costs, enhance service, and convince other departments of opportunities for profit making. Everyone in this firm is now sold on the distribution concept.

One major fact that causes young men and women to shy away from traffic and distribution is the salary scale. In June 1970 the Department of Labor issued statistics on the average annual incomes of various professional groups. Directors of personnel were earning $22,000; chief accountants, $23,000; engineers, $25,000; chemists, $28,000; and attorneys, $33,000. However, the average annual salary of top traffic, transportation, and distribution managers was below $15,000. A June 1970 report of the College Placement Council showed that in 1969–1970 monthly average salary offers to candidates for bachelor's degrees was $702 for graduates in distribution, $836 for accountants, $902 for chemical engineers, $849 for industrial engineers, and $827 for physicists.

Steady if belated progress is being made in the training of traffic and transportation personnel. For example, a Curriculum Development Workshop on Transportation Career Education, attended by twenty-five selected educators and industrial traffic managers throughout the United States, convened in Chicago early in August 1971. The U.S. Office of Education and the U.S. Department of Transportation sponsored this workshop. For three days the participants suggested logical subject matter to be incorporated into curricula for students who had completed high school or two years of college and were seeking career opportunities in transportation.

Following final editing of the material which the group assembled, the curricula finally adopted will be sent to more than 4,000 educational institutions throughout the United States who will be encouraged by the Office of Education and the Department of Transportation to teach the proposed subjects.

Before the Chicago meeting, the Office of Education conducted an extensive survey which revealed that trained personnel in this occupational category are in extremely short supply and that a strong demand exists for these courses. The federal government has already set aside approximately $100 million to help finance this overall educational plan.

The American economy must adopt enlightened approaches to physical distribution in order to meet intensifying competition of products of Japan, Germany, Canada, and other countries. At the same time the United States must comprehend this compelling, but little understood, principle: Every dollar this country spends for foreign goods eventually returns to the United States for the purchase of our own products. Protectionism is the road to economic ruin. The logical road to profit in foreign trade is to produce and sell goods at lower unit cost than other countries and to purchase from those countries the goods that they produce at the greatest comparative advantage.

On August 15, 1971, President Nixon ordered drastic action to halt inflation, the results of which will vitally affect the domestic and foreign trade and commerce of the United States. The country was suffering from a rapid increase in unemployment, a fast-rising level of prices, a decline in the value of the dollar, a growing unfavorable balance of trade, and an even faster-growing unfavorable balance of payments with foreign countries. To halt these ominous trends, Mr. Nixon took the following steps:

1. Ordered the freezing of wages and prices for a 90-day period and called on corporations to extend the freeze to dividends.

2. Asked Congress to enact the Job Development Act of 1971, which would grant a 10 percent tax credit for investment in new equipment to generate jobs, raise productivity, and make American goods more competitive in foreign markets.

3. Proposed repeal of the 7 percent excise tax on auto-

mobiles, which would mean the sale of more new cars and would, in turn, create more new jobs in the automobile industry.

4. Directed a $4.7 billion cut in federal spending to offset loss of revenue from these tax cuts.

5. Ordered a 10 percent cut in foreign economic aid.

6. Directed Secretary of the Treasury John Connally to suspend convertibility of the dollar into gold and pledged full cooperation with the International Monetary Fund in setting up a new international monetary system.

7. Imposed an additional tax of 10 percent on goods imported into the United States, calling this tax "temporary" to insure that American products will not be at a disadvantage because of an unfair exchange rate.

Whether these actions will or will not fully attain the objective the president seeks, they have warned exporters, importers, domestic and foreign banks, and governments around the world that the United States is determined to restore economic stability at home even if it requires long-range controls to do so.

The likelihood is that the United States will ultimately find markets in Communist bloc nations. One-half of the world's population lives behind the Iron Curtain, and these millions of empty stomachs and unclothed backs will eventually engage in intensive trade with this nation. Some East-West trade is already a reality, and PDMs of the United States should alert their firms to the potential advantages of this trade. One does not have to endorse the political philosophy of nations in order to establish economic relationships with them, any more than the United States had to adopt communism when it was Soviet Russia's ally in World War II.

Following a secret trip to China in mid-1971 by

Henry A. Kissinger, assistant to the president for national security affairs, Mr. Nixon announced that the United States would reestablish trade after a 21-year mutual embargo and boycott of each other's goods and services. On June 10, Mr. Nixon listed the products which we might export to China. They included automobiles, stoves, refrigerators, industrial machinery, and raw materials such as textiles and rubber.

President Nixon also announced the removal of bans on goods imported from China and nullification of the requirement that U.S. ships must haul at least half of this nation's grain exported to Russia, eastern Europe, and China. This action, the administration forecasts, will open a $300 million market for American wheat to the Soviet Union alone.

American industry's first reactions to these presidential edicts were conflicting. For example, the Chrysler Corporation thought that we had been correct all along in refusing to do business with countries which prohibited our trade. The American tobacco industry reacted favorably. The textile industry, already troubled with cheaper imports of competitive goods from Japan and other Asian countries, responded unhappily to the president's proposals.

Improvements in Railroads

In the 1970s there will be revolutionary shifts in the proportion of freight that each mode carries. The transfer of ton-miles from rail to motor, water, and airway routes has already been noted. The transition in the 1970s will dwarf the intermodal shifts that have occurred since the end of World War II.

Rail freight ton-miles will exceed a trillion ton-miles in 1975, as against 705 million in 1965. Railroads will continue to attain greater efficiency through improved technology. Unit train operations already include high volumes of such items as sulphuric acid and grain and will carry expanded varieties of other commodities. Railroad companies will continue to develop special freight cars. New, larger, all-purpose flatcars capable of handling containers, piggyback trailers, or conventional flatcar loads will begin service shortly. Only one-fourth of existing freight cars have roller bearings. Shortly that proportion will approach 100 percent. The 8,000-horsepower railroad diesel engine is not far away. DOT is developing an induction motor to operate trains up to 300 miles per hour.

In track research the railroads will emphasize new types of high-strength steel for rails. Studies are being made of vacuum-degassed rail, which will have a cost advantage over control-cooled rail. Railroad research departments are continuing studies of hardened steel for installation on curves. These researchers are probing into the feasibility of concrete ties and new clips and fastening devices to bind the steel rails to those basic track supports. Ultrasonic devices are pinpointing faults inside the steel of railroad tracks. New techniques are being developed to assure that cross ties do not sink into rock ballast along the route.

Programs for efficient tracing and expediting of cars are continuing and are producing welcome results. Thirty-three Automatic Car Identification systems have been installed in North America. Railroad management has established a central computer in Washington, known as Tele-Rail Automated Information Network or TRAIN, which is intended to transmit data regarding interchange

Future Prospects for PDM

of freight cars throughout the United States. When completed, this program will allow railroads to direct car movements more efficiently and to respond more quickly to demands for cars.

Another device is the Universal Machine Language Equipment Register (UMLER), which is fast becoming a valuable source for policing freight cars. The plan is for UMLER, which compiles per diem and mileage data and information for publication in *The Official Railway Equipment Register*, to spread throughout the entire rail carrier industry.

For thirty years deficits from intercity passenger service have been a thorn in the side of the railroads and shippers who must compensate the carriers for those deficits in the form of high freight rates. Improvement of highways, growing truck freight volume, introduction of jet passenger and cargo planes, urban congestion, and other developments have caused passengers to desert rail transportation. For example, the number of rail passenger travelers and commuters dropped from 326 million in 1960 to 250 million in 1970.[1]

It is not merely high fares that drive passengers from the railroads. In fact, gasoline priced at 40 cents a gallon or 2.7 cents per mile, plus other automobile costs, put that cost per mile well over the 3 cents per mile for a railroad ticket. The clinching reasons for diversion from rail to air and automobile passenger travel are time and convenience. Those advantages caused rail passenger train-miles to shrink from 2.2 billion in 1960 to below 1 billion in 1970.

The Railroad Passenger Service Act of 1970 assigned to a new corporation called Amtrak responsibility for operation of intercity passenger trains between points which the secretary of transportation designates. Amtrak is a quasi-public corporate entity intended to return passenger travel to the rails and to relieve those lines of huge financial deficits which the operation of nearly empty passenger cars imposes on railroads and the shipping public.

Individual railroad companies operate Amtrak's trains over their own routes in accordance with preadopted schedules. Amtrak has hired 100 office workers, bought 1,200 used railroad cars, and permits the individual railroads virtually complete control over Amtrak's operations.

The National Railroad Passenger Corporation (Amtrak's official name) plans to cut the number of passenger trains from 360 to 184 and to move those trains over 21 routes serving 114 cities with populations of 100,000 or more. Amtrak estimates that the 184 trains will serve 85 percent of the nation's urban population. The enabling statute permits Amtrak members to discontinue all other intercity passenger service. Under the various contracts with individual railroads, NRPC pays the carriers negotiated fees for use of their personnel and facilities. Railroad companies also pay into Amtrak cash, service, or equipment based on formulas related to their loss from passenger train operations.

One important saving Amtrak is expected to achieve is elimination of unnecessary passenger terminal stations. Specifically, at Chicago it expects to substitute one terminal for the five now operating there. It is also expected that the corporation will stand the expense of rebuilding tracks in sections where the poor condition of such tracks now requires slow movement of trains.

However satisfactorily Amtrak may resolve the rail passenger problem, it will not remove the myriad other dilemmas and difficulties the railroads face. Passenger trains produce only 5 percent of railroad revenues. Thus, if the entire cost of Amtrak were borne by the federal government, that payout would solve only one-twentieth of the railroad dilemma. Freight movements, which constitute 95 percent of the rail lines' maladies, must be thoroughly explored to put railroads on a sound economic footing.

An influential organization known as the National Association of Railroad Passengers seriously questions the wisdom of Amtrak's policies to date. NARP has testified before Congress that further appropriations to Amtrak would be wasteful unless the corporation quits subsidizing badly run railroad operations, assumes its full responsibilities, and does the job it is supposed to do.

One year after birth of the government-supported corporation those passenger trains that were efficient remain efficient, those that were inefficient remain inefficient. In the meantime, Amtrak has gone deeply into the red. Its managers maintain that to achieve success they need more public support, money, and time. They declare that when Amtrak arrived on the scene rail passenger travel was on its deathbed, and that it was impossible to attain instant success.

Some of the charges made against Amtrak's operations are these: (1) the separate railroads (not Amtrak) give priority to their own freight trains over those of Amtrak; (2) passengers purchase tickets based on an archaic formula devised in 1909, fares vary illogically, and making reservations is difficult; and (3) train crews work for and are paid by the individual railroad, and Amtrak has no authority over them.

Of the 1,200 passenger cars which Amtrak purchased

from the railroads for $16.8 million, most are between twenty and thirty years old. Another fault is that the railroads are not responsible for repairing Amtrak's equipment unless the NRPC specifically orders the repair and itself pays the bills.

Through October 1971 Congress had appropriated to Amtrak grants and loan guarantees totaling $140 million. However, most proponents of Amtrak doubt the sincerity of the government's commitment to the program. For example, a comparison with other transportation expenditures shows that the federal government each day spends $127 million for highway construction and each year $530 million for aviation projects.

Antipollution forces have compelled the railroads to consider operation of a gas turbine engine. The turbine mechanism, which engineers have been refining and perfecting for the last fifteen years, burns fuel at higher temperatures and therefore more cleanly than diesel engines do, and emits only minuscule quantities of noxious nitrous oxide and smoke. The biggest drawback of the turbine is that its operating costs exceed those of diesels because the former must run at full power for best performance.

Despite heroic attempts by the railroad industry since 1946 to reachieve prosperity, the carriers have failed to attain that goal. For example, a publication of the Association of American Railroads (R&E Series No. 666) shows that for the second quarter of 1971, twelve of the nation's sixty-six Class I carriers had deficit net railway operating incomes. Only fourteen of these carriers had net railway operating incomes exceeding $10 million. They included such superb properties as the Norfolk & Western, Union Pacific, Southern Railway, Chesapeake &

Ohio, and Louisville & Nashville, which are mainly transcontinental or coal-carrying lines with first-class management and deep concern for the interests of their stockholders and customer-shippers.

Fewer than ten and possibly only four or five railroad corporations have a rate of return on investment anywhere near 5 percent. Despite some improvement over 1970, the fact is that innovations, rationalization programs, and other attempted improvements of the nation's railroads are simply not paying off. The United States has never been closer to government ownership and operation of its railroad system than it is at present.

The Trucking Industry

During the 1970s the trucking industry will keep pace with other carriers in competitive power. The industry has come a long way in the past 20 years. Railroad ton-mileage dropped from 56 to 41 percent between 1941 and 1968. Simultaneously trucking expanded its ton-miles from 16 to 22 percent. Public, as against family, ownership of motor carriers will expand, and by 1980 there may be fewer than 1,000 truck lines, as against 15,396 in 1967. There will be a cascade of mergers resulting in virtual disappearance of small one-owner trucking companies. Another development will be increases in operating authorities granted by the Interstate Commerce Commission and liberalization of state and federal highway regulatory requirements. By the end of the 1970s double-bottom trailers will operate on all highways throughout the 48 continental United States.

Far from being a federally subsidized industry, the truckers not only contribute to the growth of the nation's economy but also pay their way in taxes for highway construction. Trucking informational systems are embracing computers and using radio and otherwise updating their communications media. In the next decade there will be much closer functional integration of motor carriers, shippers, and receivers and more intercarrier cooperation, both within and between modes.[2]

The trucking industry is increasing sizes of its trailers, power of its tractors, and loads per trailer. Some oppose these trends. However, pertinent congressional committees have closely scrutinized the industry's proposals and should eventually come forward with solutions that will assure that they do not reduce safety on the highways.

Other Advances

Pipeline transport will probably grow at a faster and more impressive pace than any other surface mode. A striking breakthrough will be application of pipeline transport to products other than petroleum and natural gas. For example, commodities such as coal will be piped in slurry form, and as capsulization develops, solids in watertight capsules will move via pipeline incidental to movements of liquids.[3]

Water transport has long been a key means of moving goods. However, America's present merchant marine policy condemns this country to further deterioration as an ocean power. This nation's leadership in design and construction of containerships and roll-on/roll-off vessels is pointing the way to progress that other countries are exploiting and the United States is ignoring. Our shipbuilders and foreign merchants are failing to take full advantage of these novel vessels.

An important breakthrough in improvement of the inland waterway system was completion in 1971 of a navigable route to Tulsa, Oklahoma, and erection there of a large and efficient public-use waterfront terminal. The new port, which was financed from the proceeds of a $20 million bond issue, gives Oklahoma and Arkansas a link via the Arkansas River with the Mississippi River and the water commerce of the world.

Construction at Tulsa of a $1.5 million, fully equipped bulk storage facility was recently approved. Included in the complex are a bulk fertilizer warehouse, a bagging and storage building, a bulk fertilizer conveying system, two railroad spurs, access roads, and a parking area.

The first barge of freight to reach this new port contained 650 tons of newsprint manufactured and loaded at Bowater's Calhoun, Tennessee, paper mill. The tow arrived at Tulsa on May 7, 1971, after a journey of 1,130 miles. It is a matter of historical interest that *The Oklahoma Journal* in Oklahoma City received the first ton of freight unloaded at the new river port.

There are severe discriminations against the United States in ocean steamship rates to and from the Far East. For example, freight rates are a higher percentage of total delivered costs United States to Japan than Japan to United States. In addition, Japan applies import duties on a CIF basis, whereas the United States import duties are applied to the ad valorem value, with exclusion of cost, insurance, and freight. Some of the prejudicial results against this country, as gleaned from tariffs on file with the FMC, are as follows: electric motors, United States to Japan, applicable duty is $72.50 a measurement ton, from Japan to United States, $48.50; electric hand tools, $90 versus $54.50; refrigerating equipment, $57.75 versus

$37.25; plastic sheets, $85 versus $41; and copy machine chemicals, $76.25 versus $45.25.[4]

Affected American businessmen have advised the Japanese that these disparities are unjustified. As the result of the clamor against such prejudicial charges, investigators in the United States and Japan are making a joint study to determine the extent of these inequities. Interestingly enough, Japan's ministry of transportation does not acknowledge that any disparities exist.

The Marcona Corporation of San Francisco in partnership with the Dravo Corporation of Pittsburgh will shortly adopt the so-called Marcona flow system for transport of a wide variety of commodities and marine applications.[5] The process permits savings by loading bulk materials into pipelines in slurry form for transport into ocean steamers, dewatering for stability during ship transport, and finally, repulping into liquid for pipeline discharge at destinations.

This undertaking will generate new land-based application to any material which can be turned into slurry for movement from one locale to another. The process can be applied to virtually every major mineral operation.

The Marcona plan cuts conventional bulk ship loading and discharge costs by about 60 percent, eliminates massive conveyor systems, multimillion-dollar, deepwater port facilities, and dust and other air pollution problems. It also eliminates mechanical handling and is unusually flexible.

The Marcona system will encourage development of as yet untapped mineral deposits around the world which heretofore could not be mined because of prohibitive transportation costs.

In mid-August 1971 the El Paso Natural Gas Company announced plans for the world's most ambitious coal gasification plant. The $250 million facility will be the first to produce quality synthetic gas from coal for distribution through a pipeline. The company has acquired recoverable coal deposits of about 900 million tons in the vicinity of its pipelines, and additional coal is rumored to be available in the region.

Strangely enough, the first known predecessor of the Railway Express Agency was a man named W. F. Harnden, who in 1839 started carrying small packages in a hand bag between New York and Boston. Within two years Henry Wells instituted a similar operation between New York and Buffalo. Thereafter Wells and William Fargo extended the service from Buffalo to Chicago. By 1850 Wells-Fargo had instituted small package service between New York and California across the Isthmus of Panama.

From the Civil War until 1918, stock companies dominated the express business, and Adams Express, a corporation, operated in the Northeast, Southern Express in the Southeast, and Wells-Fargo between the Midwest and the Pacific Coast.

In addition to merchandise, express companies carried gold, silver bullion, securities, and jewelry, and was the only means of transport of such high-value traffic. They also issued express money orders, dealt in foreign exchange, cleared customs, bought goods for the account of customers, and filed legal papers.

In 1885 the Supreme Court concluded that the railroads were obligated to furnish express service. The Interstate Commerce Act of 1887 brought railroad express operations under national regulation but left unregulated the more extensive operations of separate express companies.

During World War I the railroads consolidated their

separate express organizations and in 1929 established a single Railway Express Agency, Inc. (REA). In the financially difficult period between 1946 and 1959 the railroads deemphasized their express operations, and beginning in 1959 the ICC authorized the REA to route traffic via truck, bus, and other modes of transportation.

Railway Express has a simple rate structure. It applies first-class rates on articles generally, and second-class rates on food, drink, and less-carload commodity rates. Recently it instituted container rates applicable to loads up to 3,000 pounds. Rates on palletized shipments in units of 600 up to 2,000 pounds are related to the container rates. Reduced rates on combined shipments often fall below rates of motor carriers and freight forwarders, which usually publish lower rates than REA on conventional package shipments.

The REA aims to handle heavier loads to augment the smaller parcel traffic. The intrusion of REA into added types of commodities, rates, and services has brought vigorous protests from motor carriers, freight forwarders, and air carriers.

The express company's management believes that no other carrier pays sufficient attention to shippers of packages which weigh around 50 pounds. Since other transporters are apparently shunning these weights, REA in accepting them offers shippers a service not otherwise available.

To augment their policy of speedily delivering small packages, REA has inaugurated the so-called Silver Bullet, a program which delivers shipments from origin to destination within a specified time throughout the nation. Thus shipments proceed from Atlanta to Baltimore, Cincinnati, Memphis, Tampa, and Miami within 48 hours.

Future Prospects for PDM 157

An express consignment moves via nonstop trailers on schedule whether REA has accumulated 51 or 50,000 pounds.[6]

Judicious mechanization is a key feature of newly designed REA terminals. A typical express motor carrier terminal is labor-intensive; that is, if the volume increases, the terminal employs more men. Employment of added human hands is expensive because labor costs increase faster than the volume of freight handled. At the other extreme is full automation, which can save money at high volume but which becomes intolerably expensive if volume flags.

REA chose the middle ground between labor-intensive and machinery-intensive terminals. Its system is built around conveyors which carry packages to be transferred from incoming to outgoing vehicles. Cargo items too heavy for the conveyors are handled conventionally. Of course, movement on the conveyor is cheaper which accounts for emphasis upon 50- to 100-pound packages.

At truck doors of its modern terminals, REA utilizes conveyor arms which extend up to 34 feet into a truck trailer for fast unloading. Powered incline conveyors carry the cargo from the extended conveyor to a conveyor loop above. As the cargo moves off the conveyor, every package is coded with its destination and the number of the loading door of the truck headed for that destination.

Gravity conveyors lead to doors where outgoing vehicles are parked. There are three classes of doors, namely, those for intercity, local, and Silver Bullet delivery. In a representative terminal this mechanical conveyor equipment totes up to 2,200 packages an hour. The system operates so speedily that a package received at an REA terminal can be aboard a departing motor carrier trailer within 30 minutes.

REA has also shaped up control of pickup and delivery. Dispatchers, informed by radio of frequent call-ins, know locations of drivers, and can assure emergency pickups and deliveries. The system makes it nearly impossible to slight any express truck-delivery requirement.

Meanwhile, REA holds a spectacular priority in air cargo. For example, of all air freight and express items, only mail takes precedence over air express. Twelve percent of air express items reach major cities the same day they are dispatched, 70 percent in 24 hours, and 95 percent in 48 hours.

The REA's emphasis upon service has effected the desired results. For example, the Atlanta Silver Bullet operation now handles 1,200 outbound loads daily, compared to 300 three months ago, and the daily volume is still growing. The REA is on the upgrade following a decade-long decline in tonnage and revenue.

However, REA is not out of the woods financially. The dismal truth is that the agency's deficits continue to grow despite the company's innovations and determination to find a profit-making niche for itself. For example, in 1969 the operating revenues of the REA equaled $269,600,000, operating expenses were $265,700,000, and the corporation's operating ratio was 98.5 percent. That year the agency lost $23,778,000 as against losses of $2,-425,000 in 1968; $12,841,000 in 1967; and $617,000 in 1966. In 1965 it made a profit of $989,555.[7]

Freight forwarders. In the 1970s the shipping public must reckon with freight forwarders, who plan to institute major changes in their strategy, particularly in handling small shipments. Congress is almost certain to enact legislation to lift restrictions that currently block railroads and forwarders from establishing an intermodal relationship. For example, one flaw in the present statute is a prohibition against performance by freight forwarders of services beyond terminal areas. Forwarders utilize short-haul truck lines to serve ultimate destinations, but truck line mergers are gradually destroying availability of such service. The unfortunate result is that forwarders must pay increased local truck rates, whereas long-haul truckers continue to enjoy the lion's share of the division of revenues between short-haul and long-haul motor carriers. Cooperation between railroads and forwarders should eliminate this injustice.

Another inequity, which will probably disappear, is the fact that freight forwarders cannot purchase regulated truckers but regulated truckers can purchase freight forwarders.

Eighty percent of consignments which freight forwarders move weigh under 500 pounds. The ICC's recent report on forwarders (ex parte 266) recommends a change in regulation of this type of carriage in order to keep the forwarder industry economically healthy. The ICC will explore terminal operations, freight scheduling versus delivery times, and other aspects of forwarder operations. The U.S. Departments of Transportation, Justice, and Defense applaud the commission's approach, which may eventually enable forwarders to expand their operations.

Pertinent legislation before Congress concerning forwarders (H.R. 6242), proposes negotiations between railroad and forwarder management regarding rates which forwarders pay railroads. The intent of this bill is to allow freight forwarders to expand less-carload tonnage. If this bill is enacted, freight forwarders will become a much more significant entity in physical distribution than they are at present.

Forwarders claim that if they are not able to continue shipping small packages via rail routes, the annual revenue loss to the railroads will exceed $167 million because of the diversion by freight forwarders from rail to truck delivery. In 1970 freight forwarders paid the rail lines $170 million to haul forwarder freight, which is a significant revenue.

Mail has for years been one of the main methods of intercommunication inside and outside the United States, rivaling the telephone, telegraph, radio, and television. It has also been one of the major movers of small packages domestically and around the world.

However, as a handler of small packages, the U.S. mail has never been outstandingly efficient. With massive shifts of the domestic population and a growing need for improved delivery of small freight items, the United States mail service has unfortunately deteriorated at the very time it should have improved.

No wonder then that as of July 1, 1970, the president signed into law the Postal Reorganization Act of 1970, establishing a new mailing system called the United States Postal Service. The USPS must by inheritance operate the thousands of overly crowded and inadequately mechanized facilities of the post office, and its employees must work with the obsolete properties which the post office department willed it.

Even in its infancy the organization is meeting the challenges that face it and making improvements in mail delivery. As it moves into high gear, the postal service has a number of things going for it. For example, it has a

$10 billion budget for fiscal 1972, and the experience of 741,000 postal employees. Also available for transport of mail are common carrier airlines, air taxi services, highway routes, railroads (100 trains now carry the mail exclusively), and steamship lines.[8]

The USPS obtains mail contracts by advertising for competitive bids. It no longer must (as the post office had to do) gain the Interstate Commerce Commission's approval of those agreements. This spring the U.S. Postal Service began overnight service of airmail between major cities.

Many USPS offices within a 600-mile radius of the mailer of letters or parcels now receive this service. Others will not do so because of geographic factors or lack of intercity volume between certain cities.

As for rail, the new postal service estimates it will move close to 300,000 piggyback carloads of mail in 1971 on reliable, consistent, economical schedules. One of the vital routes is the Santa Fe's Super-C between the Midwest and the West Coast. The Super-C makes a 40-hour run between Chicago and Los Angeles, carrying trailers and containers of bulk mail at a cost below that of ten years ago. Along this route mail trailers flow onto and off this train from and to off-line points. The train acts as a backbone of the mailing system, serving almost two-thirds of the United States.

The Burlington Northern operates the Pacific Zip between the Midwest and the Pacific Northwest, a distance of 2,181 miles. The schedule calls for a speedy 40-hour run between Chicago and Seattle. The United States Postal Service estimates it will realize an annual saving of $600,000 from the Zip operation alone. The Southern

Railway and Illinois Central provide scheduled high-speed mail train runs, mostly piggyback, on north-south routes.

As for the highway aspect of USPS, the postal organization operates regularly scheduled twin trailer service between New Orleans and Los Angeles, a distance of 1,974 highway miles. A connecting series of highways operates from Seattle to Alaskan cities, and to Portland, Denver, Dallas, and Houston. The majority of bulk mail now moves by truck trailers. But the outmoded terminal units are not geared for the majority of trailer loadings. In fact, the original post office terminal which USPS inherited was designed to function as a central business geared to old-fashioned railroad passenger trains which moved on leisurely schedules compared to those of Amtrak, air, bus, and truck lines.

USPS is now constructing high-grade, industrial-type buildings at 33 locations for the handling of bulk mail. The new facilities will handle annually 50 million sacks of second-class mail, 60 million sacks of third-class mail, and one billion parcels of fourth-class mail.

Last year the post office reported that 37 million letters and one million parcels went to the Dead Letter Office. Each dead letter is a potential complaint. To achieve best use of USPS, it is imperative that physical distribution managers alert their companies to the need for correct addressing, good packaging, and zip coding for every letter and parcel sent through the postal service.

Containerization. Nothing in sight will contain the container. It is the transport sensation of modern times. These ingenious rectangular chests will at a hastened pace achieve hundreds of breakthroughs to improved distribution. However, excess paper work has imposed handicaps upon U.S. container transport. Merely to list the documents international container shipments generate in the United States would require a sheet of paper 12 feet long and 11 inches wide. Foreign exporters have no such unnecessary and cumbersome document burdens.

To date there have been only halfhearted attempts to achieve through intermodal container movements. The key step is to develop single-factor rates on general cargo from point of origin to point of destination. However, jurisdictional issues confronting the Interstate Commerce Commission, Federal Maritime Commission, and Customs Bureau have slowed container shipments through the seaports. As already noted, this nation's regulatory environment is archaic and out of step with technological change.

Correct documentation is one of the foremost aspects of good physical distribution management. There is no apparent reason for delay in accepting a new simplified system due to become effective on January 1, 1972. The resolutions which the National Committee on International Trade Documentation have adopted are as follows: (1) on January 1, 1972, its members will put into effect the United States standard master bill of lading for international trade; (2) the new bill will have an open masthead with no preprinted carrier identification; and (3) where parties other than shippers assume responsibility for providing bills of lading, members of the NCITD will urge their agents to furnish bills of lading which comply with the U.S. standard master.

The following documents will be aligned with the new U.S. standard master bill of lading: commercial invoice, certificate of origin, special cargo policy, delivery instructions, dock receipt, shipper's export declaration, and notice of exportation of articles with benefit of drawback. The position of Sea-Land Service, Inc. is that modernization of ocean ships will be the theme of the 1970s. Sea-Land believes that water transportation companies will concentrate on larger and speedier vessels, quicker turnaround, and fuller utilization of equipment. This will lead to reduced charges for shippers and higher operating productivity for water carriers.

Heretofore airplanes have moved a minuscule segment of the nation's express and freight tonnage. With mature development of jet cargo carriers, which can lift thousands of pounds, air transport will eventually compete with highway, rail, and possibly even water transport. For example, airlines will attract from these three modes many tons of high-value and perishable merchandise.

Under the leadership of the Water Transport Association, the nation's regulated motor, rail, and water carriers have submitted to President Nixon a joint program of transport regulation. The WTA, AAR, and ATA seek two important objectives—encouragement of substantial investment to improve carrier productivity, and expansion of the nation's total transport capacity 100 percent in fifteen years.

For the first time in history, the three national associations contend that they will cooperate to achieve equity among all the major modes of transport. They ask, for example, that water carrier rates on dry bulk commodities and motor carrier rates on livestock and agricultural commodities, both now exempt from regulation, be placed under regulation in order to attain competitive equality. Thus, the truck and barge lines, in an unprecedented joint declaration, recognize the unfairness of these exemptions, which the railroads do not and never have enjoyed.

Terminals. Terminal interfaces must face up to the demands of this bold decade. At present airline cargo waits for hours between subsonic jet flights. Motor freight stands idle day after day in truck terminals before and after intercity hauls. Rail equipment, empty and loaded, waits in yards and at industrial doors for weeks before and after line-haul movement.[9] Every terminal delay, whether an hour or a day, adds costs to transporters and the public.

In the 1970s two contrasting types of terminal complexes will emerge. One will be the intermodal layout, a superterminal with acres of land under one roof. It will have an air and water port, and all modes of transportation will service it. The intermodal complex will be fully mechanized, capable of handling a one-pound parcel, a 35-ton container, and dry and liquid bulk commodities with ease. This type of terminal will also exchange U.S. mail between airplanes and trucks. It will inventory a specific industry's stock, repair a diesel locomotive, and provide accommodations for over-the-road trucks waiting for the next day's trip.

The second type of terminal will be the special-purpose type, requiring a relatively small amount of land for performance of specific services. It will be a gathering facility for small shipments serving, for example, one airline or one railroad.

Transportation Systems

During the next decade fully integrated transportation systems, like Fruehauf Corporation, will become commonplace and vastly increase efficiency of physical distribution in domestic and foreign trade. Fruehauf, which was founded in 1914, is organized along functional lines and is active in North America and in 10 foreign countries. The highly complex firm introduced its unique total transportation concept in 1964.[10] It is engaged in all modes of transportation except air. Fruehauf manufactures on a mass production basis trailers of all types, rail cars, vessels, shoreside equipment such as cranes, docks, and floating drydocks, containers, and equipment shelters. With 101 branches in the United States and Canada the company offers a wide variety of services.

In order to insure true container intermodal capability, Fruehauf has designed a new chassis to adapt American Standards Institute (ASI) and International Standards Organization (ISO) containers to over-the-road operations. Fruehauf's flexi-quad railroad car was the first one designed for rail transportation of piggyback trailers and flexi-van and conventional containers exclusively or in combination. The concern also developed and fabricated the famous Big John aluminum hopper cars for hauling dry materials like cement, grain, and chemicals in bulk.

Paceco, a division of Fruehauf, has erected more container-handling port cranes than all other manufacturers combined. Fifty-seven Paceco Portainers now move freight over 34 world ports. Paceco cranes installed aboard ship are an alternative means of loading and unloading at ports of call that have no shoreside unloading systems.

To expand Fruehauf's commitment to the total transport concept, the corporation recently acquired the Maryland Shipbuilding & Drydock Company of Baltimore. Located on a 76-acre tract, it is a modern shipyard with facilities for large-ship conversion and repair. For example, the shipyard can convert into a modern containership a conventional C-2-type vessel. Also, it can "jumboize" or double the carrying capacity of vessels.

By acquisition of Fischbach & Moore, Inc., Fruehauf now installs complete materials handling systems. The United States Postal Department has accepted new product developments of Fruehauf to solve the mounting problem of handling mail. Fruehauf's test operations are maintained around the clock. Typical of this capability is the tractor-trailer dynamometer, a device that enables engineers to simulate road driving of a tractor trailer through millions of miles under absolute control conditions.

Interpool, Incorporated, a wholly owned subsidiary of Steadman Industries Limited of London, England, provides a worldwide, fully integrated transportation system with a multiple variety of services, including inland transportation by rail and truck, cartage and side-transfer services, and maintenance-supervision of container interchange. Interpool also provides auxiliary equipment, including side-transfer units, delivery trailer chassis, and demountable container legs.[11]

From the standpoint of the shipper Interpool creates substantial freight savings. Its rail container rates are competitive with and in many instances lower than truck rates and are based on 40-foot trailerloads. To ship only two 20-foot containers on a flatcar, which is the most that the 85- or 89-foot flatcar can handle, means that the shipper must pay as much for a 20-foot as for a 40-foot unit. Interpool facilities can carry four containers on a flatcar. Thus the freight bill for the car is distributed among four units, rather than two (or at best three) units, and the freight cost is reduced substantially.

Another approach to total transportation is through voluntary associations exemplified by the International Cargo Handling Coordination Association (ICHCA), founded in London in 1951 for the purpose of encouraging efficient cargo movement. Its membership includes owners of goods, consignors, consignees, as well as carriers by air and sea, together with shipping, forwarding, customs, and insurance agents. Location of ICHCA offices at seaports was natural because of concentration of merchandise at the docks. Today there are over 1,700 ICHCA members in 70 countries. Among the present membership are stevedores, shipowners, shipbuilders, port operators, air carriers, freight forwarders, insurance interests, packing experts, civil engineers, consultants, naval architects, and manufacturers.

One of the major achievements of the ICHCA is free international interchange of information. ICHCA has set up a communications and documentary system based on the international central office in London.

There are two types of memberships in ICHCA—corporate and private. ICHCA also has a library membership, which enables colleges and universities to obtain technical publications at low cost. Corporate members can consult ICHCA's central offce at no extra charge. Should inquiry demand wide investigation, the central office can call upon the aggregate knowledge of the whole membership. Other professional bodies may also be called upon for information.

As an established nongovernmental organization, ICHCA holds consultative status with the United Nations. The cargo organization has sent its secretary-general to visit home companies in all the 19 countries with national committee memberships in ICHCA. There is a constant flow of members through the central office in London. This keeps contacts personal and up-to-date and feeds back valuable information to ICHCA. The association is not a consulting firm, but by an exchange of knowledge and by sharing problems, the members achieve real coordination, although those involved may be half a world apart. Neither the central office nor individual members pretend to have remarkable knowledge. However, the aggregate of knowledge and experience to be found in the total membership is significant.

A Parting Challenge

The above pages have only scratched the surface of physical distribution. Respect for PDM will uncover sources of profits that many enterprises are now overlooking. More scientific analysis, especially of the systems approach, intermodality, regulatory reform, and use of new techniques, particularly computerization, is necessary. Examples cited herein of successful application of PDM techniques and descriptions of technological advancements among the various modes should not mislead anyone to the conclusion that the national economy is moving speedily toward ideal physical distribution goals. The examples cited are a fraction of what should have occurred long ago and a much smaller fraction of what should take place within the near future if the world's economic productivity is to advance sufficiently to assure social justice for all people.

References

1. Bill Keller, "Amtrak—Vision or Visionary," *Progressive Railroading*, May–June, 1971, p. 19.

2. "G.E. Symposium: Carrier Strategies for the '70s," *Traffic Management*, August 1970, p. 53.

3. John P. Doyle, "Looking into Transportation and the '70s," *Handling and Shipping*, January 1970, p. 56.

4. "American Shippers Seek End to Rate Discrimination in Far East Trade," *Traffic Management*, July 1971, p. 19.

5. "Revolutionary Slurry System," *World Ports*, August 1971, p. 29.

6. John F. Spencer, "Has the Express Company Found Its Magic Formula?" *Handling and Shipping*, July 1971, p. 52.

7. *Transport Statistics in the United States for the Year Ended December 31, 1969, Part 1, Railroads* (Washington, D.C.: Interstate Commerce Commission, 1970), p. 356.

8. H. G. Becker, Jr., "USPS . . . It's New, Now, or Never," *Handling and Shipping*, July 1971, pp. 57–59.

9. "State-of-the-Art Reports on Technology and Air, Highway, and Rail Transportation," *Handling and Shipping*, January 1971, pp. 48–63.

10. *Total Transportation* (Fullerton, Calif.: Fruehauf Corporation, 1968), p. 4.

11. Peter Hunter, "Interpool Bids to Capture Pooling Market," *Containerisation International*, July 1969, p. S5051. See also Charles S. Carew, "Interpool Container Leasing Cuts Costs for Carriers and Shippers," *Handling and Shipping*, March 1969.

Index

A&P Food Stores, 30
AAR, see Association of American Railroads
Abitibi Paper Co., Ltd., 63
Acadia Forest, 123–124
Acme Fast Freight, Inc., 48
air freight, small shipments by, 74
airlines, in transportation system, 40
air parcel post, small shipments by, 75
airports, shortcomings of, 67
air transportation, improvements in, 97
AJF Industries, 24–27
American Association for the Advancement of Science, 9
American Association of State Highway Officials, 89
American Bankers Association, 9
American Bar Association, 9
American Chemical Society, 9
American Institute of Certified Public Accountants, 9

American Medical Association, 9
American Smelting and Refining Co., 118–122
American Society of Traffic and Transportation, 6, 8–9
American Standards Institute, 94, 166
American Trucking Association, 12–13, 76, 88
American Waterways Operators, 13
Amtrak (National Railroad Passenger Corp.), 147–150
Association of American Railroads, 12–13, 107, 110, 150
associations, founding dates and memberships of, 9
AST&T, see American Society of Traffic and Transportation
ATA, see American Trucking Association
Atchison, Topeka & Santa Fe Railway, 100, 107, 120
  Super-C service of, 161

172 Index

Automatic Car Identification Systems, 146
automatic pressure-control conveyors, 135
automation
 of dock facilities, 93, 125
 in railway transport, 41
AWO, see American Waterways Operators
BAD, see Business Assistance Division
Balanced Foods, Inc., 47
Baldwin–Lima–Hamilton Corp., 120
banana industry, packaging in, 35–36
bargaining ability, lack of in physical distribution management, 15–16
BIC, see Bureau of International Commerce
Boeing 747 cargo plane, 97
Bone Valley, Fla., phosphorus industry at, 116
book industry, packaging in, 36–37
Bowater Organization, 63, 68, 103
Bricker report, 68
British Steel Corp., 131
Brown, Virginia Mae, 73
Bureau of International Commerce, 17
Burlington Northern Railroad, 161–162
Business and Defense Services Administration, 17
Business Assistance Division, U.S. Commerce Department, 17

CAB, see Civil Aeronautics Board
California, strawberry production and distribution in, 137–138
Capital Projects Division, U.S. Commerce Department, 17
Cargill, Inc., 136–138
cargo planes, 97
"carnet" system, 78
carrier(s)
 ICC favoritism toward, 11
 influence of over shipper, 8
 liability standards of, 17–18
 lobbyists for, 13
 physical distribution manager's prejudice and, 7
 total revenue of, in small shipments, 74–75
Carrier Corporation, total logistics system of, 26
carrier selectivity, 76
carrier traffic officials, camaraderie among, 7–8
CASL, see Committee of American Steamship Lines
Celanese Corp., 125
Census Bureau, U.S., 68
Central of Georgia Railway, 83
C-5A cargo plane, 97
Chesapeake & Ohio Railroad, 150–151
China, Nixon's trip to, 144–145
Civil Aeronautics Board, 10, 18
CML, see Container Marine Lines
coal gasification plant, 154–155
College Placement Council, 142
college students, PDM courses for, 70–71
Commerce Department, U.S., 17–18, 115
Committee of American Steamship Lines, 13
company image, physical distribution and, 5

Index

computer
  in delivery service operations, 58–60
  in order-planning system, 24–25, 134–136
  in physical distribution management, 78–79, 131–133
  in total logistics system, 26–27
computer processing, in market-oriented firms, 125
computer systems, in transportation, 67
Congress, U.S., transportation legislation fiascos in, 13–14
Connally, John, 144
Consolidated-Bathurst, Ltd., 63
Consolidated Freightways, 85
consumer-oriented firms, distribution in, 134–136
consumer packaging, 28–30
  see also packaging
consumer power, growth of, 29
container, dimensions and construction of, 94–95
containerization
  dock labor and, 56–58
  future of, 162–165
  improvements in, 94–97
  in Japan-to-Europe commerce, 101
  in land-bridge freighting, 97–102
Container Marine Lines, 18
containerships, 57
control information, in physical distribution, 2–3
Corps of Engineers, U.S., 93
cost(s)
  of foreign trade documentation, 77
  inventory, 50–51
  inventory-holding, 22
  mailing, 60–62
  ordering, 22
  transportation, 32–33
creativity, lack of in physical distribution manager, 5–6
Crown Zellerbach Corp., 63
Customs Bureau, U.S., 163

Data-Verter order-entry system, 59–60
Dead Letter Office, 162
Defense Department, U.S., 10
delivery services, in physical distribution, 58–64
Diamond Crystal Salt Co., 47
diesel engines, high-speed, 92
diesel locomotive, future of, 146
Digitronics Corp., 59
distribution, physical, see physical distribution
distribution parks, 49
dock facilities, automation of, 93
dock labor, containerization and, 56–58
dock management, 53
documentation, 77, 163–164
DOT, see Transportation Department, U.S.
double-entry accounting system, shortcomings of, 23
Doyle, Gen. John P., 68
Doyle report, 68
Driscoll Strawberry Associates, 138
Druce, Miles, see Miles Druce & Co., Ltd.
Du Pont de Nemours, E. I., & Co., 47, 124

El Paso Natural Gas Co., 154–155
excise tax, repeal of, 143–144

Index

Fair Packaging and Labeling Act (1966), 28
F.A.K. (freight-of-all-kinds) rate, 99
farm-oriented firms, distribution in, 136–138
FASTRAND unit, 132
FDA, see Food and Drug Administration
Federal Coordinator of Transportation, 68
Federal Maritime Commission, 12, 18, 79, 95–96, 163
Federal Trade Commission, 28
fertilizer, commercial, 115
FFA, see Freight Forwarders Association
Fibre Box Association, 109
Fischbach & Moore, Inc., 167
fixed order quantity, vs. fixed order time, 23–24
Florida, phosphate rock in, 115–119
Florida Cross-State Canal, 72
FMC, see Federal Maritime Commission
Food and Drug Administration, U.S., 28–29
Food, Drug and Cosmetic Act, 30
foreign trade documents, 77, 163–164
Fortune, 67
forwarding, pending legislation on, 159–160
freight
  damage to, 106–109
  railroad, 40–41
freight cars, damage-free, 83
Freight Forwarders Association, 13
freight forwarding, improvements in, 158–162
freight-of-all-kinds (F.A.K.) rate, 99
Freight Loss and Damage report, 109
Fruehauf Corp., 165–167
FTC, see Federal Trade Commission

gas turbine engines, 92
General Logistics Corp., 134
Gibson, Andrew E., 101
Government Accounting Office, 91
Great Lakes shipping, 44, 52, 98
Great Northern Paper Co., 63
gross national product, 1
Gulf Coast shipping, 98

Harnden, W. F., 155
Harris, Oren, 14
Harris Bill, 14
Hartke, Vance, 11
Heinz, H. J., Co., 49
highways, damage to from trucking, 91
highway transportation, improvements in, 85–92
House Interstate and Foreign Commerce Committee, 14
House Ways and Means Committee, 14

IBM 360 computer system, 60
ICC, see Interstate Commerce Commission
ICHCA, see International Cargo Handling Coordination Association
ILA, see International Longshoremen's Association

Index 175

Illinois Central Railroad Co., 81
image, in physical distribution, 5
import tax, 144
industrial packaging, 30–32
 see also packaging
inland waterway system, 43
 improvements in, 92–94, 153
International Business Machines Corp., 66–67, 127–128
International Cargo Handling Coordination Association, 168
International Longshoremen's Association, 54–57
International Paper Co., 63, 123–124
International Standards Organization, 166
Interpool, Inc., 167
Interstate Commerce Act, 15, 76, 81
Interstate Commerce Commission, 7, 10–11, 18–19, 40, 69–70, 74, 78, 81, 151, 159–161, 163
 favoritism in toward carriers, 11
 member qualifications of, 11–12
Interstate Highway System, 42, 72
 improvements in, 87–90
inventory, size of in relation to sales, 23
inventory control, 50–52
inventory cost, 50–51
inventory-holding cost, 22
inventory planning, order cycles and, 24
ISO, see International Standards Organization

Japanese shipping industry, 101, 153–154
Jet Air Freight, 128
Jewel Tea Companies, Inc., 30, 33
Johnson, Lyndon B., 14, 55
Justice Dept., U.S., 19

Kennedy, John F., 13
Kimberly-Clark Corp., 63
King Soopers, Inc., 30
Kissinger, Henry A., 145
Krug, J. A., 72

Labor Dept., U.S., 141
land-bridge freighting, 97–99
 uncertainties of, 100–102
liability, variety of standards in, 17–18
Litton Systems, Inc., 98
lobbyists, carriers' influence with, 13
logistics, physical distribution and, 4, 26–27
longshoremen
 containerization and, 56–58
 number of, 53
loss and damage, transportation and, 102–111
Louisville & Nashville Railroad, 83, 104, 151

MacMillan Bloedel, Ltd., 63
mailing costs, 60–62
management, physical distribution responsibility of, 1–2
 see also physical distribution management; physical distribution manager(s)
Marcona Corp., 154
Maritime Commission, see Federal Maritime Commission

176   Index

market-oriented firms, distribution in, 124–134
Marshall, Alfred, 38–39
Marshall Plan Report (1947), 72
Maryland Shipbuilding & Drydock Co., 166–167
materials handling, automatic, 125
McKinsey & Co., 2, 4, 98
Metroliner service, 69
Miles Druce & Co., Ltd., 131–134
mining industries, distribution principles in, 115–122
Montgomery Ward & Co., 60–62
motive power, improvements in, 92
motor carrier terminals, improvements in, 92
motor transport, 42–43
 see also truck(s); trucking industry
Mueller report, 68
multiple trailer operations, 90–91
Murphy, Rupert L., 73

National Association of Railroad Passengers, 149
National Committee on International Trade Documentation, 163
National Highway Safety Bureau, 89–90
National Railroad Passenger Corp. (Amtrak), 148
National Sugar Refining Co., 56
National Tea Co., 30
Nelson, Gaylord, 88
newsprint
 automated warehouse for, 105–106
 damage to, 104–106
 demand for, 62–63
 prices and sales of, 63–64
 see also paper industry
New York Shipping Association, 54–55
Nixon, Richard M., 143, 145, 164
Norfolk & Western Railway, 83, 99, 150
NYSA, see New York Shipping Association

ocean steamships, as freight carriers, 39
ocean transport, 44
 improvements in, 94
Office of Education, U.S., 142
Oklahoman, The, 105–106
order cycles, inventory planning and, 24
ordering costs, 22
order planning system, 21–24
 computerized, 24–27, 134–136
Owens-Corning Fiberglas Corp., 49

Paceco Portainers, 166
Pacific Intermountain Express, 85
Pacific Zip service, 161–162
packaging
 accessibility in, 31–32
 in banana industry, 35–36
 in book industry, 36–37
 consumer, 28–30
 consumer vs. industrial, 31
 defined, 27–28
 design in, 32–34
 industrial, 30–32
 loss and damage in, 109–111
 polystyrene inserts in, 38

Index 177

pricing and, 33
protection through, 31
sales and, 34
of stereo cassette players, 37–38
in total physical distribution system, 34–38
transportation costs and, 32–33
Paddle and Saddle Sportswear, 34
Panama Canal, 93, 98
Pan American Highway, 42
paper industry, distribution in, 123
    see also newsprint
parcel post, small shipments by, 75
Paul Bunyan Box, 138
PDM, see physical distribution management
Penn Central Company, 11, 83–84
phosphate rock, mining of, 115–119
physical distribution, 1–20
    components of, 21–64
    control information in, 2–3
    cost of, 1
    delivery services in, 58–64
    economics of, 3–4
    effectiveness in, 2
    inventory control and, 50–52
    loss and damage in, 102–111
    packaging and, 27–38
    paper work problem in, 19–20
    personnel competence in, 3
    principles and practices of, 114–138
    scope of, 4–5
    stevedoring in, 52–58
    storage and warehousing in, 44–49
    vs. total logistics system, 4, 26–27
    transportation and, 38–44
    vest-pocket centers for, 49
    worldwide scope of, 16–17
physical distribution department
    bargaining ability of, 15–16
    ineffectiveness of before regulatory agencies, 11
    influence of on transportation legislation, 12–15
    low ranking of, 10
physical distribution management (PDM), 1
    components of, 21–64
    computer in, 24–27, 78–79, 134–136
    courses in, 70–71
    current problems and opportunities in, 66–111
    documentation in, 77, 163–164
    future prospects for, 140–169
    in mining industry, 115–122
physical distribution manager(s)
    creativity lack in, 5–6
    insufficient training of, 8–10
    overspecialization by, 6–7
    prejudice for particular carriers, 7–8
    shortage of, 140–141
    shortcomings of, 5–10
piggybacking, 85, 129, 146
    future of, 161–162
pipeline transport, 43
    future of, 152
Plough, Inc., 125–127
polystyrene inserts, in packaging, 38
Ponce de Leon containership, 57–58

178 Index

Port Ilo, Peru, 121–122
Postal Reorganization Act of 1970, 160
Pressed Steel Tank Co., 128–131
Price Co., Ltd., 63
price and wage freeze (1971), 143–144
pricing
 package design and, 33
 profit margins and, 29
professionalism, in AST&T, 9
profit margins, pricing and, 29
Puritan Fashions, Inc., 34

queue theory, 134

RAGMOP (Random Access Generated Mail Order Processing), 59
rail freight ton-miles, improvement in, 146
railroad(s)
 centralized traffic control of, 82–83
 encouragement from, 99–100
 freight rate structures of, 84–85
 freight ton-miles of, 146
 improvements in, 145–151
 low-level transcontinental rates of, 99–100
 government ownership of, 84
 storage-in-transit by, 46
railroad corporations, consolidation of, 83
railroad-forwarder management, legislation on, 159–160
railroad industry, decline of, 40–41
railroading, improvements in, 80–85, 145–151
Railroad Passenger Service Act (1970), 147–148

rail travel, super-high velocity, 67
rail unit trains, 80–81
Railway Express Agency, Inc., 12, 73, 75, 155–158
railway transport, 40–41
Rapistan, Inc., 134–135
raw-material-oriented firms, distribution in, 122–124
REA, see Railway Express Agency, Inc.
red tape barrier, 19
regulatory agencies, ineffectiveness of physical distribution management before, 11
Rent-A-Train plan, 81
Rosenthal, Benjamin, 30

Safeway Stores, Inc., 30
St. Louis Southwestern Railway, 48
S&H Green Stamps, 134
Santa Fe railroad, see Atchison, Topeka & Santa Fe Railway
Scott, H. H., Inc., 37
Scott Paper Co., 108–109
Seaboard Coast Line Railroad Co., 116–117
Sea-Land Service, Inc., 164
shipments, damage to, 17–18
Shuford Mills, Inc., 32
Silver Bullet program, of Railway Express Agency, 156–158
Sinclair-Koppers Co., Inc., 38
small-shipment carriers, total revenue of, 74–75
small shipments, as transportation problem, 73–77
Southern Pacific Railroad, 111, 120
Southern Railway Co., 12, 40, 83, 103, 150

Index

Southland Paper Mills, Inc., 63
Sperry & Hutchinson Co., 134–136
Spiegel, Inc., 58
Steadman Industries, Ltd., 167
Steelcase, Inc., 125
stereo cassette players, packaging of, 37–38
stevedoring
    dock labor and containers in, 56–58
    labor-management strife in, 53–54
Stop & Shop Companies, Inc., 30
storage and warehousing, 44–49
    small business requirements in, 48–49
strawberry producers, distribution by, 137–138
Suez canal, 44
    improvements in, 93
Supreme Court, U.S., 11, 155

Taft–Hartley Act, 55
TDCC, *see* Transportation Data Coordinating Committee
Technical Impex Corp., 36
Tele-Rail Automated Information Network (TRAIN), 146–147
teletype (TWX), in order-planning system, 25
terminals, future improvements in, 165
TOFC (trailers-on-flatcars) rates, 85
Toquepala (Peru) project, 121
total logistics system, conversion to, 26–27
Trade Simplification Bill, 19
traffic department, physical distribution and, 4
traffic managers, lack of training among, 9–10
Traffic World, 107–108
trailer operations, multiple, 90–91
trailers-on-flatcars (TOFC) operations, 85, 129
Trak-rak system, 105–106
transportation
    government research in, 68–70
    improved technology in, 80–97
    inland water carriers in, 43–44
    loss and damage in, 102–111
    motor, 42–43
    physical distribution and, 4, 38–44
    pipelines in, 43
    problems of, 66–80; *see also* transportation problems
    railway, 40–42
transportation costs, package design and, 32–33
Transportation Data Coordinating Committee, 78–80
Transportation Department, U.S., 10, 15, 19, 68–69, 78, 98, 130
Transportation for People Fund, 88–89
transportation industry, changes in, 39–40
transportation legislation
    fiascos in, 13–14
    jaundiced view of, 20
    number of bills in Congress for, 13
    physical distribution management's influence on, 12–15
transportation problems
    airports and, 67

Index

transportation problems (*cont.*)
  distribution courses and, 70–71
  documentation and paper work as, 77–80
  freight-carrying capacity and, 71
  highway network and, 67
  ICC cynicism and, 69
  Interstate Highway System and, 69, 72
  research in, 68
  road congestion as, 72
  small shipments as, 73–77
  transportation systems, future improvements in, 165–169
Transport Internationale Routier, 78
truck(s)
  highway damage by, 91
  improvements in equipment for, 86
  private, 125
  trucking industry, future prospects for, 151–152
  trucking service, common-carrier, 86
  truck lines, loss and damage payouts by, 102–103
  twin-trailer operations, 91

Union Pacific Railroad, 99, 111, 150
United Cargo Corp., 99
United Parcel Service, 74
United States, as land-bridge, 97–102
United States Postal Service, 160–162

unit loading, 103
Universal Machine Language Equipment Register (UMLER), 147

vest-pocket distribution centers, 49
Volpe, John A., 87

wage and price freeze (1971), 143–144
Walrath, Lawrence K., 73
warehousing, 44–49
  for newsprint, 105–106
  public, 45–48
  small business and, 48–49
  vest-pocket centers for, 49
water transport, 43–44
  future of, 152–154
Water Transport Association, 164
Watson, Thomas J., Jr., 66
Weeks report, 68
Wells, Henry, 155
Wells-Fargo Co., 155
Western Electric Co., 49
Westinghouse Electric Corp., 5–6
Williams, J. B., Co., 247
Worcester Moulded Plastics Co., 38
work stoppages, in stevedoring operations, 53–55
World War I, railroad consolidations and changes since, 145–146, 155–156
World War II, freight-carrying capacities since, 71